# Christ Is in Me

The Hope of Glory/Victory

## The Autobiography of Salma Carunia Carter

An orphan girl's journey of faith, hope, courage with divine miracles. Raised in the Dohnavur Fellowship in India, finally becoming an American and *a missionary to all*.

SALMA CARUNIA CARTER

ISBN 979-8-89345-344-7 (paperback)
ISBN 979-8-89526-735-6 (hardcover)
ISBN 979-8-89345-345-4 (digital)

Copyright © 2025 by Salma Carunia Carter

All rights reserved. No part of this publication may be reproduced, distributed, or transmitted in any form or by any means, including photocopying, recording, or other electronic or mechanical methods without the prior written permission of the publisher. For permission requests, solicit the publisher via the address below.

Christian Faith Publishing
832 Park Avenue
Meadville, PA 16335
www.christianfaithpublishing.com

Grateful acknowledgment is made for the following:

Amy Carmichael's poetry/lyrics are taken from *Mountain Breezes: The Collected Poems* of Amy Carmichael, published by CLC Publications, Fort Washington, Pennsylvania, USA, and used with permission. All rights reserved.

The Dohnavur Fellowship Corporation grants permission to Salma Carunia Carter to print photographs that belong to the Dohnavur Fellowship in her autobiography.
http://www.amycarmichael.org
http://www.friendsofdohnavur.org

Printed in the United States of America

I want to tell my story to the world—the secret of my charming personality! The secret is *to know* the mystery of God's divine presence, which is "Christ is in me, the hope of glory!"

*To whom God would make known what is
the riches of the glory of this mystery
among the Gentiles, which is Christ in you, the hope of glory.*

—Colossians 1:27 KJV

Thou in me dwelling And I in Thee One!

The evidence of the indwelling God (I John 4:15) …is the fundamental ground for our Faith and Victory. (I John 5:4)

Salma's mother (Amma) Amy Carmichael

# DEDICATION

I would like to dedicate this book to many people who played a great part in my childhood and teen years when growing up at the Dohnavur Fellowship.

The missionaries who served a lifetime, rearing, teaching, and caring for us orphans.

In my story, you will learn why Aunt Helen Bradshaw (Premalu Sittie) and Aunt Margaret Wilkinson (Nura Sitttie) deserve special mention. In addition, other leaders and house mothers, such as my beloved Kirubai, Rajarathinie, Amithal Accal, Lola, Rajamacottie, and Shanthie Arludasan, who loved me dearly and gave me hope to go forward in my life.

I also dedicate this work to my many Dohnavur sisters: Mani Accal, K. Leela, Devashanthi, Anihala, Rajaseeli, Ponmalar, Ruhinie Emmanuel, Amirtha Devairakkam, Inbarani, Saroruha Richard, Uslia Naveenaseelan, Davarual, Urani Borloz, Sunithie, Navarathinie Raja, Sarovinda, and Kamalavalli Carunia. A special note of dedication to Dr. Ponnalari Carunia who was like an elder sister to me. I cannot forget to mention some of my schoolchildren who were under my care at Wynberg-Allen School in the Himalayas: Harpawan Narang Kukreja, Jyotsna Verma Sharma, Linda Kelsang Yacob, and the staff: Mr. and Mrs. Amani Thomas, Hugh and Ruth Bradby, and Ms. Irene Rudling.

Several hundred of my sisters and brothers spent their lifetime at Dohnavur working for the young orphan children. Many of the missionaries and most of my sisters and brothers have now passed over to live eternally with Christ.

# CONTENTS

Acknowledgments .................................................................ix

Chapter 1:  Salma Carunia's Home ........................................1
Chapter 2:  Let Me Tell You about My Home! ......................10
Chapter 3:  Life in Our House: The School Compound ............50
Chapter 4:  Back to School .........................................74
Chapter 5:  The Missionaries .......................................92
Chapter 6:  Nura Sittie .............................................119
Chapter 7:  Christina ...............................................146
Chapter 8:  Life in Dohnavur .......................................164
Chapter 9:  The Adolescent Years: 1959 to 1965.................173
Chapter 10: My First Day Out of My Dohnavur Home! ..........231
Chapter 11: Life as a Timothy at Boarding School .................240
Chapter 12: Period of Uncertainty ................................268
Chapter 13: Bangalore, South India .............................291
Chapter 14: Bible Seminary .......................................309
Chapter 15: Institution Life: Every Day New Experiences .........323
Chapter 16: A Job at Last! In the Himalayas .....................343
Chapter 17: Tibetan Children .....................................352
Chapter 18: A Very Big Responsibility ...........................361
Chapter 19: A Great Prophecy Comes through Mr. Thomas......372
Chapter 20: The Trials and Miracles in Making My Passport .....382
Chapter 21: Another Revelation: God's Intervention ..............404
Chapter 22: At Last! A Visa to Study Abroad ......................411
Chapter 23: Arriving in America with Only One Dollar Left!....416

Notes and Endnotes ............................................................425
Postscript.............................................................................439
Published Works and Articles ..............................................443

## ACKNOWLEDGMENTS

My story could not have been finished in proper form and better language without the help of several others whom I wish to thank. The initial editing was done by Neal Ostman, CPA in Texas, U.S.A. with the assistance of Dilip Chouguley, LLM, and Ini Chouguley, BEd, MA, from India. Mary Anne McLean from our book club (First Presbyterian Church, Chicago Heights, Illinois) initiated the idea of putting my stories on paper some thirty-five years ago. Also, my thanks to Dr. Jacky and Rosie Saunders, PhD in England, U.K. Special thanks to Richard Hatch in Irving, Texas, U.S.A. for his great help in arranging the pictures presented.

Above all, in both regards, "This is the Lord's doing; it is marvelous to our eyes" (Psalm 118:23).

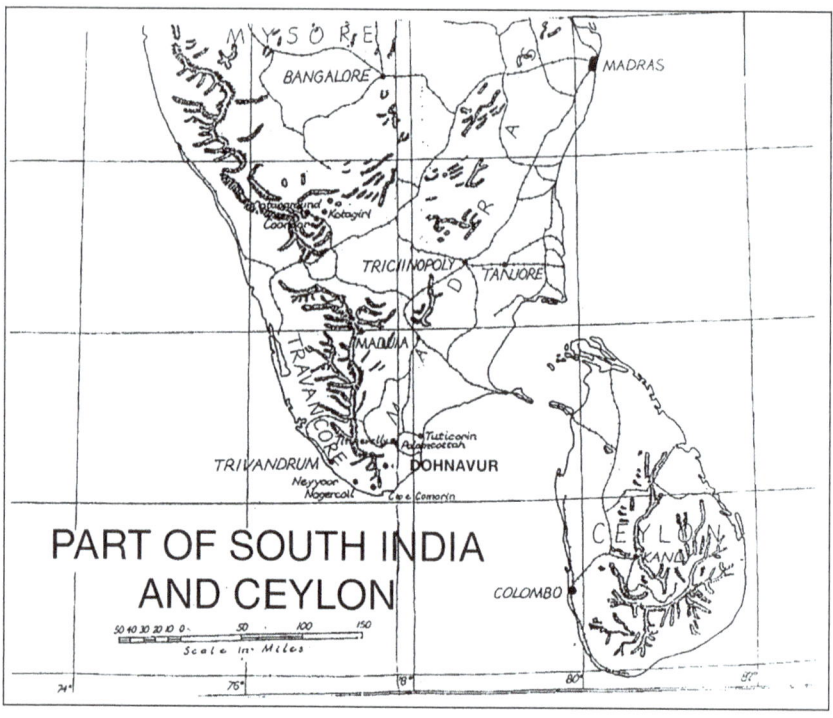

Dohnavur Fellowship map, showing where
Salma Carunia and many other orphans were raised in the
fellowship's children's home by Amy Carmichael.

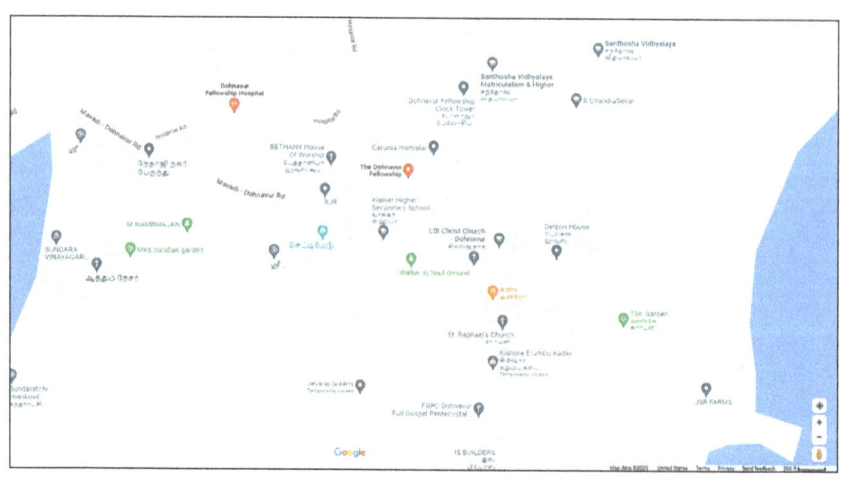

# CHAPTER 1

## Salma Carunia's Home
### The Dohnavur Fellowship, Tirunelveli District, Tamil Nadu, South India

*Not a single sparrow can fall to the ground
without your father's knowing.*

—Matthew 10:29

*The pen is mightier than the sword.*

—Edward Bulwer-Lytton

(Heb. 4:12; Isa. 49:2; Rev. 2:12)

My story began when I was placed in the hands of Amy Carmichael who founded the Dohnavur Fellowship in 1901; she was known as Amma (Mother). To know me, I must tell you about the special place where I grew up, the Dohnavur Fellowship, a Christian orphanage in South India. You will learn about its founder and the missionaries who dedicated their lives to saving and raising unwanted and forgotten little children. This book will also tell you how my sisters, brothers, and I lived and learned, and all of the miracles that have happened to me, and now I am able to tell my story to the world.

At Dohnavur, the missionaries were our mothers, fathers (for the boys), teachers, and trainers. All gave selflessly of their time and lives. Some were as loving as any true mother, and a few took a special interest in little Salma, but I am getting ahead of myself.

The Dohnavur Fellowship has always been a beautiful place. I will describe its flowers, trees, and the bungalows where I lived, played, worked, and slept. This all happened with my fellow orphan sisters. We grew up together, and you will learn of those who were close to me. As an orphan at Dohnavur, I had many wonderful sisters with whom I have maintained a lifelong relationship.

## How I Became Salma

Once upon a time, on November 29, 1944, a baby girl was brought to the famed missionary Amy Carmichael. The baby weighed less than three pounds. Amy took the child in one hand and said, "This child's face is very peaceful." It was during the dreadful time of the Second World War. She named the child Salma; *Salma* means "peace" (*Shalom* in Hebrew; in Arabic, it is *Salaam-Alaikum*; in Tamil, it is *Salam*). This is the key word in the polite and proper greetings of *shalom, shalom aleichem (Jewish), as-salamuy 'alaikum (Islamic)* (they mean, "peace be upon you").

I was ten years old when I found my name in the Bible in 1 Chronicles 2:11–12 KJV: "And Nahshon begat Salma, and Salma begat Boaz, and Boaz begat Obed, and Obed begat Jesse…David." This is the lineage of Jesus Christ, our Savior.

## Who Brought Me to Amy Carmichael? Evu!

Evu, a Dohnavur fellowship girl, had been given in marriage by Amy as per the custom of arranged marriages in India. She lived with her husband, Mr. Sanjeevan, in the nearby town Palayamkottai, about two hours' bus journey from Dohnavur. The town was developed and prosperous, for many years ago, an Indian king had lived there in his castle (*Kottai* means castle in Tamil).

## CHRIST IS IN ME

Amy had asked Evu to watch for children needing a home. Evu faithfully brought many babies and little children who had lost their parents to the orphanage. This gave many children a chance to have a richer life and avoid starvation or other dangers. In those days and even today, life in India was very hard for the poor and unprotected. Evu brought many children to this lovely place. However, the babies always had to be approved by Amy Carmichael to enter the fellowship.

Evu brought me to Amy Carmichael's bungalow. After Amy had given me a name, I was taken to the large baby nurseries and put into the care of my dear Mother Kirubai, the Tamil name in English translated as Grace. Amy hired wet nurses from the surrounding villages, who would come around the clock to give their milk to the babies of the fellowship. They also had medical checkups twice a week at the Fellowship Hospital. At this time, this was performed by British doctors and nurses.

Thanks to the care and love of these people at the Dohnavur Fellowship, I survived! I have no regrets that my father gave me away to the famous missionary Amy Carmichael, for I would not have survived without special care and help. And I am glad I had a very clean, healthy, and happy place to live, learn, and grow. I am very privileged to have been raised at the Dohnavur Fellowship, which I call my home!

When I was fifteen years old and getting ready to go to boarding school, I got my birth certificate which showed I was born on November 23. Since I learned about my birth date, I have looked forward to celebrating my birthday on November 23 every year. But the Dohnavur Fellowship celebrates only the coming day and never the birthday. The only exception was the birthday of Amy Carmichael, which is celebrated even today on December 16, with a great feast for the whole family. For many years, it was celebrated on the field where the clock tower stood. See picture on page 159.

When I was in my late twenties, I found out that I was born as the fifth child in a family and had four brothers. My father was a judge in the big town of Palayamkottai. My mother died giving birth to me. I weighed less than three pounds and had little hope of surviving. My father didn't know what to do. Under these circumstances, the British doctor at the hospital told him about Dohnavur

Fellowship, the children's home, where I could be cared for and be safe, so my father agreed. Evu was called to the hospital. On November 29, 1944, when I was six days old, she brought me to the Dohnavur Fellowship. Traveling by bus, she arrived at sundown and went into Amy Carmichael's bungalow and gave me to her.

I learned all this because Evu, who brought me to Amy Carmichael, talked about me with her close friend, Tara. She was one of the senior ladies who worked in the Dohnavur Office. Evu had warned Tara that this information should be kept secret to protect the children. One day, Tara told this secret to her friend Sendu, who told me when I was in my twenties. She passed away in August of 2024 at age 91.

Whenever Evu visited the fellowship, she rested at her friend Tara's house. Evu would always send a message to the children's compound to fetch me. I would run to her and get a big hug. She enjoyed seeing me as I grew up. I was a very active child, always climbing trees and running around. She would kiss me, give me some small gift, and then off I would go and climb the trees again. In fact, we had the most beautiful hundred-year-old tamarind trees all around the compounds.

Entrance to Dohnavur Fellowship. Evu entered through this gate with baby Salma, who was only six days old, and brought her to Amy Carmichael.

Deva Arul and Salma Carunia (right) at age nine sitting with their slates outside the fellowship home school. They used sea urchin spines as quills to write with.

Dohnavur Fellowship became Salma's home, along with all of Amy Carmichael's children, called Starry Cluster, for they are many.

## Who Was the Amazing Amy Carmichael (1867–1951)?

(The following is from the book *Amy Carmichael of Dohnavur Fellowship* by Frank Houghton, first published January 1, 1953, and some of the pictures are taken from the book *Lotus Buds* by Amy Wilson Carmichael, Keswick missionary, first published in 1909.)

Amy Carmichael was born at Millisle, In County Down, Northern Ireland, on December 16th, 1867. In 1895 she came to India as a missionary. She studied the language at a village in the Tirunelveli District, Madras State. In 1901 a seven-year-old girl, who had run away from a Hindu temple, was brought to Amy. She discovered by inquiry and research about the Devadasi system. "Devadasi" means servant of God, Deva (GOD) Dasi (servant). This was an ancient religious practice or custom in the southern part of India started in the 7th Century. In which a girl in her pre-puberty was dedicated to worship and serve a deity in a temple for the rest of her life. She would be 'married' to the deity. In addition to taking care of the temple and performing rituals, these women also learned and practiced classical Indian artistic traditions such as dances and classical music. Their social status was high. Devadasis were respected members of the society as it was believed that they are eternally married, one who is never widowed. And their presence in marriage ceremony for the purpose of making mangalasutra (mangala, holy, auspicious. Sutra, thread, a necklace that the groom ties round the bride's neck) for marriage was considered auspicious and compulsory.

But this religious practice deteriorated during medieval period. Because of their financial problem they became mistress of royals and rich men. The devadasis were exploited by the rich, powerful upper-class people and on the other side their economic needs did not allow them to leave, ultimately, they were driven to prostitution. Amy was convinced that God had brought these facts to her knowledge with a purpose, so that she should rescue and make a home for the Children who, for this or any other reason, were in danger of immoral exploitation.

Moved with their plight Amy founded the Dohnavur Fellowship to provide a safe haven for these girls. In the coming years she was joined by missionary Men and Women from various countries except the United States of America. The devadasi system was abolished by law in 1988.

Amy kept the record of 'her children' confidential. This was for fear that their relatives or temple authorities might come later and claim them, especially once the child reached the age for marriage. For it was then a common custom in India for parents to arrange the marriage of a 10 to 12 years-old child.

Amy Carmichael's home in Northern Ireland, where she lived with her parents.

Amy's family with her mother

Amy as a teenager

Amy's children, Salma and Devarul

Salma at age 19

Amma (*mother* in Tamil), the amazing Amy Carmichael.

Amy Carmichael's bungalow in Dohnavur Fellowship, in South India.

## CHRIST IS IN ME

This is the gate that children were brought to Amy Carmichael's bungalow when they were saved from perilous situations.

...Neither wasting nor destruction within your borders;
But you shall call your walls Salvation, And
your gates Praise. —Isaiah 60:18

# CHAPTER 2

## Let Me Tell You about My Home!

In 1901, Amy Carmichael started an orphanage and children's home in the small village of Dohnavur, Tirunelveli District, in southern India, called the Dohnavur Fellowship to provide a safe haven for the thousands of girls who were in danger and needed a home. Later, it started to take boys in 1918. Amy took the Tamil name, Anantha Carunia. The children of Dohnavur Fellowship took Amy's Tamil name as their surname. The boys use Anantha (happiness) and the girls Carunia (kindness) after their first names.

Dohnavur Fellowship was always a family, never an institution. Amy was the mother, loving and loved by all. As the family grew, its activities grew: babies' nurseries led to a dairy farm, rice lands, fruit and vegetable gardens, tailoring, kitchen, laundry, workshops, weaving—a model village spread over four hundred acres of land, even a mission hospital.

Upon arrival in Dohnavur, Amy Carmichael gave everyone a Tamil name. The missionary ladies were called Sitties (Tamil for *auntie*), and the men were called Annachies (Tamil for *elder brother*). The local women who joined Amy initially and, later, the girls who grew up in the fellowship and took up fellowship work were called Accal (*elder sister*). There was also quite a big group of boys who grew up in Dohnavur and offered their services to the fellowship and remained bachelors. They were also called Annachies and lived in Vanacharbu, working in different areas such as agriculture, workshops, hospital, and boys' school. They received no salaries, only a small allowance for personal needs. Everyone was dressed in blue-colored clothes. The ladies in saris and blouses and the men in veshti (lungi) and open-neck vests.

All the children also had blue uniforms. Children from two years to five years old wore strap knickers. The children ages six to eleven years old wore sleeveless dresses. Those twelve years and older wore a wonderful blue sari. All the dresses were made from cotton and would last for years! Our own Dohnavur Fellowship people made them, men and women, who worked on a loom, weaving our clothes and other goods like sheets and towels. The children of each age group all dressed the same, no differences.

Amy felt this would help all the children to be treated the same—no one getting more and no one being left out, no partiality.

There were three babies' nurseries, and each had two or three helpers, for in those days, they may have had about fifty babies under two years old. I was a six-day-old baby given to Kirubai (Grace) Accal, who cared for me and loved me very dearly. The whole fellowship always wondered why Salma was so special, especially since Grace had raised or looked after hundreds of babies who had gone through her hands and nursery; she faithfully worked there for forty-five years. Her bed was outside the nursery, where she and her assistants would rest, sleeping when they could, at night or during the day, rising when they heard the babies crying. The babies are kept in a white cotton linen hammock, hung from the roof, which can be rocked. See picture on page 39.

When I outgrew the milk of the wet nurses, and as cow's milk was hard to come by, Amy's friends in England sent tins of Glaxo milk. I survived. When I left Grace's nursery and went to the children's compound, I was allowed to go back and visit her only every Sunday evening for an hour.

Grace and I bonded as though she were my mother. She loved me dearly till her death in 1974. She had the joy of seeing me grown-up and educated. I went to a Bible seminary and then to work as a dean in an English school (Wynberg-Allen) located way up north, in the Himalayas. I would see her one last time when I came home on vacation from this position.

Salma (left) at age forty-three with Sangarue (middle), who was her wet nurse from six days old until she was eight months old. When Sangarue went to the hospital to get medicine, Anihala, Pharma D (right), brought her to meet with Salma, who was home in India to visit Dr. Ponnalari in 1989.

## How the Fellowship Compounds Were Arranged when I Was a Child

Six compounds in which about five hundred children lived according to age and gender. The first had baby nurseries for both boys and girls from a few days old to two years old. After that, from age two till they finish grade 2, girls lived in the Square and the boys in Vistara. They were looked after by accals (elder sisters). When they reached grade 3, the girls lived in two compounds, the Round and Samadhanam. The boys lived in Vanacharbu, which means "open fields of woods." Here, they were looked after by the Annachies, and I have heard them saying they miss the accals who raised them from babies to 8 years old.

Boys and girls never mixed even though fifty to sixty small boys who lived in Vistara went to the same home school called Jeevananda. This school was for kindergarten to second grade. The boys and girls each had separate classrooms. After that, from grade 3 to 7, the girls attended Jeevalia and the boys Vanacharbu School. All three, Jeevananda, Jeevalia, and Vanacharbu, were called home schools.

In the center of the compounds stood a church, which Amy called the House of Prayer. It had a high tower with tubular bells. One of the girls would climb up the tower stairs to play the designated songs as we entered the church. And again, after we all said the last prayer: "Blessing, and glory, and wisdom, and thanksgiving, and honor, and power, and might, be unto our God forever and ever. Amen" (Revelation 7:12). Songs were played daily at 6:00 a.m., 1:00 p.m., and 9:00 p.m. to mark time.

This helped the children learn the songs which became more meaningful as they grew older. They helped strengthen one on the journey into adulthood. Children were encouraged to memorize the scriptures, especially the Psalms; they had been set to various tunes. Every Sunday, we sang them at 7:00 p.m. in the singsong service. To me, it was the stronghold of my soul. God's words became written on my heart and in my head and helped me in my life's journey. I still sing them often. "Thy word is a lamp unto my feet and a light unto my path. I have sworn and will perform it that I will keep thy righteous judgments" is one of my favorite passages from Psalm 119, which has 176 verses. As a schoolgirl, I memorized many Psalms but only part of Psalm 119!

## Your Coming Day

Amy Carmichael celebrated the day she adopted us, called the Coming Day. I celebrate my Coming Day every year on November 29.

Everyone's Coming Day was celebrated on the nearest Sunday. Then, in the House of Prayer, they would call out your name and pray for you. This was very special. When I was a young child, I happily waited for my Coming Day to visit my mother, Grace, in her cottage. I would spend more time with her on that very special day.

Sunday started with an English service at 9:00 a.m. After the service, the missionaries and everyone came from the compounds of the fellowship to greet the Coming Day girl at her cottage.

We wore a little sari, which would be blue, green, purple, or pink colored. We put jasmine and pink rose flowers around our heads that looked like crowns and had such a beautiful fragrance. The house was even more decorated on that day, by the head of the household, with beautiful vases full of colorful flowers, all giving off natural perfume. The wonderful scent of pink cabbage roses would permeate the entire cottage.

The Coming Day girl went to Amy's bungalow at 8:00 a.m., before the church service, and got to choose a little gift from the Coming-Day cupboard, such as a small decorated plastic dish or container. Then Amy's helper, Neela, gave the girl a small paper bin with the hard candies. The Coming Day girl got two for herself and each child in her cottage got one. This was special as we did not get hard candies except for Christmas and Easter. On glorious Christmas Day, each child received ten candies; on Easter, each child got eight candies. Because we weren't treated to so many sweets, I never had a big urge to eat them, and at seventy-nine, I still have good teeth and no cavities!

Amy let us visit her until she had a second fall and became a complete invalid in 1931, when she was sixty-four and had just bought a house outside of the fellowship grounds for the missionaries to learn Tamil. She went to inspect the house one evening, walked to the backyard, and fell in a hole being dug for the outhouse. This damaged her hip, and she became bedridden and lived with a lot of pain for the next twenty years. She used those years to write many books and poems. Her workers would set them to music. Visit http://dohnavurfellowship.org for more information.

Interior of Amy Carmichael's bungalow. On the wall to the left is mounted the head of a tiger that was endangering the children's cottages one night. When Amy became bedridden, a bed was placed in the middle of this room, where she spent the rest of her days writing books, poems, and songs for her children, and letters to her friends abroad.

## The Square, Children's Compound

When children reached two years of age, they were sent from the babies' nursery to live in the children's compound called the

Square. It was called this since the cottages in this area were built around the meadow in that fashion. We lived in the Square until we were six to seven years old. There, Amithal Accal raised me. She taught us many things, such as how to dress and eat with the fingers of our right hand, for up to that time, everything was done for us. We were washed, fed, and dressed by the ladies. In India, the left hand is never used for eating food as it is used for cleaning the bottom after attending to nature's call.

Amithal Accal taught us the creation story and a song about it. Eight children, all about the same age, were in my group: Saro, Tara, Usila, Jeya, Satya, Chella, Jeyavalli, and me. I learned the creation song quickly as Amithal sang it for us every night at bedtime. It told of how God created heaven and earth in the beginning, and in six days, he created all things. I liked the song and kept singing, "Let there be light"; that's what happened on the first day. Before then, nothing existed. Then God separated the light, called it the day, and the dark, night. On the second day, he divided the water. On the third day, the dry land appeared, and he separated the sea; on the fourth day, the sun and moon were created. As a child, I could see the sun in the morning and the moon and stars at night, as I often slept outside on the house's veranda. Because there were no electric lights or city lights, the sky was dark, and I could see the countless stars shine and twinkle! Therefore, at a very early age, I learned how things came to be, as it was taught to us from the Bible.[1]

I loved the words, "The grassland appeared. The fruit trees came up," for I could easily relate to it as we had many trees in our children's compound. In the middle of the square, there was a large meadow where we played daily. We had fruit trees of papaya, mango, and custard apple growing in our backyards. See "Imitation of Christ" by Dr. Ben M. Carter at http://www.drbenmcarter.com and also available on www.christianfaithpublishing.com.

---

[1] See the website www.christianfaithpublishing.com for my late husband's book, *The Defective Image: How Darwinism Fails to Provide an Adequate Account of the World.*

# Red Velvet Bugs!

In the rainy season, in that green meadow, there occurred a miracle! Small red velvet bugs would suddenly appear from the ground! They were crawling everywhere—thousands of them! Each had six soft legs. Its back seemed like velvet, soft and cushioned, very bright red, contrasting with the blue evolvulus lace flowers. Those flowers were part of the morning glory family and seemed like nature's velvet. They were very pretty blue.

When these little red velvet bugs appeared, we children would run around, catch them, keep them in a little box we got from the missionaries, and place them in our pockets.

Years later, I discovered that those little boxes originally held the missionaries' toothpaste from England. Today, when I look back on my childhood times—playing in the meadow—it seems I was in a little heaven.

Another amazing bug came during the season from October to February: a beautiful neon-green golden-headed beetle with pincers for jaws; they would appear on the tamarind trees. We would catch them, put them in the small cardboard box, and then place some sand and tamarind leaves, which they liked to eat. We would then wait for them to lay eggs!

The bugs' legs had small hooks like a grasshopper's legs, so they would easily fasten on our blue dresses.

## Growing Up

Everything changed suddenly. Our house mother, Amithal, got a new set of two-year-old girls. This meant it was time for us older children to move to another cottage. At age five, we were given a blue sleeveless dress that reached our knees. It was a big promotion for us little girls, leaving behind our strap knickers. We ran around and showed it to everybody; we were so happy to have grown a little older and started kindergarten.

## Jeevanantha: The Joy of Life

Let me take a moment and explain our education system. The home school, from kindergarten to second grade, for children aged five to seven, was known as Jeevanantha. Lola supervised the first and second grades.

The middle school from grade 3 to grade 7, which you will hear about later in my story, was called Jeevalia. The child's age when leaving middle school may vary because some children have to repeat a grade. After passing seventh grade, if considered a good prospect, you went out of Dohnavur to boarding school from eighth to twelfth grade for the Secondary School Leaving Certificate Examination (SSLC). After this, almost everyone received vocational training as nurses, teachers, or typing. Very few got a college education.

Those who could not pass seventh grade stayed in the fellowship, where they performed hard work for the rest of their lives. This was almost my fate.

The missionary home school had very strict rules and regulations, supporting a strong foundation for education. The exams were conducted monthly and at the end of the terms. Passing marks were 50 percent in every subject. At the end of the year, one had to score an average of 50 percent in each subject to be promoted to the next grade.

One day, as usual, Kareema Accal, my kindergarten teacher, was telling us a Bible story. She often used a flannel board, on which you could attach paper cutout figures, as a teaching tool. The story that day was about Jacob, who dreamed that he saw a ladder reaching from earth to heaven (Genesis 28:12), which was illustrated with a picture of a ladder. I was listening intently and looking at that picture. It fascinated me to see how those angels went up and down on a big ladder while Jacob slept. At the top, I saw somebody standing with glory all around, and that was God! And at that little age, I wanted to reach God! Later in my life, I realized that I had to climb up this spiritual ladder.

Then we learned a song about this story: "We are climbing Jacob's ladder. We are climbing Jacob's ladder. We are climbing Jacob's ladder, soldiers of the cross!" Although I did not understand what a soldier of the cross meant as a five-year-old, I just knew I wanted to climb up the ladder and reach out to touch God.

Suddenly, I realized all the children had left for lunch, but I sat still, gazing at that picture, wishing I could fly like an angel to reach God. It never left my mind.

Also, at five years old, I had an amazing dream. It happened like this. Mevara Sittie (Miss Lilian Crowley), a Canadian missionary, would come every evening to take us for a walk. She would often take us to the west-side dairy farm, where the fellowship had coconut groves, a wonderful place to walk. When we were heading to the dairy farm, I held her hand, and we went around the fence. Suddenly, she stopped as our clock tower started to strike six o'clock, for everybody was required to stand where they were and pray every time the clock tower hit the hour. That was something Amy Carmichael wanted her family to do.

The clock tower also regulated our lives, for no one had a wristwatch. Our Big Ben clock tower could be heard for miles! A large gong was also hung atop the silo at the east farm to announce the work hours. A worker would climb the ladder to ring the gong every day at 6:30 a.m. and again at 5:30 p.m. This would signal to all the workers living in the villages around the Dohnavur Fellowship could come to work on time and leave for home in the evening. They worked in our compounds from 6:30 a.m. to 5:30 p.m. with a lunch break from 11:30 to 2:30 p.m. On Fridays, they would line up at the office house to get their wages in cash, which in those days were sometimes seven to ten annas for the week's work.

After the six strikes of the clock tower and the prayer, we continued and walked around the dairy farm when Mevara Sittie stopped to show us something. That's when I saw my vision! I saw an angel with wings on the top of the roof. And he wanted to show all the children how he could fly. Could this be due to hearing about Jacob's ladder in class? Since then, I have always wanted to fly and soar with the angels to go upward to heaven. Then the angel shouted and said, "I will show you how to fly," and then he flew off while I watched and finally disappeared.

At 6:15 p.m., as we returned home, after saying good night to dozens of cows when everybody was coming around the Wicket Gate, I waited under a neem tree. Suddenly, I saw the angel again, sitting on a branch above my head. So I talked to him, asking, "How could I go to heaven?"

He said, "You could someday go to heaven if you are a good girl."

At that time, Mevara Sittie looked back and told me to hurry up, so I ran to join the group.

I never forgot this vision. When I woke up the next morning, I ran to the house mother and told her that I had seen an angel, and he said that if I was a good girl, I could go to heaven one day. That was the understanding of a five-year-old child: to be a good girl, but this dream is still vivid in my head. And that place where it happened and even the same trees are still standing there in the dairy farm at my home in India, in the Dohnavur Fellowship.

I also remember another story in the kindergarten scripture class, illustrated with the flannel graph pictures. It was about Elijah, who went up to heaven in a whirlwind of chariots of fire. I always wanted to go up into heaven whenever I saw white cloud puffs in the blue sky. I wanted to go up because I thought God was up there, just like when I saw him on the flannel board in the story of Jacob's ladder. I sat close by the flannel board and saw Elijah going up to meet the Lord. I was deeply moved and decided I wanted to go to God. But could I go in a whirlwind? I trusted and hoped I could also go to God that way. "As for God, His ways are always perfect" (2 Kings 2:1). See picture on page 47.

One day, Saro, Usila, Tara, and I were playing in the meadow on the jungle gym with a big wooden slide. We were climbing up, sliding down, and running around. I still remember it was five minutes before 10:30 a.m. We were standing under the slide, and I asked God, "In my little faith, please let me come up like Elijah." So I leaped from my feet, and can you believe it? I went three or four feet up to the top of the slide! And fear came over me! Then, I was dropped down slowly, and all the girls around me saw it, but I don't know whether they understood what had happened. I remembered how Peter became afraid while walking on water at Jesus's command and began to sink, so Jesus said to him, "O you of little faith, why did you doubt?" (Mathew 14:29–31). After a time, about 10:30, a lady named Champuka, the helper in our house, came near the slide and said, "It's time for you girls to come and drink some water," so we all went back home.

I have never forgotten how I leaped three or four feet above the ground level. It was my little faith! That faith I still have kept. It was given to me at this very early age by hearing and seeing the scripture stories: how God took Elijah up and how Jacob's ladder led to God. Those things are very important for a child: to grow up to be trusting God.

Another story that left a deep impression on me was when the kindergarten teacher told us about the ten virgins (Matthew 25:6), "Behold the bridegroom is coming, go out to meet him." The bridegroom is coming! The teacher told the story: five had oil, but five foolish virgins did not have oil to replenish their lamps. Now this situation was understandable to us, for in the villages at that time, we used hurricane lanterns, which we had to fill with oil daily. This must be done every day because that was the only source of light during the whole night. When children needed to get up and go to use the chamber pot, they had to have light to see the way. It got pitch-black after 7:00 p.m., and we could not see anything in front of us. Then there was no electricity in rural India.

But this is a bigger picture: the bridegroom coming is our Redeemer, God. The ten virgins were all waiting for the bridegroom but did not know when he would arrive. Five virgins were unprepared; they did not keep oil in their lamps. Then suddenly, at midnight, a big voice called out, "Behold the bridegroom is coming." I found it very surprising that the five without the oil, even though they had time, didn't get prepared. So they were begging the others at the last minute, saying, "Please give us some oil" (Matthew 25:1–13).

As I have grown older, I understand who is coming: the bridegroom is the Holy Spirit! We need to ask God to fill us with His Holy Spirit. One must receive it from God. As a child, I understood that we must be ready, and even to this day, I am very much alarmed at the thought of being unprepared. It was a good lesson for me in my early childhood. Now that I drive a car, I do not like seeing my tank nearly empty. I fill the gas tank in my car when it gets to half of a tank, so I am ready to go anytime. I recall my kindergarten Bible story time and never thought I'd have my own car and be driving in America one day!

How deep was the impact of these Bible stories in my childhood days? This is illustrated by another incident concerning a missionary at Dohnavur, Devasamathanam Annachie (Godfrey Webb-Peploe), an Englishman and Cambridge graduate who was a coleader with Amy Carmichael, would come to the children's compound to play with us. I remember running to his house in the boys' compound; he always carried me on his shoulder. He was very tall, six feet, six inches. He would even give us rides on his bicycle. We loved him like our father.

In 1949, one day, when we children were all playing at our house, the church bell started pealing. The song it played was "Forever with the Lord." They announced to the family that someone had gone to be with the Lord! Everybody wanted to know who it was. Then we found out that Devasamathanam Annachie had passed away. How sad, very sad, we children realized he wouldn't be coming to our cottages to play with us anymore.

His funeral occurred in the afternoon; they bury the body on the same day in India. Champu'ka, the lady looking after us, was crying while sitting on the windowsill. (All the other adults were at the funeral in the church.) Now, there were about eight of us children in that house. So I summoned all the children and said, "Let's play the game of bridegroom." I told them all to go into an alcove far away in the house, and I would stand in the middle and shout, "The bridegroom is coming!" Then you all must run past me and through the big door into the main room. And I said, "The door is now open," but when I say, "The bridegroom is coming," everybody must rush past me because I'm going to shut the door. Whoever is left behind cannot meet the Bridegroom, the Lord. So they all agreed, and we played the game. To my surprise, Ponnamai, the oldest, was left behind when I shut the door. She took it so seriously that she started crying, thinking she was not ready to enter into heaven!

And later, when I grew up, Champu'ka, the lady who had been taking care of us, told me, "You were a real comfort. When you were only a five-year-old and everyone was mourning the loss of Devasamathanam Annachie, you played the bridegroom game, and that comforted and made me happy." So you see, even as a child, I was conscious of God very much and wanted to go to heaven. It was all because the Bible stories were read to us children daily.

Godfrey Webb-Peploe, an English missionary who graduated from Cambridge University in England. He worked with Amy as coleader overseeing the boys' compound from 1926 until he passed away in 1949. I know that one day I will see him in heaven.

Christmas was the most eagerly awaited event in our childhood. We would get up very early on Christmas Day; children, as a rule, got up at seven o'clock, but on Christmas Day, we were woken up at five o'clock! We put on a little woolen vest, for it was cold. We carried the handmade shades that covered the hurricane lanterns just like the pictures of shepherds in the fields watching their flocks or Mary and

Joseph by the manger. And we would all go around the compound, singing our Tamil Christmas songs and carols. Amy's first generation had written these songs of children. We would do the same on New Year's Day. These are part of my wonderful happy childhood memories.

## Premalu Sittie (Helen Bradshaw)
## Missionary from Liverpool, UK

We children went to a big bungalow to eat breakfast and lunch. Premalu Sittie, in charge of the Square, served us porridge in the mornings and rice in the afternoon. We would then go to Veera Accal, who would put some rasam or sambar on it. About eighty to one hundred of us ate together under her supervision, and we had to finish all the food in our bowls before we were allowed to go. Many would return for a second serving, but sometimes, I could not finish even the one bowl of rice. Premalu Sittie would see to this, and being so kind, she would take me to her house which was in the same compound. There I would stand in her backyard with my rice bowl and allow the birds to help me empty it. Then I would show her the empty bowl, and she would let me go home.

At noon, she would go and eat lunch at the bungalow where all the missionaries ate their food, which was prepared by the butlers. The missionaries ate Western food, including bread and butter, which we never ate. We children ate only Indian food, rice and curry cooked in coconut oil on the wood fire. No baking was done for the Indians in those days!

Premalu Sittie loved me dearly. I still remember that she often let me play with dolls that came from England in her house. She also made a scrapbook for me, and I would choose a picture to stick in it every evening. She encouraged my interest in nature. As a little girl, I always held her hand in the evenings when she took us children for a walk outside the fellowship campus.

I knew that Premalu Sittie loved me dearly, and I loved her very much, for when the time came to choose the books from the children's library in her house, I always chose the same book. It was a book with a picture of the rainbow on its cover. I would take it home every time and enjoyed looking at all the colors on the cover. Today, it seems that she knew this was the way to occupy the lively (mischievous) and always active Salma.

Later in my life, a very sad day came when my beloved Premalu Sittie retired and returned to Liverpool, England. She had come to work at the orphanage in December of 1916 and finally retired in 1952. Then she was gone forever. She was my first English mother who loved me dearly, and I never got to see her again because she passed away on March 29, 1972. I am very much looking forward to seeing her again in heaven.

# First Punishment

In 1946, the Dohnavur Fellowship built a printing press, and a Swiss nun, Naveena Sittie (Sister Paula Frei), started running it. It was used to print exam papers for the home school and other things. We children liked her because she gave us a cocoa party on the terrace of her printing press every Saturday at 4:00 p.m. We enjoyed it very much. But one of my visits to the printing press, as a six-year-old, was under most unhappy circumstances.

It so happened that Premalu Sittie (Helen Bradshaw) had a fish tank on her veranda. It was always partially covered with a wooden plank, just a little opening for the fish to breathe. I liked Premalu Sittie very much, and sometimes when I could visit her, I would wait at her door on the big veranda. One Friday evening, as all the other children were going for a walk, my house mother, Ananthie Accal, told me I should go to Premalu Sittie's house and wait at her door.

When I got there, Premalu Sittie took me to the veranda and showed me a dead fish covered with ants! She asked me, "Did you take this fish out of its glass fish tank and leave it on the floor?" I said, "I did *not do it*." I had no idea how it came to be on the floor, and I was also shocked to see a dead fish on the floor.

She then held my hand and led me to the printing press building. Naveena Sittie, a Swiss nun and Helen's friend, sat at her desk. They spoke in English, which I did not understand. Naveena Sittie told me to go and sit in the corner. After ten minutes, she called me over and asked me to show her the palm of my left hand. Then suddenly, she applied press ink to the palm of my hand with a small brush and told me to go and sit in the corner again. She got busy with her work while I waited and waited, holding my left hand tightly closed, afraid to look at my palm. Finally, after what must have been about half an hour, she asked me to go over to a big sink and wash my hand. I went to the sink and saw a pedal that I used, stepping on it with my foot and leaning forward to get my hands into the sink. I was amazed to hear and see the rush of water! I realized this when I pressed the pedal repeatedly. Finally, I tried to wash my palm, but the black press ink would not wash off!

    Naveena Sittie told me to go back to the corner. She came over and told me my sin was like the black ink on my palm. Only the blood of Jesus can wash it away. I was not paying much attention to the second part of her preaching. I knew I did not catch or throw the fish on the floor. I had no sin to be cleansed. But I began to wonder about my wildness. I always climbed on every tree in the compound, shouting and singing loudly. I never knew how to stand or sit still as I was always busy, for instance, trying to catch butterflies in the day and fireflies in the evening. See endnotes on page 426-427.

    When I returned to my house, I was very confused and sad. But as a little child, I had no real voice to say, "I did not do it!" Later, I remembered seeing a cat in her house, which used to roam around there, and once I saw it sitting on top of the wooden plank on the fish tank. But I did not recall when I was accused of killing the fish. We grew up thinking that the missionaries could do no wrong, and above all, we were never to question them. Eventually, the spot faded off my palm. But before that, my joyful nature returned, and I played and sang as before from the top of the trees that were almost touching the sky.

    The children returned from their walkabout at 6:30 p.m. Since there were fifty to seventy-five of them, they had not missed me. I came back about the same time. I did not want to show them my hand, which would not have interested them anyway, as we all just wanted to have our glass of milk and go to bed by seven o'clock. In those days, the children were in bed by 7:00 p.m. and up by 7:00 a.m.—no TVs or other distractions. This way, we had a good full night's rest, as growing children need sleep. Sadly, the times have changed, for I hear of and see friends' children stay up very late. I have also observed that these children cannot concentrate for very long. I am glad my little brain got twelve hours of sleep when I was growing up!

January 1951 saw the end of Amma's (Amy Carmichael) fifty-five years of unbroken, loving service in India. For two days, she had been unconscious. Then early morning on the eighteenth, the music of one of her songs was played on the House of Prayer bells. Amma had herself asked that this be done when the time came to let us all know that she was no longer with us but with the Lord she loved. The sound reached to all parts of the compound and, as we heard the bells, mixed with our deep sorrow was comfort that the words she had written were now so marvelously fulfilled for her:

> One thing have I desired my God of Thee,
> This will I seek thine house be home to me.
> I would not breathe an alien, other air,
> I would be with Thee, O Thou, fairest fair.
> For I would see the beauty of my Lord,
> And hear Him speak who is my heart's adored.
> O Love of Loves, and can such wonder dwell
> In Thy great name of names, Immanuel.
> Thou with Thy child, Thy child at home with Thee,
> O Lord my God, I love I worship Thee.

CHRIST IS IN ME

# The Round

Until we were seven years of age, someone, usually the house mother, bathed us and brushed our teeth. We used our pointer finger to brush our teeth, for we did not have toothbrushes or even toothpaste! For cleaning teeth, the kitchen staff would burn rice husk and distribute it to each house, where the ash would be kept in a bucket in the backyard. We children dipped into it every morning and held some ashes in our left palms. We would then pick up some ash with a wet pointer finger to smear on our teeth, brushing them with our fingers! The burnt rice husks made our teeth white and made a lovely smile! Also, we would sometimes use the twigs from the neem trees, chew the ends, and brush our teeth. The villagers at that time would break up bricks, pound them into the grit, and use it to clean their teeth.

When we reached age seven, we were considered school-age children and no longer little girls. About fifteen of us, six- to seven-year-olds, went to the Round schoolgirls' compound. The cottages were positioned here around the church called the House of Prayer. Its tubular bells were the only instrument played by a girl. Other devices, such as the organ, piano, and violins, were available only to the boys in those days!

In June 1951, my time at the children's compound, the Square, ended. Then I had to go to the school compound called Round. Premalu Sittie was responsible for deciding which child went to which house mother in the Round. She felt that she could trust her beloved Salma with Lola. Lola was one of the first three children of Amy Carmichael, so she had a lot of authority and power to protect little Salma. I believe my beloved Premalu Sittie saw what was coming in the days ahead. So to save her dear Salma and give her a great chance in life, she gave her to Lola. Lola was then around fifty-two, so they stopped adding children to her family. I was the *last one* that was added to her cottage's family. At that time, Lola had twenty-four other children for whom she was responsible.

On June 1, 1951, I arrived at the Round compound. It was a Friday evening, and there was a great crowd standing in front of a large hundred-year-old tamarind tree to welcome the newcomers. Each child is assigned to one of the house mothers to stay in their house. Each house is named according to Revelation 21:19–20 after the twelve foundation stones (precious stones) of the city wall of New Jerusalem.

Lola was also the compound's (Round) leader, for she was one of the first children to come to Amy. Lola arrived on January 13, 1901, when she was three. At that time, Amy had two other girls, Preena and Leela, and Lola joined them. Amy raised them as her children. When Amy passed away on January 18, 1951, her first generation of children were given senior positions of authority. They each carried out Amy's work fulfilling different roles and responsibilities.

As I will tell you later, Lola was a great protector and protected me from many harsh punishments from the school.

Lola came to meet me with her twenty-four children! I was one of the last girls to join her family. She asked Ponnalari to take me by my hand and bring me into Lola's family, and now there were twenty-five of us. Lola had two helpers. Ten girls stayed with the house mother, Leelarathina, at the house called Onyx. I stayed with Lola and the fifteen of us at the home called Carnelian. If anyone quizzed us about the twelve precious stones in the Bible, we could proudly recite them, for we memorized them. Premalu Sittie would come to Lola's house to see me every evening and kiss me good night!

Lola was known for her strictness, and any misbehavior was met with punishment. Lola's last set of children consisted of Ponnalari, Pushpaveni, Santhaevu, Pramotha, Jeevanathi, Jeyavanthi, Neelanathie, Lavanaleela, Prealulla, Dayaseelie, Dayamani, Davarul, Jeyavallie, Jayapushpam, and me. The last four were the same age as me. The others were two to three years older. I had lots of help with those older sisters, and our love for each other grew as much as, if not more than, blood sisters.

In this compound, one felt like a grown-up. Now I had to do everything by myself. When I was in the children's compound, a helpmate lived with the house mother in each house. These two ladies took care of us. They bathed and dressed us, brushed our teeth, and combed our hair. They would even wash our clothes every day.

When we needed to heed the call of nature, the children used a chamber pot (bucket), and the helpmate lady would even wash our bottoms with water. I had to learn to use the outhouse at the new Round school compound! (No more chamber pots except during the nights as the houses were locked at 9:00 p.m.)

The lavatory was a hole, six feet by eight feet wide and six feet deep, on which were laid two wide planks—that was it! One had to learn to stand on these planks and then squat carefully.

This wasn't very comforting for a six-year-old to see what looked like a bottomless pit! Thankfully, some older girls helped me learn how to use it. Indian custom is to wash our bottom with our left hand while pouring water from a mug held in the right hand, then always wash our hands, which makes us feel clean again.

There was a heap of sand next to the lavatory block pit, and when finished, you had to throw some sand into the hole. Once the pit filled up, they dug the next one. Now all that remained was sand, and nature's recycling occurred.

What a luxurious life I am living in the Western world, where most homes and buildings have indoor toilets! Even after a hundred years of existing, the Dohnavur Fellowship has an indoor bathroom only for visitors, no toilet paper, and the children still use water to clean.

The bungalows in the Round compound were beautiful and secure homes for us. All the Dohnavur houses/bungalows are built with red bricks because the sand at the foothills of Red Lake is reddish. Once the brick is made and baked, it looks pretty red. So the walls are red terra-cotta from the reddish colored earth of South India. What a beautiful contrast to the mass of greenery and blossoms outside! There are gardens next to and around the bungalows. Many have blooming oleanders of various colors. Their crimson, pink, and white flowers spread a sweet perfume. There are also red, pink, and white flowering hibiscus trees everywhere in the compound. A beautiful paradise of colors and smells surrounded us. The foothills of the western Ghats, also known as the Nilgiris (Blue Mountains), as a distant backdrop, making our Dohnavur home a picture-book place.

It takes a lot of hard work to keep it that way. The red floor tiles demand the most attention, for we sweep them with palm-leaf brooms or coconut leaves and scrub them with wet rags, on our hands and knees, until they shine enough that we can see our reflections.

Some children found the housework and the discipline that went with it hard to bear, especially in Lola's house.

We had two steel buckets, each with our names written on the outside on their bottom. These two buckets, with brooms and rags, became our companions from morning to evening. We learned hard work and responsibility at a very early age. Once, a guest asked what polish we use for the floor, and someone answered, "Elbow grease!"

We did not have running water either. We had to carry buckets of water from the bore wells. There were ten to fifteen houses and three to four hand pumps in each compound, and children from other houses also waited to get their turn to use the pump and fill their buckets.

It was hard to push down the thick steel pump handle. It was heavy, and I was small built. I tried to do it with all my strength, pushed it with my stomach, and stomped it with my foot to get the water to fill my buckets. Oh, what a hard time I had pumping water! There was no one to blame, for I was not growing as fast as the others of my age. See picture on page 85.

The pipes went down about fifty or ninety feet where the spring waters flowed underground. This water was the best sweet water to drink. I lived in a place where there was this wonderful abundance, and it reminds me of a song I used to sing:

God Is Seen All Around!

> Spring waters rise, fountains flow, rivers run, and
> all declare that God is there, in meadows, dressed
> in green, and God is seen all around.

The path around the houses also needed to be swept clean after sprinkling water to keep down the dust. Never was rubbish left around the house! It all looked clean year-round, for we little girls kept it clean, and as we grew older, we were assigned more places to clean around the compounds.

Dohnavur is full of beautiful plants and flowers that are a constant joy to the family. They demanded lots of watering. With our two buckets, we girls drew this water from the large cistern and carried it to the gardens and plants around our homes. The cistern's water came from wells in the vegetable garden. We would water the plants after school every day except Sundays. Lola had many plants around her house and a lovely rose garden with bushes in large pots. No one could ever be idle at Lola's house, for she had work for us all day long, from 5:00 a.m. to 5:30 p.m., except for school days!

Like the houses, our roofs were made with locally available materials. They were constructed with palmyra palm tree wood, a hard and durable timber. Here, we have acres of land filled with these trees. Many grow up to ninety feet tall! This is the official tree of Tamil Nadu. In Tamil culture, it is called a celestial tree because its top has broad palm leaves which look like a crown. This tree is highly respected as all its parts can be used for many types of food. Before the invention of paper, leaves were used as parchment for writing upon in ancient times. See picture on page 156.

These are known as palm-leaf manuscripts through which Tamil language and literature were preserved and transmitted. I will tell you more about the goodness of this tree. It is one of the most remarkable trees in the world.

In our kindergarten, we learned a song about it, which goes like this: "Palmyra palm, with leaves like a crown, what do you see when you look down? (The tree replies) 'I see hills like steps of stairs and nurseries and teddy bears!'"

Another interesting fact about these trees is religion and social status. In India, caste defines you. Your caste is everything, and you are born into this station. Those of the highest caste are called Brahman, the highest Hindu caste, that of the priesthood. Contained within the ancient stone temples are many mythological carvings. All the religious text was in the Sanskrit language, which only a Brahman had the right to learn and understand.

In the evenings, we children were taken for walks; we often saw a palm tree climber go up on the tree, climbing like he would touch the sky. *What is he after? Why is he taking some clay pots tied to his hip?* we wondered. We watched in awe as he reached the top, up among the leaves. There, he changed the clay pots with the ones already hanging. Those clay pots contained the sap, sweet nectar that dripped into the jars from the trunk, which had been shaved. Sap can become toddy or arrack, an alcoholic drink. Therefore, the empty clay pots are first smeared with limestone inside. This stops the sap from fermenting and forming alcohol and prevents illegal harvesting. The sap is consumed fresh as a refreshing drink or for producing palm jaggery or gurr, which is used to sweeten everything, especially coffee. Regarding India's caste system, the palm tree climbers are called channers and are considered a low caste.

## Z Set and Lola's Children
## My Sisters!

Now I will tell you something about my sisters and what happened to them. I kept in touch with as many as possible, some of us being closer than the others, but we all loved each other as the only family we would ever know.

At Dohnavur, all the children born in the same year are called a set. As such, my set had nine other girls: Jeyapushpam, Usila, Taraevu, Davarul, Jeyarathina, Saroruha, Ponnarul, Sellananthinie, and Tarie (who went to England in 1953). We all were born in 1944 and were classified as Z set. It was the last alphabetical order of the second generation. I still correspond with or talk with them on the phone. There is a strong bond between the girls from the same set, almost like siblings.

Besides the girls from the same set, there is also bonding between the girls from the same cottage, and Lola's children I grew up with became my elder sisters.

Ponnalari was not from my set, but I bonded so well with her that I became her little sister. She was top-ranked in her school classes and was a very good person. Lola wanted Ponnalari to become a doctor and had expressed her desire to the fellowship leadership team before she passed away in 1956.

In one hundred years of Dohnavur's history, they have sent only one person to become a medical doctor. It was Ponnalari! She completed her training in seven years and became a medical doctor in 1968. She joined the missionary doctors, Karunai Sittie (Dr. Nancy Robbins) and Kiruba Sittie (Dr. Jaqueline Woolcock, who arrived in 1969) at the Dohnavur Fellowship Hospital. Ponnalari gave forty-four years of service and never earned a penny for working in the Dohnavur Fellowship! Dr. Nancy Robbins worked most of her life at Dohnavur, finally retired, and died in England at age ninety-nine. Dr. Jaqueline, who also spent years serving at Dohnavur Hospital, is living in West Sussex, England. Whenever I am on my way back to the fellowship, I try and visit her at her beach house near the English Channel. We went for a swim in the afternoons.

After I came to America, Ponnalari and I corresponded a lot and kept our sistership and friendship throughout the years. Then, after ten years, I had finally saved enough money for traveling, so I could travel to India and see her again. After this trip, I made a few more visits to see her. Ponnalari passed away in 2015 after working hard day and night. She was the only doctor at the hospital! She never got paid for this work—forty-four years of her service! I loved her dearly, as any blood sister would, and I still miss her very much. She considered her efforts as serving the Lord. Now she has entered into eternity, greeted by the words, "Well done, my faithful servant."

Pushpaveni is a very loving person but went through many troublesome days. For talking back to the principal, Bee Trehan took her out of boarding school (high school level). Punishments were very harsh in those days. Bee sent her to hard labor at the parboiling rice plant for ten years! Pushpa was a hardworking person and, in the end, finished high school after ten years of delay. She was then permitted to sit privately for the Indian government's high school examination. After this, she went to nursing school, became a nurse, and lived and worked in Dubai for ten years! I told you she was a hard worker! Finally, she returned to India and lived in Delhi until she passed away in 2008.

Jeevanathi was a capable person in sewing and stitching beautiful things. She spent about eight years working in different places in Dohnavur. After high school, she took a secretarial course at home school under Meleela Sittie (Ms. Silvia Crawly), a Canadian missionary who taught the typing class. Then one day, Jeevanathi was sent to Bangalore, where the fellowship had a hostel for young girls. There they made toys and learned to live on their own. After a year, she received a marriage proposal from a well-known family. I was with her in Bangalore when Jeeva was betrothed to Mr. Alexander. He was a high-ranking officer in the Indian army.

The wedding occurred in just a month, and she became Mrs. Jeeva Alexander. After a year, Jeeva's husband was ordered to a station in London, England. Jeeva had a son before she went to England, and she then had a daughter, Mercy, born in England. After five years, they returned to Delhi, and the children were educated in India. Jeeva's daughter went on to study at Oxford University! She then got a job teaching biology at Cambridge University. Mercy taught at Allahabad University in India, and her brother David is an officer and pilot in the Indian air force. Jeeva's life is a great story. Sadly, she passed away suddenly in 2014. I miss her too, but Mercy visited me in Texas eight years ago, and we had a good time remembering our old days. See picture on page 359.

Santhaevu was working in Delhi and had a very responsible position at the hospital. She was single, never married, and was eighty-three when she died in April of 2023. Dear Santha, I miss talking to her, for she was always busy and had much to tell.

Jeyaventhi, I saw her for the last time when she came home to see Dr. Ponnu on her deathbed. I was also there at that time on vacation from the USA. The last I heard was that Jeyaventhi passed away in 2015.

I know little about Pramotha, except that she got married and had children.

Lavanaleela was a very clever girl and always a topper in her class. She became a nurse and worked in Vellore Hospital. She was married and had two children. Lavance and Preealala went to Madurai for high school; they married and had children, but I do not know where they live now.

Dayaseeli came to see me when I visited Dr. Ponnalari before her death. She is single and eighty-one years old but told me that she does evangelistic work in Tanjavur.

Dayamani was older than me. She left the fellowship long before me and was teaching in Bangalore. She then got married and had a place built to help disabled children. I salute her for this noble deed. I understand that she passed away suddenly in 2015.

And there is no word about my dear Jeyavallie, for no one knows where she is, and I wish I could talk to her one more time as she was also my best childhood friend.

DevaArul (Arul) works with the Swedish Lutheran Mission in Tanjavur, South India. While all the other girls were separated or sent to other houses, DevaArul and I were never separated. We both were sent to Nazareth High School, where we lived at the boarding school. We stayed together in the same house when we came home (to the fellowship) on holidays. Arul took secretarial training that Meleela Sittie taught and went outside to work with a Lutheran mission. She is still working there, as I talked to her while writing this book. Arul came from a famous Mimosa family and was a very gentle-spirited girl. She is not married but dedicated to the Swedish Lutheran Mission, where she works today, at seventy-eight years of age.

Jayapushpam is still in Dohnavur as she offered to work among the children and is now retired. I call and talk to her now and then to get the news of my home. See picture on page 85.

When I was twelve years old, I read a book from the Sunday library called The Darkroom Princess about the emperor's daughter being sequestered for many months in a room full of books preparing for the final royal exam. In 1988, I took a tour with my husband of Tiananmen Square in Beijing, China, where I found the room spoken of in that book.

The Dohnavur Fellowship nursery has a legacy going back 125 years.

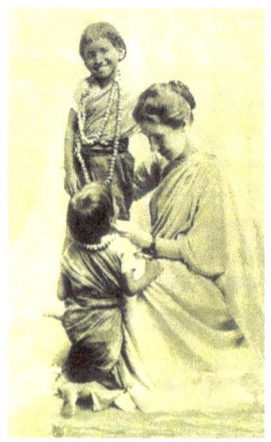

Amy with Lola (standing) and Leela. Salma became one of Lola's children, the last one to be added in June 1951.

Right to left: Missionaries Premmie, Preethie, and Preeya Sittie in 1909. The house behind them was where Salma went to receive her coming day gift and candy from Preeya Sittie.

Amy's travelling wagon.

Old nurseries were built from palm tree trunks, near the mountain where the tiger came from. Amy believed the tiger was guided by an angel back to the mountains; it was killed on the way.

Children's nursery where the tiger was prowling outside one night.

The water carriers for the nurseries.

Top right: Tara. Lower right: Evu, who brought six-day-old Salma to Amy in 1944.

Sisters Seela & Mala (2$^{nd}$ & 3$^{rd}$).

Veera Carunia (3$^{rd}$)

Pyarie & Vineetha

Arulai & Rukma

Baby's nursery.

Salma was placed in Kirubai's hands when she was six days old. Kirubai used to bathe the babies with her feet as a support to hold the babies, using a water bucket.

Helpers looking after babies in the new nursery. The hammock, made of cotton, hangs from the ceiling. Kirubaimani, on the right rocking a baby, was at the village training center with Salma from July to October of 1972.

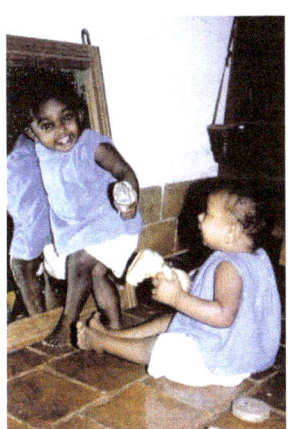
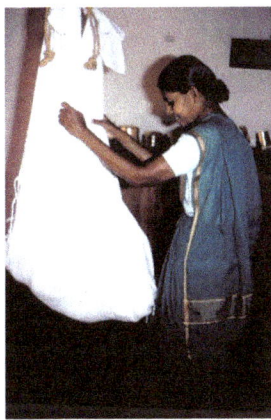

Babies playing in the new nursery built with bricks and tiles to accommodate more children taken in by Amy Carmichael.

Chandrakanthiepu Carunia (Champu'ka). See Salma's story about her helping at Salma's nursery from 1940 to 1951.

Champu'ka and her helper Sameehara taking care of babies in the new nursery, made of bricks and stone.

Suba Carunia helping at the babies' nursery, keeping them happy.

Salma Carunia visiting the babies' nursery.

Salma Carunia-Carter, age forty-three with her former wet nurse, Sangarue along with Anihala Carunia. Kirubai maintained about five hundred wet nurses to wean the babies around the clock at the nurseries, along with Pyarie (see picture on page 39) and Chellachie.

Playschool Suhanantha (full of love).

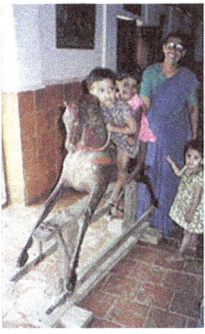

Children playing in playground. Boys wear red-strap knickers, girls wear blue.

Children riding the same riding horse Salma played on. It has lasted over one hundred years.

House mothers taking nursery schoolchildren back to their homes. This was used as a lunch area when Salma lived there as a child. Veera served lunch at that time with missionary Helen Bradshaw (Premalu Sittie).

Babies playing in the playground outside of the nursery school.

Vistara, small boys' compound (two to eight years of age).

Boys playing with Amy's dog, Lassie. Amy had two dogs, Lassie and Toots.

Children playing in the Vistara compound.

Salma standing in front of her former home, where she lived in her late twenties. Today, it is being converted into a retirement community.

Packiavathy Carunia, who took care of about three hundred boys in Vistara, the small boys' compound. She was the last house mother who took care of the last set of nine boys who arrived.

Packiavathy Accal, who took care of about three hundred boys in Vistara, the small boys' compound. She was known as a kind and gentle house mother to the boys, who miss being in her care.

Deenadayalan Anantha with his wife, Josephine, and children, Amy and Danny. He was one of Packiavathy Carunia's three hundred children. He now works for the United States government.

Deenadayalan was taught in first and second grade by Porumai Carunia, who was assisted by Salma Carunia. Porumai was a member of the staff in Dohnavur Fellowship and taught elementary school for forty years.

John Varathan visiting Salma with Deenadayalan at Dohnavur Fellowship in 1991. John was the son of Salma's friend Usila. He became a minister. When he passed away in November of 2018, the whole town mourned the loss, saying, "The preacher has disappeared."

The location near the lotus tank at the foothills of the western Ghats, where Dohnavur girls and boys go for picnics.

Coming Day.

Coming Day is marked by colorful saris being worn by girls and beautiful flowers decorating the ceremony. Each child receives a gift and two pieces of candy on their Coming Day.

When Salma celebrated her Coming Day, pink cabbage roses were provided from Seela's garden, which she wore in her hair along with jasmine. In the afternoon, Salma had lunch with Seela on that special day.

Kindergarten School Jeevanantha, the Joy of Life.

Children playing in front of the school. This is where Salma attended kindergarten.

Children playing on a jungle gym in the playground. This is the same jungle gym that Salma played on as a child.

Children waving flags and singing songs in school. Memalar was the headmistress of kindergarten from 1991 to 2016. She is now responsible for taking in guests who visit Dohnavur Fellowship.

The Square children's compound.

The square kitchen, where the workers came to retrieve food waste to take to feed the cattle. In front is a laburnum tree.

Flame of the forest.

When Salma learned the biblical story of Elijah in kindergarten, she asked God to take her up to heaven in a whirlwind while she was playing under the slide. She was under the slide just like the girl in the blue dress in the photo to the left. She experienced a supernatural miracle through her little faith, and her feet left the ground, but she remembers that her fear brought her back down. See this story earlier in chapter 2.

Salma lived in this house from age two to five and learned biblical creation stories from Amithal.

Uruthie with her children in the same house where Salma lived from age five to eight. One of her favorite games at this time was "Ten virgins, the bridegroom is coming." See story on page 22.

Navaroja with her children.

Prabavathy with her children.

# CHAPTER 3

# Life in Our House
# The School Compound
## The Round
## School Life at Jeevalia
## Grades 3 to 7

### Life in Our House

Our houses had little furniture, and we all slept on grass mats on the tiled floor. We would get a cotton sheet for covering if the weather was cool. In the morning, the sheet was folded, and the grass mat rolled up and neatly stacked on a wooden pallet. As did our sheets, each mat had our name stitched on it, so everyone used only their own.

To eat, we sat cross-legged on the floor. When I came to Lola's house, I was given a brass bowl to eat rice from, a brass plate for curry, and a brass tumbler to drink milk twice daily. My name is engraved on these three brass items I had to return when I left home for good. I was responsible for keeping my vessels clean by polishing them with the ash from the kitchen firewood. With that many children staying in one house, everyone *must* use their own vessels to eat and drink, keeping us from spreading germs to each other.

If anyone got sick, she was sent to our hospital where Karunai Sittie and Kiruba Sittie worked. From 1970, Dr. Ponnalari Carunia would examine and take care of them. We were very lucky to be cared for by the good old missionaries who gave us royal treatment. The medicine was always there for us to recover from the sickness, whatsoever it might have been. As per the medical wisdom of that age, each child had a tonsillectomy to reduce throat infections, especially in a situation like this, where so many small children were staying together. It was usually performed before they were twelve years old.

Once a girl *came of age* (this means that they are beginning to have a menstrual cycle) around ten to twelve years old, each girl was given twelve white cotton towels and waist belts to which the towel was attached. Each girl would stitch her name on the twelve towels. All of Lola's children knew how to do cross-stitch. She taught this during the summer holidays. The girls soaked their cloth towels until they had time to wash them, but always before night fell, because there was no other light except for the moonlight!

Every Saturday, a washer man or woman would come from the nearby village to take the dirty clothes to wash in the nearby mountain river.

They would be washed and dried there and brought back on the next Saturday. Therefore, stitching your name on your clothes was important because hundreds of identical items come and go to wash every week. Hygiene is crucial when a large community lives together and uses common facilities. In those times, nothing was disposable, and everything had to be washed and reused.

It took a staff of about fifty to take care of about eight hundred to one thousand Dohnavur Fellowship members and continue rescuing, nurturing children, and maintaining outreach. The children who Amy Carmichael took in were loved, cared for, and educated until they had a job or were given in marriage.

The administration was guided by senior fellowship members who each held different positions of responsibility. The areas of operation were: hospital, workshop, engine room, fields and groves, and vegetable gardens, and there were also hundreds of children at the home school. The leaders were Indian and British missionaries, but Amy's first children—Sella in Muppandal, Lola, Leela, Rukma, Paripu, and Preena—were the primary leaders.

Lola oversaw all the groves and gardens around the fellowship. She left the house by 8:00 a.m. to supervise the vegetable gardens and guava, mango, and coconut groves. When we came home during the break from school at 9:00 a.m., she would put a tablespoon full of shark liver oil, a teaspoon full of calcium, and an iron pill in our mouths every morning, just before the school prayers at 9:30 a.m. Milk was served then, and each child got ten ounces in the morning and ten ounces in the evening after supper.

Lola made sure her children were well-fed. The food from the kitchen was measured correctly and divided between the cottages according to the number of children in each cottage. There were eight large kitchens in the fellowship for preparing meals, one kitchen in each compound. The kitchens had at least five or six staff and one head cook who tasted all the curries before they were served. Only women worked in the kitchen. They came to work early each morning, starting at about 2:00 a.m., so the breakfast would be ready by 6:30 a.m. and served to all by 7:00. This allowed the children to be at school and the adults at work by 8:00 a.m.

Lunch was served at noon, and we had rice and rasam in our bowls and one or two different vegetable curries with cooked fertilized eggs (which tasted much better than non-fertilized eggs), such as an omelet or fried eggs or what we called bull's-eye eggs (boiled eggs). Sometimes, there were some duck eggs, which I liked because they had a bigger yolk than a chicken egg. We had eggs three times a week, which was a joy. Also, after lunch, everyone had a full bowl of buttermilk, which was our delight. Then we rose to wash our bowls, very satisfied and full. We sat in a circle on the tile floor whenever we ate with the food vessels in the center. We ate with our fingers on the right hand, so washing up was easy! Supper was always rice and vegetable curry. See pictures on pages 85 and 86.

I never forgot the raw eggs that we were given to us in the morning by the house helpers in the children's compound. Our helper Premalumallai would ask us to open our mouths and then crack in an egg, one apiece, and tell us to swallow it. As one of the smaller children, I could not hold a full egg in my small mouth. So she poked a hole in the shell and poured it into my mouth, and once I swallowed that, she poured the remaining egg into my mouth. This went on till we were seven years old.

Along with the egg, our breakfast was a red-colored porridge made from ragi (finger millet). Ragi whole grain was crushed on a stone hand grinder. This millet had a higher protein content than rice and was good for children. It was then cooked to make porridge and mixed with cow's milk. I worked on this stone grinder in 1959 and knew how hard it takes to grind things on it. (But this is an episode that will come later.) We were fed with the same old ragi every day for twenty years. That changed when we reached twenty-six years of age. Breakfast became rice pancakes we called dosa and idli, a rice cake we ate with coconut chutney. It's yummy! And we also got coffee in the morning; until then, we drank only water and milk.

## School: Black Mark Register, Third Grade

Muthara Sittie (Peggy Craig), a missionary from Scotland, began teaching English to the third grade and started something new. She introduced what was called the Bad Mark book in every class. If a child misbehaved, such as raising their hand out of turn, talking to the next student, or did not know the right answer, an X was entered against the student's name. We had twenty students in the class, but I bore the brunt of this new rule. The punishment for getting bad marks was severe and sometimes unbearable. You were sent to the principal's office, which is the staff room, for discipline.

The principal would then take the child with the bad marks to the broom closet where she kept her switch sticks that she broke off a tamarind tree near her office and would apply the punishment.

I must confess that I have visited that room more than a hundred times. I could get double punishment, too, for Lola was very good at her swings at home. We were very frightened of her at such times, for she was yelling and shouting at us.

We had very strict rules, and I tried to follow them, but I was a very active child. It was difficult for a young child to sit cross-legged for hours at a time; each period was for half an hour. If I tried to change position or move around, I got a bad mark, and sometimes, I would get three or four marks just between 8:00 a.m. and 9:00 a.m.! Oh! What a terrible time being such a lively child. I still remember that I had a big blister on my left leg from the hard floor.

Lola came home at 9:00 a.m. to oversee our break time. She always asked me how many bad marks I got from 8:00 a.m. to 9:00 a.m. I would shyly say, "Five…," and she would sternly say, "Make sure you don't add to that when you come for lunch." So off I ran back to school. The other girls may have one bad mark, or sometimes, the whole class gets one bad mark if the teacher finds the class disorderly. By lunchtime, I might have more bad marks.

Lola always worried about me. "Why are the teachers giving Salma so many bad marks?" she said. 'My Salma never tells lies, never steals (for it was common among the girls to steal sweets or edibles that were kept in a storage place), always keeps her things in the proper place. There is no guile in her. She is very innocent, and she does everything on time." Lola was in charge of twenty-five girls, split into two houses, and thought Ponnalari and I were the best among the fifteen girls she had with her. I believe that there was another girl she was proud of: Sittara, one of the ten who lived at Leelarathina's house.

If we had bad marks, we had to eat our lunch standing up, holding our rice bowl in our left hand, and eating with our right. Eating rice without curry was the hardest punishment, and I hated it. But sometimes, Lola showed kindness and told us to sit down after five minutes, then we could take curry on the plate.

At about 5:15 p.m., Taraleela would ring a small bell. Then we all ran to where she would distribute the snacks. Sometimes, girls were sent away empty-handed, crying as punishment for doing a poor job, missing their housework, or some other mistake, like not keeping the things in their proper place. The rule was "Everything has a place. Everything in its place." This may seem harsh and did at that time. But think how difficult and dangerous it would have been if four hundred children were allowed to do as they pleased, leave things wherever they wanted, or miss their work responsibilities.

One day, Lola came up with an idea. She got everyone a small container and gave her children the monthly portion of edible treats that came from the kitchen every month. We kept the container in our wooden locker and watched when we could, so no one stole it. We did not have a lock for the locker, which three or four girls shared together.

Some children finished all of their goodies in a week or even less. Mine lasted for a long time, for I ate very little and tried to stretch it till the end of the month till the next lot of edibles arrived. Giving each child the whole month's allotment was a way to teach self-control. Lola, as she had learned from Amy Carmichael, was always teaching moral lessons to her children. Galatians 5:22–23 says, "For the fruit of the spirit is love, joy, peace, and self-control."

Every Saturday, Lola gave a tea party for those of her children who had no bad marks for the whole week. My class teacher wrote on the blackboard that I had fifty for the week! I knew I had fifty and another black sheep, a girl named Asala, who had a total of fifty-one, beating me by one. However, Lola said Salma could come to the tea party even if she had twenty bad marks, for Lola thought the schoolteacher was unjust to me.

Later, Lola even told the other ladies working for her, "One day, when all this is past, when she has grown up, Salma will become a great person. She has good qualities. She is honest and has no guile." Maybe Lola noticed that I was deeply religious and had the proper fear of God. She also told them, "One day, my Salma will do great things and will become a great leader." And yes, I have led in teaching and spreading the gospel after six years of higher education at a famous Bible college and missionary work in countries worldwide! Later, Dr. Ponnalari and I laughed about how Lola overlooked my bad marks.

In 1954, Lola became weak and sick and was moved to a different house, for she refused to go to the retirement home. She wanted to stay close by her children. Her place was taken by a very kind lady, Rajamacottie. The first thing we noticed about "Cootie," as we called her, was that she talked very gently and softly, unlike Lola's yelling and shouting. Even though dear Rajamacottie applied the rules and regulations, her kindness overcame harshness, and we lived happily with her.

These were halcyon days for us. We were now freer to do things on our own; sometimes, I was hopping and jumping around the house and enjoying this freedom. We were moved to the house called Sardonyx, the fifth precious stone, and Lola moved to the house called Emerald, the sixth precious stone in Revelation chapter 21.

We still did our housework, swept around the house, and kept things tidy, but we could also go out and play, which we could not do under Lola's authority. Lola would find work for us all day long.

## My First Book!

As a tradition, on January 1, at the fellowship home school, every child was given a book to keep. Each house/cottage had one bookshelf, and all the girls in that house would share the bookshelf. Having your own book was a big thing for us, as *we did not own anything—everything was for common use in the orphanage.*

The first book that I got was when I was in grade 3. It was the New Testament with my name written inside. Therefore, it belonged to me, and I could take it from the bookshelf and read it as I pleased. This mostly happened when Lola's children had a quiet time in the morning from 6:00 a.m. to 6:30 a.m. Then, we sat around the house and had individual time to read the Bible and pray. We would take our Bible or New Testament to school every day, for we had scripture class from 11:30 a.m. to noon, immediately before lunch. We came to our cottages for lunch from noon to 1:00 p.m. When the clock tower chimed 1:00 p.m., we lay down and slept till 2:00 p.m. This kept us out of the heat of the day, which in Southern India is intense and could weaken young children exposed to or working in it. The sixth and seventh graders returned to school at 2:30 p.m. and the lower grades at 3:00 p.m. School ended at 4:30 p.m.

In fourth grade, all the children received the book *The Pilgrim's Progress* by John Bunyan, written in Tamil. I kept mine on the shelf along with my New Testament, which I had received for third grade. I started reading *The Pilgrim's Progress* during the summer holiday. We got a long afternoon break for that season, so we could read our books and sleep till 4:00 p.m.

## CHRIST IS IN ME

I still remember that I could not put down this book. I would turn to face the windowsill where I lay down and keep reading. Many times, I wept quietly. This book was life-changing. It allowed me to understand the struggles a Christian will face and why God's goodness is there for us! I did not want anyone to know why I was crying, for there were fifteen of us sleeping in that same house.

I was supposed to be resting in midday, but Lola was on vacation for six weeks and was not there to tell me to put the book away and nap by 1:30 p.m.

Let me tell you about this amazing book and the author, John Bunyan, and how it made things so clear to me.

*[This information is from, <u>The Pilgrim's Progress</u>, by John Bunyan, published by Penguin Classics.]*

He was born at Elstow near Bedford, England in 1628. But in 1644, the Civil War swept him up into its course as he mustered in the country militia on the Parliamentary side and was for some years on garrison duty. In about 1648, he was plunged into a religious crisis that lasted for several years and brought him to despair. His vivid imagination was possessed in a simple and terrible form by the Calvinist doctrine that all men were predestined to salvation or damnation as he battled with doubts about his faith.

After conversion to a form of Baptist/Puritan worship, he began leading unauthorized religious services. He emerged a new man converting others and comforting them with their spiritual problems. He joined a nonconformist group in Bedford. This theology was against the Church of England. November 1660, a few months after the restoration of a king in England, Charles II, who was a Catholic, Bunyan and other nonconformists were arrested. A local magistrate took him while preaching in the fields, and he was imprisoned off and on for the next twelve years in the town of Bedford.

Legend tells us that Bunyan began to write *The Pilgrim's Progress* while he was in jail. After his imprisonment Bunyan, who became the pastor of the Bedford separatist Church, also earned the nickname of "Bishop Bunyan" for his zeal in traveling to preach and to solve the personal problems of his scattered congregation. He died in 1688, just when the period of religious persecution was coming to an end.

Go to http://www.christianfaithpublishing.com and see "The Adventures of Kitten Kaboodal" (written and illustrated by my husband, Dr. Ben Michael Carter, 2019).

*The Pilgrim's Progress* is one of the most published books in the English language, with over 1,300 editions printed by 1938.

The circumstances of how this book and Bunyan's story became even more vivid in my life occurred later after I was married. In 1985, my husband, Ben Michael Carter, and I were at Aberdeen University in Scotland, UK, where he was studying theology. This was just before he got his master's degree. We were able to go to Bedford, England, to see the Robbins family. This family were known as my prayer friends. They supported the orphanage of Dohnavur Fellowship in South India. (I will tell you more about this process later.)

They took us to see a replica of the small prison, more like a cave or den, where John Bunyan was locked up and where he wrote the book, *The Pilgrim's Progress*. Little did they or my husband know that this was my favorite book I had read in my childhood. It also guided me as I was growing up, and later on, the scriptures from the Bible made me understand the pilgrimage that we are on this earth.

One item in the book sparked my imagination. Bunyan said he dreamed; behold. He saw a man clothed with rags standing in a certain place with his face turned away from his own house, a book in his hand, and a great burden upon his back. He opened the book, and as he read, he wept and trembled. Unable to contain himself, he broke out with a lamentable cry saying, "What shall I do?" Romans 7:24 says, "Who shall deliver me from this body of death?"

This made me think that man needs salvation (Romans 6:23) as life is a confrontation between the powers of light and darkness. Or changing the metaphor, the adventurous journey of the armed, Psalm 18:34, and vigilant Christian through hostile country, which is this world, the City of Destruction, and a Christian's need for the desperate flight from the City of Destruction.[2]

---

[2] See the book, *The Adventures of Kitten Kaboodal*, 2019, by Ben M. Carter, on www.christianfaithpublishing.com

CHRIST IS IN ME

# John Bunyan Story

Let me tell you about this story and how some of it meant so much to a teenage orphan girl like me!

The story begins when, at the prompting of an evangelist, Christian puts everything behind him, including his family and security. He flees from their pleading with his fingers in his ears, crying, "Life, life, Eternal Life." His sole desire is to be on the right road to the Celestial City for the book in his hand tells him that he is condemned to die and, after that, to come to judgment. Then Christian asked the evangelist, "Whither must I fly?" As he gave Christian a parchment roll, on which was written, "Flee from the wrath to come," he pointed with his finger over a very wide field. He said, "See the shining light yonder where you come to the Wicket Gate and keep your eyesight on the light and go directly and knock on the door and you shall be told what thou shalt do."

(I changed this to make it more understandable, but if the quotation was exact before, it isn't now. Hoping John Bunyan will understand.)

This gave me the idea that Jesus is the Door! See John 10:7–10: "I am the door, if anyone enters through me, he shall be saved."[3]

The second thing I noticed was that the burden upon Christian's back was heavy. It was labeled Sin!

He said this burden is sinking me to lower than the grave! He could not get rid of it. But when he reached the Wicket Gate House, he was told a way to relieve his heavy burden. A man called Goodwill told Christian, "An open door is set before thee, and no man can shut it. Now I will teach you about the way thou must go. Look before thee, and you see the narrow way, and that is the way thou must go, which was cast up by the patriarchs, prophets, Christ, and his apostles, and it is as straight as a rule can make it. This is the way thou must go" (Psalm 5:8; Hebrew 12:13).

---

[3] See the book, *The Door*, 2004, by Ben Carter, www. christianfaithpublishing.com.

"As to the burden, be content to bear it until thou comest to the place of deliverance; for there, it will fall from thy back itself." Then Christian went on this path and came to the highway, up which Christian was to go.

However, this way is bordered by a wall fencing on either side. This wall is called Salvation. So Christian kept going this way. He walked with the burden and then ran, with great difficulty, because the load on his back was heavy.

He ran thus till he came to a place somewhat ascending. Upon that place stood a cross and, a little below, a sepulchre. When Christian came up to the cross, his burden loosed from his shoulders, fell off his back, and began to tumble down till it came to the mouth of the tomb, where it fell in, and therefore, it was no more!

At this part, I liked what happened next:

> Three angels appeared to Christian, saying, "Peace be to you," and the first one said, "Thy sins are forgiven," and the second angel stripped him of his rags and clothed him with the change of raiment. The third angel set a mark on his forehead (we Christians have our foreheads marked with a cross using baptismal water when we are baptized) and then gave him a scroll with a seal upon it, and bade him to look after as he ran towards the Gate and that he should give it in at the Celestial Gate.

This part of the story made me want to get baptized immediately. However, at Dohnavur, one must bring a good report after being at the boarding school for one year in order to be baptized. At this point, I had years before I could achieve that goal. So I consoled myself by singing the song we learned, "At the cross, where I first saw the light, and the burden of my heart rolled away. It was there by faith I received my sight, and now I am happy all the way."

# CHRIST IS IN ME

The next thing that impacted my life was how Christian fights Apollyon, the demon who came to meet him in the Valley of Humiliation.

Christian tried to defeat the demon with a drawn sword in hand and wearing the armor of God. However, he was forced to put away the sword and betake himself another weapon called All-Prayer. So he cried, "O Lord, I beseech thee deliver my Soul." Christian won the battle with Apollyon, the devil, by calling upon his Lord and Savior.

This fight with Apollyon gave me an idea of where I can go when trials and temptations come, as we see in Ephesians 6:10–17, "Put on the whole armor of God, that ye may be able to stand against the wiles of the devil. Therefore, the Sword of the Spirit is the Word of God." In the beginning, the Word was God. It is written, AI (Genesis 1:1, John 1:1). "Who has the greatest intelligence?" (1 Corinthians 3:18–23). Apart from God, nothing can exist!

Yet another incident I read was about the Valley of the Shadow of Death. This place had a deep ditch on one side and mire on the other, haunted by the same voices and noises as an obsession with personal guilt.

Christian was walking on the narrow path between the ditch, and the wicked ones got behind him. As he traveled in this sad condition, sometimes, he heard the voice of a traveler going before him, shouting and singing, "Though I walk through the valley of the shadow of death, I will fear no evil for thou art with me." Christian was glad and knew that someone who feared God was also in this valley as well as himself and that God was with them in this dark and dismal state, and now he had company to travel together. By and by, the day broke, and he saw the hobgoblins, satyrs, and dragons of the pit all afar off, and after the daybreak, they came not nigh.

From this, I could understand how the Bible tells us to walk in the light. Psalm 4:6 and Psalm 18:28 say, "The Lord my God will enlighten my darkness for Thou wilt light my candle." We all sometimes walk through this valley with our sorrows and pain, which can only be overcome if we put our trust in the Lord who will be our refuge in times of trouble (Psalm 46:1). The next thing which consoled me, as I was reading about this horrible valley that Christian passed through, was the friend and companion he found whose name is Faithful, quoting the scripture from Psalm 23:4.

They both walked and came to the town called Vanity, and they had to pass through the Vanity Fair where people were asking questions as they went along. They met a man called Worldly Wiseman, who tries to convince them to take up residence in the village of Morality under the care of Legality and his son, Civility. Mr. Wiseman stands for the temptation of the world, and his corruption is suggested by an air of social importance with which he invests himself. In the end, Christian's companion Faithful met with martyrdom for his defense of Christianity! But the good news was that another man named Hopeful joined Christian, and they became travel companions on the way to Celestial City.

This taught me to stand firm for the truth even unto death. Second Corinthians 1:4 says, "For by Faith ye stand." Job 19:25 says, "For I know that my Redeemer lives." I have learned a strong lesson from this story of Christian, and this verse is already carved on my grave site beside my husband.

Mike passed away June 5, 2005, and lies at Restland Cemetery, Dallas, Texas, USA, awaiting the final victory of Christ!

Ours the cross, the grave, the skies. Hallelujah!

Mike with Salma in Dohnavur.

Salma being comforted by her best friend, Marilyn Kolker.

Salma at Mike's graveside.

Salma and Mike's gravestones at Restland in Dallas, Texas, USA.

## The Mystery of Resurrection

This mystery was revealed to me on November 29, 1959, at age fifteen, which is "Christ is in me, the Hope of Glory!" (Colossians 1:27).

*Behold, I tell you a mystery: We shall not all sleep, but we shall all be changed, in a moment, in the twinkling of an eye, at the last trumpet. For the trumpet will sound, and the dead will be raised imperishable, and we shall be changed.*

—1 Corinthians 15:50

# CHRIST IS IN ME

*For the Lord Himself will descend from heaven with a shout...*
*and with the Trumpet of God; and the dead in Christ*
*shall rise first and we shall be with the Lord Forever!*

—1 Thessalonians 4:16

Another big lesson I learned from the story of the Doubting Castle. When Christian and his companion Hopeful were weary after walking the whole day toward the highway, they fell asleep in the nearby meadow. There is a castle called Doubting, and it is owned by the giant, Despair. As the giant was taking his morning walk at the meadow, he caught Christian and Hopeful sleeping on his grounds. He shouted at them, and they told him that they were pilgrims who had lost their way. But the giant took them into his castle and locked them up in the dark dungeon and beat them up day after day. Now the pilgrims became very discouraged, and Christian wanted to take the giant's counsel and die rather than live in the dungeon, which was the easy way out.

But Hopeful reminded him that to commit murder upon this body is to kill body and soul at once. It is easy to go to the grave but not to hell where the murderers go. Hopeful encouraged Christian, saying, "Let us be patient and endure the trouble for a while for the giant Despair may die with the fits (seizures) that he gets or may lose the use of his limbs when he comes to beat us in the morning and evening. Maybe he forgets to lock the door or something, and we can escape." They were there without food from Wednesday till Saturday, and on Saturday evening, Hopeful found the key to the gates of the dungeon, but there were three more gates that they need to open before coming to the castle's last rusty gate. The key that opened the Doubting Castle's doors was the Word of God, as Hopeful found a small book of promises in his pocket. When the last rusty gate opened, it made a big noise, and the giant came running to catch them, but he had a sudden fit and lost the use of his limbs and fell down! The pilgrims escaped and found the path to King's Highway and engraved the warning sign on the steps of the meadow for the other pilgrims who would pass that way.

Many times, we struggle to get out of our troubles and trials. However, if we have faith in God, who promised us that He will deliver us from them, we can get out of the Doubting Castle and set on a journey homeward or upward as we are the pilgrims. They would pass through the world that way.

Now the lasting impression of this book was how Christian and Hopeful reached the City of Gold.

This happened as they came to the border of heaven as they were entering the country of Beulah Land where the air was very sweet and pleasant, and they heard the singing of birds and saw the beautiful flowers. They found a garden with orchards, vineyards, and the garden gate opened into the highway, and the gardener told them this is the King's Garden and they were planted for the solace of the pilgrims. Christian and Hopeful refreshed themselves with the dainties, and here they tarried and slept as it is called Beulah Land.

Sometimes I feel I am in the Beulah Land, as being in America. It is such a land of plenty—things that I never had before I came to the USA. I will tell you all the troubles and trials that I have endured in my life to get here in the coming chapters. When I was on the other side of this world, growing up in an orphanage and not having any material things, I desired them. However, now that I could afford them, I found that they are as vanity of vanities, and I want them no more and am learning to be satisfied in that which God has blessed me with. I have learned to say that God is everything, and He is all in all to me. Redemption is the greatest gift to me from God, and any amount of money cannot buy the peace and joy that I have now. Romans 3:24 says, "Being justified freely by his grace through the redemption that is in Christ Jesus."

When Christian and Hopeful woke up, they were told to go up to the city, but the city was pure gold, and they could not face it because of the sun's reflections upon the city. They asked the two angels to go up with them, but the angels answered, "You must obtain it by your own faith." Then Christian and Hopeful went on together till they came within sight of the gate. Here, they saw the river, and there was no bridge to cross it, and the river was deep, and the angel said to them, "You must go through the river or you cannot proceed to the last gate which is the gate of Heaven."

The pilgrims asked if there was any other way to the gate but were told that none but Enoch and Elijah had trod that path since the foundation of the world, nor shall, until the last trumpet shall sound. Christian was more frightened and looked this way and that way, but no way could be found that they might escape the river. This is called the last crossing of River Jordan before the Israelites went into the Promised Land. Now they went into the river, and Christian began to sink and, crying out to his friend Hopeful, saying, "I sink in deep waters, the billows go over my head and all the waves go over me!"

Hopeful tried to encourage Christian, saying, "Be of good cheer, my brother, I feel the bottom." But Christian seems sinking and could not keep his head up. Hopeful tries to comfort him, saying that he sees the gate. Christian was troubled with thoughts of sins that he committed, and one sees that guilt is the cause of us going under.[4]

> Guilty, vile, and helpless we…Bearing shame and scoffing rude,
> In my place condemned He stood; Sealed my pardon with His blood.

## Hallelujah! What a Savior!

Hopeful said to his friend, "Be of good cheer, Jesus Christ maketh thee whole." Christian cries out with loud voice, "Oh I see him again!" and he tells me, "When thou passeth through the waters, I will be with thee, and through the rivers, they shall not overflow thee" (Isaiah 43:2). Christian therefore found ground to stand upon and the rest of the river was shallow, and they crossed over. Now upon the bank of the river, on the other side, they saw the two shining men again who were waiting for them and took them to the

---

[4] Please see www.christianfaithpublishing.com, and learn more from my late husband's book, *The Clay Supper*.

city that stood upon the mighty hill. They told them they will see no sorrow, sickness, affliction, and death anymore, for the former things are passed away. "Behold God makes all things new." Then Christian and Hopeful were taken through the golden gate to meet their Redeemer, Lord Jesus Christ.

As I read this amazing book, weeping quietly, I felt I had found the purpose for my life. Even though I was only ten years old, I was determined to make this pilgrimage toward my Redeemer and sing:

> None other Lamb, None other Name, None other hope in heaven or earth or sea,
> None other hiding-place from guilt and shame, None beside Thee.
> My faith burns low, my hope burns low; Only my heart's desire cries out in me,
> By the deep thunder of its want and woe, Cries out to Thee.
> Lord, Thou art life, though I be dead; Love's fire Thou art, however cold I be,
> Nor heaven have I, nor place to lay my head, Nor home, but Thee.
>
> (Christina Rossetti)

Here I say the evidence of the indwelling God (I John 4:15)… is the fundamental ground for our Faith and Victory. (I John 5:4)

The Round, Jeevalia schoolgirls' compound.

This compound is called the Round because the houses are built around the church in the middle. The church is directly in front of Salma's house. At summertime, in the moonlight, Salma played the stories that she read from *The Pilgrim's Progress* as a game. The children were allowed to play between 7:00 p.m. and 8:00 p.m. while there was still moonlight. When I returned home in 2010, Kanahanitie, who had polio, told me that she enjoyed our time playing the game of "Pilgrim's Progress" in the evening moonlight as children.

In 1931, when Amy was sixty-four years old, she had an accident that confined her to her room for the next twenty years. These are five of her most trusted workers, who had been with her for many years, who then took on leadership roles.
Top left to bottom right:
Rukma, leader of the square.
Paripu, in charge of round compound and Jeevalia.
Lola, in charge of gardens as well as first and second grade.
Leela, in charge of small boys' compound. Preena, Amy's first child. Salma personally knew all of them, as they interacted with her life. She also knew Preena, who ran away from the Hindu temple and became Amy's first child and, later, became an educator.

Lotus buds: Lola's children.

Lola oversaw the raising of around five hundred children. Salma was the last, arriving in 1951, five years before Lola passed away in 1956. The last twenty-five children stayed with Lola until 1956, when kind mother Rajamacottie took over.

Left: Dayamani (age nine).
Devarul and Salma (age nine).
Jeevanathie (age twenty-five).

Left: Ponnamai Carunia and Salma Carunia.
Dr. Ponnalari Carunia.

Sittara Carunia.

Beloved gentle housemother,
Rajamacottie Accal.

The flower, vegetable garden, and mango grove growing behind the house where Salma was raised and worked in. Salma enjoyed seeing migrating birds and mongoose in her backyard. The mongoose is the cobra's only natural enemy.

Left: Jackfruit tree. Upper left: Narthai (bitter orange, used for making pickles, juice, and marmalade, and eaten as is. It is a great source of vitamin C). Upper right: Mangoes. Lower left: Tapioca roots. Lower right: Red bananas. Below: The road to God's garden, where Salma worked for years.

Lola sometimes took children in her care to see the TVS garden, where the jackfruit grows. Salma sometimes saw large jackfruit, as large as fifty pounds! The jackfruit tree pictured above was growing in the forest, near our holiday house on the mountain.

# CHAPTER 4

## Back to School
## Fifth Grade

My teacher, Navarathinie Carunia-Raja. Her hope
and trust in me (Salma) were crushed!

On the first day of fifth grade, we all ran to the Jeevalia school to place our books (we called them "pile") in our assigned place at the long writing desks. We would take them from the cupboard where they were kept at night and pile them on our designated spots, where we sat on the floor cross-legged. My seat was in the third row. After that, we all rushed to the big blackboard on which our names were written in alphabetical order, as we all were eager to see our assigned class duties.

Everyone wanted to get the duty of bell ringer as a gong hung in this classroom. Navarathinie, our fifth-grade teacher, had written "class leader" (class captain) beside my name. I could not believe it and kept trying to see whether I was reading it correctly, for there were twenty-five others in the same class. Yes, it was written next to my name: class leader, and I ran home very happy, thinking what an honor for me to be a class leader.

This kind act of the teacher, Navarathinie Carunia, showed that she had faith and belief in me. She must have seen me very differently from other teachers. It gave me a real big *hope and courage* to continue my life against the fiery darts and high waters.

Alas! My happiness was short-lived because things changed when we all returned to school at 8:00 a.m.! While sitting down in front of our bench in our classroom, our headmistress, Christina, and the two missionary English teachers, Evu Sittie (Evelyn Bowden) and Vimba Sittie (Eleanor Backhouse), entered the classroom. When they saw my name on the board as class leader, they held their heads in their hands and began shaking them with disapproval. They told Navarathinie not to make me the class leader. I was crushed.

Instead, Angelie was chosen as the class leader. Angelie was one of the few students who lived with her parents in the fellowship. She did not live as one of us orphan girls. She had certain privileges. For example, let me tell you about her good fortune by explaining the writing tools we had for class.

All students were given one pencil to use for a full semester. It had our names carved on it, and we carefully put them on the class teacher's table at the end of the day. The teacher would sharpen them in the morning and return them to us to use for the day. It had no eraser on the tip, and we had no separate erasers! We were forbidden to erase anything we wrote. Some girls tried to use the stone we would put on the top of our book pile, but they found that it only tore their paper!

At the end of the semester, the teacher would measure each pencil in the class and award a prize to the student with the tallest pencil. Now every time, this award goes to Angelie. In those days, I did not understand how. She had all the same assignments we did. But now, I realized she used a pencil her parents gave her to save the school pencil. No one seemed to know she had an advantage.

After just one semester, our dear teacher, Navarathinie, was taken away from us when she was given in marriage to a man in Madurai, who was also a teacher. She was only twenty-two at the time and very attractive. Many men had been asking for her hand in marriage. In those days, the fellowship would try to have its adult children married and have an outside career. Otherwise, they would stay and work at the fellowship. So they gave her in marriage. It was not considered necessary even to ask her if that is what she wanted.

She was *gone*! I was very sad about her departure to a faraway place. But then, married girls came home to deliver their first baby as was the custom.

She returned home for her first delivery and named her baby Margaret, which was the English name of Ms. Wilkinson, who was one of the great missionaries who brought modern education to the fellowship.

On July 25, 2023, I talked with her on the phone, and later, her grandchildren sent me the photos you see above. She had forty in her family, including grandchildren and great-grandchildren.

Today, at seventy-nine years old, I am so grateful and salute my dear teacher Navarathinie, who, I realized later in my life, had faith in me and gave me *hope and courage* to continue my home school life, despite the many unjust punishments that I endured.

She saw what Lola had seen in me when Lola predicted that Salma would be a leader one day! Navarathinie is ninety-three years old. She still lives in Madurai and has five children, along with many grandchildren. Two months ago, I heard that her first child Margaret has retired. Navarathinie still calls me from time to time, asking me to come and visit her in Madurai. When I go to India next time, I must do this. On October 30, 2024, her granddaughter Jeni told me she is thriving at age 93!

After writing this part, I called her in India and discussed my life. Since she left me in the fifth grade, much has happened. But the kindness she had shown me was something I remembered, and I thanked her for her faith in me. This helped me to have hope in life, come what may, when facing the storms of life in my early teenage years at the home school.

I had to repeat the fifth grade and was now in the same class with younger girls. Fifth-grade children received a personal Bible on New Year's Day, January 1. All fifteen children living in Lola's house shared one bookshelf! As you can imagine, sometimes, when children were grabbing for their books, which were piled up high on one shelf, some were dropped on the floor or otherwise mishandled. Lola knew how careful I was with my things, so she told me that my Bible could go to her table where she kept her devotional books! So my Bible was kept where no one else could touch it.

We had a scripture portion card from Scripture Union, from which every child was to read a daily portion, for which we all went to the House of Prayer. Sellamma, who looked after the church and prepared it for Sunday services, would open it and switch on the lights at 5:30 a.m. Then all of us young schoolgirls, about eighty in number, would run to the church from our houses, find our little place, and read till 6:00 a.m. Every Sunday, when assembled at the school assembly hall before English service, the fifth to seventh-grade children would recite the Sunday Collect (from the English prayer book) which we memorized during the week.

I wanted to take my new Bible and run to the church to read it with the other children in the mornings. But it was being protected on Lola's table in her little prayer room.

I slept next to Lola's bed. So when it was still dark at 5:30 a.m., I crawled under her bed and then over the windowsill into the little room to reach my Bible. I would sneak like this each morning to get my Bible and read with the others. (Especially chapters from the Old Testament that fascinated me!) However, I knew that I must return it to her table before 6:30 a.m., which was when she bathed.

## Lola's Glory Day
### August 23, 1956

In August 1956, Lola took ill and was taken to the fellowship hospital. On Thursday evening, I came home from the playground and started to light the hurricane lanterns. (It was always my chore to fill them with kerosene oil in the afternoon after lunch.) It was now almost 6:30 p.m., and my evening chore was to light the three hurricane lanterns for the house and one to take to where Lola lived. I took the lamp and went to Lola's house. I was surprised to find her friends Leela, Rukma, and Paripu, Amy Carmichael's first children from 1901, gathered at Lola's house and wondering what was happening. I put the lantern in between the two doors as usual, called "good night" to Lola, and turned to go when Leela called my name and said, "Salma, you must shine for the Lord just like this little lamp you brought." Then I saw our fellowship van, Silver Queen, come to Lola's house, and Dr. Nancy Robbins (Karunai Sittie) took Lola to the hospital.

I ran back to our home and stood with the rest of Lola's children. Then, there were just seven of us. We stood at the front of our house and saw Lola taken to the hospital by the doctor. At 7:00 p.m., we all ran to the school to do our homework till 8:00, but some of us wondered about Lola. Usually, when we returned after doing our homework, Lola would have pudding for me. She would get this pudding from the missionaries' bungalow kitchen and always kept some at the bottom of her dish for me. No pudding awaited me on that night or thereafter, and Lola's house was closed.

Our house mother, Rajamacottie, would go to the hospital every morning and evening to see how Lola was doing. Lola would go in and out of a coma. But when her childhood friends came, she was often able to talk to them. Paripu, now the fellowship's leader, told me that Lola kept asking for me.

Unfortunately, we children were not allowed to go to the hospital. They said Lola kept asking the doctor, "Will my Salma go to boarding school, and will you send her to high school?" I think it showed that Lola was still worried about my schooling.

Lola knew I needed to be educated to do the great things she already felt were ahead of me. I was her last child, and she had great hopes for me.

In the second week of her hospitalization, Lola kept calling out for me. Finally, on Thursday at about 10:00 a.m., someone came to the school to call all the children of Lola. We were told to go to the hospital with our house mother, Rajamacottie. The walk took us about half an hour. We went inside the hospital and arrived at Lola's ward. Rosema, the nurse, summoned us in, and we stood before Lola's bed. The nurse told Lola, "Your children are here to see you."

Lola looked around but was quiet. Suddenly, Lola asked, "Where is my Salma?"

So the nurse asked me to come forward. I hid behind Ponnamai, who was taller, because, as a little girl, I was afraid of her authoritative presence. When I came forward, Lola looked at me and said, "Salma, I will not come home anymore. Be a good girl, so they can send you to boarding school." And then her voice sank.

This left me very confused and scared. Lola was dying, and I was being left behind to swim through the much-troubled waters, for I was only eleven years old. After that, Lola did not talk to anyone and went into a deep coma. She passed away on August 23, 1956. It was the birthday of Jeyavallie, another of Lola's children. I can never forget that day, Lola's glory day!

Lola's children were taken to the church where her body was in view. She wore a white sari with an orange border that she always wore on Easter Sunday. I stood beside the body, still in disbelief. I was sad that she was gone. She was always stern but fair, and she was my protector from troubles in school. On the other hand, I was happy that our kind house mother, Rajamacottie, was with us now, for she dealt with us with much kindness.

Children were never allowed to go to funerals. However, this time, Lola's children were allowed to go to the graveyard called God's Garden. This is where they buried all the members of the Dohnavur Fellowship who lived there. It was my first time to witness the death and burial of a person, and this was my own beloved Lola. The tubular bells in our church tower played "Forever with the Lord."

> Forever with the Lord, Amen, so let it be
> Life from His death is in that word
> 'Tis immortality
> Here in the body pent. Absent from Him I roam
> Yet nightly pitch my moving tent
> A day's march nearer home
>
> So, when my latest breath
> Shall rend the veil in twain
> By death I shall escape from death
> And life eternal gain
> Knowing as I am known
> How shall I love that word
> And oft repeat before the throne
> *That resurrection-word, That shout of victory, Once more,*
> Forever with the Lord
>
> (James Montgomery, 1771–1854)

## In the Sixth Grade

I passed fifth grade on the second attempt and went to the sixth grade. My name was on the blackboard in the classroom with others, but next to my name were lots of black marks, which meant I would be punished. I and others with black marks cleaned and swept the school compound with brooms every Saturday. We used rags to scrub the red tile floor of the classroom, where we sat cross-legged on the floor in front of a wooden bench where we kept our books.

Up until the fifth grade, we could only use a pencil. Now, as big sixth graders, we had the privilege of using a wooden pen holder and ink. The bench we used in the sixth and seventh grades had an inkpot hole at both ends. Each child was given a wooden pen holder. This was a wooden shaft with a small metal nib at the end. We also had blotting paper to soak and dry the extra ink or ink drops on the paper.

We were happy to use this holder and would carefully dip the nib into the inkpot. We felt like we were now grown-ups. Writing in our exercise books with ink was serious schoolwork! However, this could bring trouble. If one were not careful, sometimes, the pot would tip and spill ink on the bench and the floor. Man! Then everyone on the bench got black marks!

There was a large tamarind tree just outside the school, and we would pluck its leaves to help scrub up the spilled ink. There was no room for accidents. We were held responsible for our actions. Sometimes, if your pen nib split or broke, you would not get a replacement without doing some kind of detention.

One day, my friend, Jeyavallie, told me that she had invented a nib for the pen! She made this out of the pod of a plant that grew outside our classroom. The pod's tip was pointed, which gave her the idea that we could dip that into the ink bottle and write. Sure enough, one day, my pen nib broke. So I tried the nib of the dried pod, which I plucked through our classroom window, and it was a success! Sometimes, nature will give you the answer.

When we reached sixth grade, all the children had to learn to swim. Each class was assigned an afternoon swimming lesson. Evu Sittie (Evelyn Bowden) will take our swimming class at 2:00 p.m. in the large open irrigation well. It was about fifty feet across and very deep; as children, we thought it was maybe one mile deep!

About twenty terraced stone steps led down to the water's edge. The twenty girls in the class would get in the water while the teacher sat at one end on the stone steps. She could not always see everyone in the water all the time. When we swam, we usually went from one side to the other where some bamboo lines (ropes) hung down. We grab these to rest. The swim dresses, very loose one-piece jumpers, often too big that would hang below the knees on some and had to be tied with a string around the waist. One day, while swimming on the far side of the well, I was holding the bamboo line.

Suddenly, I saw someone struggling, trying to swim up, but she couldn't because of her tangled swim dress. I quickly dove under, got hold of her swimming dress, and pulled her up. It was my best friend, Jeyavallie! I let her rest by hanging on to the bamboo line and then helped her to the steps. It was lots of fun swimming in the garden well.

I have many good happy memories of those times. Sadly, this generation of fellowship students can't swim there, for the well went dry due to years without rain. It may be worse that they likely do not know how to swim!

Jeevalia School, home school from third grade to seventh grade.

The fourth grade classroom where Salma learned about Niagara Falls in 1952.

Salma visited Niagara Falls in 1998. It was a dream come true!

Teacher Amirtha Devairakkam, BA, BEd, supervising the exam hall. On the wall to the left, you can see the gong used to mark the end of each class period. When the bell rings, the students remain seated, and the teachers change. All of the students wanted to ring the gong, but it was assigned to a specific student. There was only one clock in the entire school (seen above in the upper right), and this was back when no one had a wristwatch.

This is the same fifth grade classroom where Salma studied with teacher Navarathinie, who gave Salma hope for the future and helped her to advance in her studies and her life.

Salma was short and thin, so she tried to pump the water with her stomach, just like the girl in the picture. This is how the children bathed, sitting or standing under the spout.

Jeyapushpam Carunia, who grew up with Salma in Lola's house, became part of the staff, taking care of the children.

Tarabai Carunia feeding the little one while the other children are eating from the brass bowl with their right-hand fingers.

I scrub my pots, I scrub my pans,
I scrub my brazes and my cans,
For work is such a jolly thing,
it makes one want to sing!

# CHRIST IS IN ME

When each duty crowds the other
Through the sultry days,
Plant a little flower of patience by our way.
When the slothful flesh would murmur,
Ease would cast her spell,
Set our face as flint till twilight's vesper bell
(Amy Carmichael)

Hate not laborious work, joy, joy is in it.
Do not thy duty shirk, joy, joy is in it.
Welcome the daily round,
on and be faithful found.
On and thou shalt be crowned
Joy, joy is in it.
(Amy Carmichael)

Playing the tubular bells in the House of Prayer tower.

Packiaveni Carunia, concentrating as she plays a song on the tubular bells.

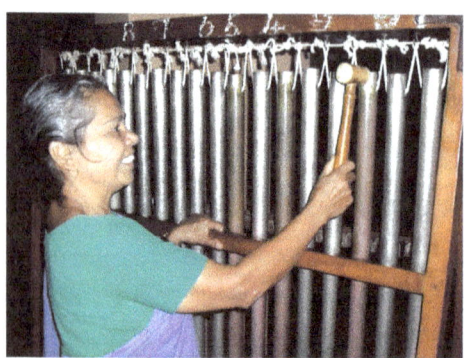

Memalar Carunia, joyfully playing the chimes. This has been one of her duties from 1991 to the present day.

Shanthie Aruldasan reverently playing the vesper bell in the 1940s and 1950s.

Amirtha Carunia and Ezekiel Devairakkam on their wedding day on February 12, 1993.

Nalaiya and Nesarani on their wedding day.

Mimosa's grandson, Rajamanian, and great-grandson, Albert Rajkumar Devairakkam.

# CHAPTER 5

## The Missionaries
### Men Are Called Annachie, Ladies Are Called Sitties

The Australian missionary, Arul Sittie (Kathleen Grant), was responsible for the kindergarten at Jeevananda. Every Monday at playtime, 11:30 to noon, she organized the playing of musical instruments. She made sure that every child in first and second grade would have a chance to play an instrument.

We would stand in a long line, leading to where the devices were handed out. The first two students in the line got to play the drum. We would all run to get in the front line, for everyone wanted to play the drum!

We children all liked the music time very much because we played instruments such as triangles, tambourines, cymbals, etc. She treated all the children the same and never showed partiality.

She came to help in Dohnavur Fellowship in June 1927 and returned to Australia when she retired in 1961. I liked her because she played the organ at the kindergarten school and for the children's meetings. On Saturday evenings at 5:30 p.m., she would take some of the children in first and second grade to sing evangelistic songs for the patients in our hospital. We, the children, liked it very much because we got to play some musical instruments, which were always kept at the kindergarten school.

Now I must tell you about the coleaders of the Fellowship, Devasamathanam Annachie (Godfrey Webb-Peploe) and Devanesan Annachie (John Risk).

Godfrey Webb-Peploe was in charge of the boys in Vanacharbu from December 1926. He was elected as coleader with Amy Carmichael in 1927, but he suddenly passed away on February 19, 1949, while serving at Dohnavur Fellowship. I heard that he was a good cricket player at Cambridge University in England.

Then Devanesan Annachie (John Risk) (who I understand came to India during the Second World War and had been the ship's captain) was requested by Amy to work in Dohnavur Fellowship. He came and helped her, working in the boys' compound.

In 1949, after Devasamathanam Annachie, the coleader, passed away, Amy asked Devanesan Annachie (John Risk) to be her coleader, and he agreed.

Two years later, when Amy passed away in January 1951, Devanesan Annachie became the leader of the fellowship, and Ubaharie Sittie was elected as a coleader.

We all loved Devanesan Annachie like a father. As little girls, we would go to his house, in the boys' compound, on our Coming Days (birthdays), and he would give us a ride on his bicycle. On Sunday afternoons, he played with us for an hour at his home. We enjoyed afternoon time playing with him at his house.

It was in his house that I saw a typewriter for the first time. He put me on his lap, guided my fingers, and showed me how to type my name on his typewriter, which I can never forget. I never thought in 1949, one day I'd have my own typewriter, let alone the computer I have now (personal computers had not even been invented in 1949).

Devanesan Annachie passed away suddenly in February 1962. It was a somber day for everyone, as we loved him so much. The news was even delivered to all those who were away at boarding schools throughout South India. So it was a very sad day for all of the children and students at Dohnavur Fellowship.

SALMA CARUNIA CARTER

# About Our Rice Farms

Tholan Annachie (Norman Burns), an Australian missionary, was in charge of the farms. We had a lot of Jersey cows, which gave hundreds of gallons of milk daily. They milked the cows twice daily, and each child got twenty ounces of milk daily.

He was also in charge of our eight hundred acres of rice fields and other crops and was responsible for bringing the grain into the granary after the harvest. There would be hundreds of sacks of rice taken from the fields to the granary, covering fifty to seventy miles, by bullock carts. At times, late in the night, we heard the bells tied around the necks of the bulls pulling the carts on the country road in the pitch-dark as they neared our granary.

The rice stalks had to be cut from the field, then gathered, and winnowed (shifted) on the same day to separate the grain. This was performed by hand, and everyone hoped for a windy day to help blow the chaff away. After all of this hard work, it was ready to bag and ship by the carts into the fellowship granary. See picture on page 161.

Tholan Annachie rode his bike at the back of the last of twelve bullock carts to protect it from thieves. Sadly, there were people in the jungle areas where the carts passed, ready to take the rice any way they could. This was an impoverished area, and people were always looking for food.

But this food was for one thousand orphans, so Tholan Annachie guarded it with all his might until it was safely put away in the granary and locked up. From here, Seela Carunia saw that the rice was parboiled and the husks were removed by pounding on a mortar stone with long wooden pestles, which had metal attached at the end. She then distributed the rice sacks to the seven kitchens according to the head count in each compound. Later on, machines replaced this hard manual labor.

Santha Sittie (Lorna Burns), wife of Tholan Annachie, worked as a nurse in the boy's compound, Vanacharbu. I knew hundreds of those boys were grateful for her love and kindness; she looked after them when they were sick. They both retired in 1964 and returned to

Australia, Tholan Annachie passed away in 1994, and Santha Sittie passed away in 1996.

Sirappan Annachie (Mr. Philip England) was an engineer who came to Dohnavur in December 1931 and worked in the workshop. There was no electricity in Dohnavur Fellowship in those days. He built a large generator that brought electric lights to the fellowship hospital so they could also do emergency surgery at night.

He also built a large cistern on the hospital's roof, connected to each ward by pipelines and a tap that worked with the leg pedal. This provided running water. The nurses filled the cistern daily by pumping water using a hand pump attached to a long pipe that went into a very deep well. When I was doing the first year of nursing training, we younger student nurses had to take turns operating the hand pump to fill the tank. We tried to do it before the sun's temperature rose to 120 degrees during the summer.

Sirappan Annachie also built two bridges across a swift-flowing mountain river to reach Naraikadu, the estate owned by Dohnavur Fellowship in the western Ghat mountains. The bridge is still standing today. He was married to Joan England, who had come to the fellowship in October 1928 and worked in the main office. They had two children, Tara and Tarie, both born in the Dohnavur Fellowship hospital. Tarie was born on November 19, 1944, and was four days older than me.

Tarie and I became friends, but Tarie left for England in February 1954 when she was ten. Her ship sailed through Suez Canal. I missed her much. After over forty years, I met her in 1994 in Edinburgh, Scotland, the UK.

This happened when my husband Mike Carter was doing his PhD at the University of Edinburgh from 1992 to 1995. Tarie came to see me, but we felt sad as our childhood had all passed without seeing each other. I was fifty years old then.

Later, when I was again in England in the summer of June 2018, Tarie came to stay with me as I was visiting a Dohnavur missionary, Dr. Jacky Woolcock (Kiruba Sittie). Tarie and I had three good days to catch up on each other's lives.

Tarie became a rector, is now retired, and lives in Wales. She has three children and four grandchildren. Her parents stayed and worked in Dohnavur, India, till they retired. They went back to England in 1968 after forty long years of service at the fellowship.

Tarie was ten when she left her parents and Dohnavur. She would miss her home and couldn't visit them for many years. After all this time, when we met again, she told me, "Salma, at least you have the Dohnavur Fellowship to call home. You can go there anytime to see the Indian housemothers who took care of you while growing up in Dohnavur in South India." (After 2000, she was able to visit Dohnavur Fellowship at any time.) Now I feel for her loss and thank God for the happy home where I grew up. Everyone knew everyone. It was *one* great, *big* Dohnavur family.

## The Missionary Doctors and Nurses

Dohnavur Fellowship was filled with beautiful children. The doctors and nurses worked tirelessly to maintain our health. Many girls and boys raised in Dohnavur were trained as nurses by the missionaries. See the picture on page 107.

Anyone who fell ill was sent to the fellowship hospital and admitted into separate wards reserved for the fellowship girls, boys, and adults. It was called the Family Section.

The hospital was built in 1927 and was named Place of Heavenly Healing. It had several wings for the outpatients with a tower in the center. Later, a men's section was added after some male doctors came from England to work at the hospital.

When I came as a six-day-old baby, the doctor was Devamitthiran Annachie (Murray Webb-Peploe). He was the elder brother of Devasamathanam Annachie (Godfrey Webb-Peploe), who worked with Amy in 1926. Devamitthiran Annachie married Miss Oda, who was from Holland. They had twins born in the fellowship hospital. But they left and went to England for their children's education.

Peruthavie Sittie (Dr. Christian Rogan) came from Edinburgh, Scotland, UK, in October 1934 and became the Dohnavur family doctor. She retired in 1968 and went back to Edinburgh, Scotland.

It was a great pleasure to see her again in 1992–95 when my husband Mike Carter did his doctorate in Christianity in the Non-Western World at the University of Edinburgh. Every Saturday afternoon, we went to her house for high tea and enjoyed sharing old memories of the Dohnavur Fellowship.

Manosanthi Sittie (Sister Anna Milt) came from Switzerland in December 1932. She was in charge of the hospital and was known as a very strict person and ran a tight ship. However, I remember one sad incident the day before her birthday: Sunday, December 6, 1957. That Sunday ended up being spent in a sad and dark mood.

We children were assembled on Sunday morning at the school assembly. They told us that someone who worked in the hospital had gone into the pharmacy room to take something. This room was open with the door ajar, as nothing was locked up in those days. That person was also seen pumping water from the nearby hand pump but was not questioned why she was around the operation theater and X-ray room at 9:00 p.m. After all, she did work in the pharmacy, and people were not very suspicious in those days. This lady returned to her nurse's quarters and was later found dead in her room.

Later, we discovered that she wanted to get married and asked Manosanthi Sittie (Sister Anna Milt) for permission. In those days, a marriage needed to be arranged and approved. Sittie said no and told her that she needed more helpers to work in the hospital because the number of patients was increasing yearly. So the helper wanted to do something drastic to spoil Manosanthi Sittie's birthday celebration. Manosanthi Sittie could not celebrate her birthday on that Sunday. The private funeral was held at 5:00 p.m., and we children went for a long walk outside the fellowship. Manosanthi Sittie retired in December 1958.

We also had some more missionary nurses, such as Nurani Sittie (Sister Erna Stuwe). She came in 1929 and retired in December 1956; Uthara Sittie (Sister Hulda Sauter) arrived in December 1933 and retired in 1962; Ubasanthie Sittie (Lucette Collingwood) came in February 1938 and retired in February 1966.

There was also a couple named Kaitunai Annachie (Dr. Ronald Taylor) and his wife Ronnie Sittie (Stella Taylor). They had a small dog called Helpie.

When I was four to seven years old, I used to play with it, for they brought it to the children's compound. They came in January 1948 and went back to England in January 1951. We children missed playing with their little dog, Helpie.

Then there was Thiral Annachie (Terence Addenbrook), who worked in the X-ray room. I remember him always wearing the purple hospital workers' uniform like Indian men's wraparound.

Dayaseelan Annachie (Dr. Angus Kinnear) worked from January 1940 to 1948, but I do not remember him much, for I was only four years old when he left.

Surgeon Dr. Ben Walkey arrived from England in July 1950 and performed many operations with Peruthavie Sittie (Dr. Christian Rogan) and Karunai Sittie (Dr. Nancy Robbins). In 1952, he married Muthara Sittie (Peggy Craig), and they were transferred to a rural hospital.

## Karunai Sittie
## Our Doctor and How I Obtained My Sponsors

Karunai Sittie (Nancy Robbins) came in February 1946 and became the Dohnavur family doctor in 1950. She held that role for the next twenty-seven years. Therefore, I grew up under Karunai Sittie's care. When we came home from boarding school for the holidays, she was the one who gave us full medical checkups.

When Karunai Sittie came from London, Rajarathinie Accal was the family's head nurse in the clinic. Karunai Sittie was learning Tamil, and Rajarathinie was a great help to her. Karunai Sittie lived in the bungalow near Rajarathinie Accal's residence. The babies' nursery was right across from the clinic. This way, the babies did not have to be taken to the hospital a mile and a half away.

Rajarathinie was a great friend of Kirubai (Grace), who was taking care of me then. Rajarathinie introduced me as a one-year-and-several-months-old baby to Karunai Sittie, as each child in Dohnavur

Fellowship had to be financially supported by a sponsor (referred to as "prayer friends"). Karunai Sittie wrote to her brother Rolland and his wife, Agnes Robbins, and they became my sponsors. I learned this once I grew up and wanted to contact my sponsors, but this wasn't easy. All information about the sponsors was kept secret at the fellowship's office in Wimbledon (the London office), England.

At that time, I did not know I would meet them in England one day! My wish was fulfilled when we went to Scotland for my husband's study at Aberdeen University in 1985. We made a trip to Bedford, England, to see my sponsors (referred to as "prayer friends" in Dohnavur Fellowship), for I managed to get their address from Karunai Sittie when she visited the youth hostel in Bangalore, India, in 1966 while I was there.

They were delighted to see me, the real person for whom they had prayed and supported when I was growing up in the orphanage. The Robbins took us to Cambridge and other places, especially to see a replica of the prison/cave of John Bunyan, who wrote *The Pilgrim's Progress*. Little did they know, this was my favorite childhood book

When Karunai Sittie (Dr. Nancy Robbins) was first tasked with overseeing the babies and small children, things about their behavior puzzled her. Their play was unimaginative and tended to be late developing, as they were late in learning to speak. This seemed to happen even though the babies were loved and well cared for. What, she wondered, was the reason for this?

Was it due to keeping the same-age children together in the nursery and moving them to live together again at the next level in the school compound? Did keeping them all in the same age group limit their learning? She thought this was so unlike a real family scene where children of different ages lived together. So she added two-year-old babies to each group.

As an example, two-year-old Packiaveni and Manomani and two six-year-old girls, Jeyapackiam and Sameehara, were part of my family with our house mother, R. Cottie. In addition, Amaravathi, a nineteen-year-old adult, was also moved to live with us to help R. Cottie with those youngsters.

These little girls brought us much joy as we watched them growing up, and Amaravathi became their house mother and moved out to her own house with them after two years of being with us.

I loved Packiaveni very much; she always ran to me when she saw me. Today, she telephones me as we still have that same sisterly love for each other. As I was writing my story in April 2019, I woke up and saw that she had called me. When I called back, my dear Packiaveni wished me a happy Easter. I was thrilled to hear her voice and talk with her, even though she was far away in India while I was in America.

Pakia offered thirty-five years of her life to help raise children in Dohnavur Fellowship. She was in charge of the large sewing room, where they prepared children's dresses, tunics, and so forth. She was then thirty years old and still dedicated her life to caring for the children at her house in Dohnavur Fellowship. She retired at age 65. My dearest Pakia passed away on September 5$^{th}$, 2024 at age 68.

Karunai Sittie (Dr. Nancy Robbins), whom I have known all my life in India, retired and returned to England in 1977. In England, I saw her for the last time in 2012 on my way to my home Dohnavur Fellowship. She passed away in 2014 when she was ninety-nine and a half years old.

Meleela Sittie came to the fellowship from Ottawa, Canada, in July 1946. Her elder sister, Mevara Sittie (Lilian Crawley), came to work in the Dohnavur Fellowship two years before her in August 1944. They both worked in the main office. Meleela Sittie became a personal secretary to Nura Sittie (Margaret Wilkinson) in 1959 when Nura Sittie became the leader of the fellowship.

Meleela Sittie also worked in the school office and conducted lower grade typing classes for the girls who did not pass the government exam at the secondary school level. Later, even those who had passed the government exam at the high school level were added to her typing class. This allowed them to continue practicing typing until they could get a seat at teacher's training or nursing training institutions outside the fellowship. Unfortunately, in those days, it could take a bribe to get a seat in the government training schools—the fellowship would not pay bribes! Therefore, it would take time for the orphan children of Dohnavur to be admitted into training schools.

In 1924, a missionary doctor from Ireland, Ubaharie Sittie (May Powell), came to work at Dohnavur. After Amy's accident in 1931, Ubaharie Sittie became the leader along with Devasamathanam Annachie (Godfrey Webb-Peploe), as it pleased Amy Carmichael to declare an Irish woman leader after her. Ubaharie Sittie was a strict administrator and ruled the first and second generations with an iron fist. She retired in October 1964 and returned to England, where she passed away in July 1991 at a long-term care home in Cheltenham, England.

Kiruba Sittie (Dr. Jacky Woolcock) was the last missionary to come to Dohnavur Fellowship. She came in November 1969, retired in June 1987, returned to England, and resides at Shoreham-by-Sea at West Sussex near the English Channel. I would visit her in England whenever I went home to India. She is the kindest and most broad-minded missionary I ever knew. I can talk to her about anything without fear, and she listens. Her picture is on page 109 (lower right photo, in blue sari, at Dohnavur Hospital).

Dr. Ponnalari, one of our own fellowship girls, led the hospital once the missionary doctors retired and returned to their home countries. She worked there for forty years, day and night, without a salary or any payment. She did it voluntarily until she entered into the joy of the Lord on February 2, 2014. As she heard the words:

> Well done, my faithful servant, as she fought the good fight and had finished the course and kept her faith. The Lord awarded her with the crown of righteousness. (2 Timothy 4:7–8)

# SALMA CARUNIA CARTER

## *PAUL HARRISON AWARD 2008*

The Paul Harrison Award is the accolade of the Christian Medical College, Vellore to alumni who have rendered selfless, steadfast and significant service to the neglected and the disadvantaged in the area of health care. Dr. Ponnalari Carunia from Dohnavur Fellowship Hospital, Tutucorin and Dr. John Cherian Oommen from Christian Hospital, Bissam Cuttack in Orissa are being presented the awards this year. I will read their individual citations.

The life story of Dr. Carunia is inextricably linked with the Dohnavur Fellowship which was founded in the latter part of the nineteenth century in Pannavilai village in the Tirulveli District of Tamil Nadu by the well known Irish missionary, Amy Carmichael. This institution has continued to be a home for hundreds of destitute, unwanted or orphaned children, especially girls. Its Fellowship Hospital is a charitable medical resource in this rural region for all manner and kinds of health needs. The core of the institution is a fellowship of dedicated individuals who live out their lives in service without remuneration except provision for their basic needs. From her infancy, Ponnalari grew up in the Fellowship where her educational proficiency eventually led her to medical studies in the Christian Medical College. She has been described by her contemporaries as a "sincere, conscientious and humble student with manifest Christian devotion". She graduated in 1966.

Dr. Carunia was posted to the Dohnavur Fellowship Hospital as part of her service obligation and there she has chosen to remain, accepting the austere and arduous life style and the responsibilities of the core fellowship. In her early years at the hospital she was inducted into the valuable skills of multicompetent care by the medical missionaries who had manned the hospital till Ponnalari arrived there as the first Indian volunteer. As her experience grew and medical sciences advanced, she built on her knowledge and skills. But she has continued to provide multicompetent holistic care in a profession that has overwhelmingly veered towards specialisation. Rural surgery is an essential part of her work and when she felt the need for additional skills in anesthesia, she returned to Vellore for a short period of training. Indeed that has been her only "sabbatical" from the rigours of her chosen career. Most of the time working single handedly, she has helped to develop the hospital into a 70 bed facility.

Realising the highly circumscribed life of Dr. Carunia, some of her expatriate classmates organised a special reunion for her. Here is how one of them describes that experience: "We had an opportunity to see our classmate after 40 years and to hear first hand of the stories of her life as a rural doctor. Many of us had done so well academically and professionally. But we were indeed proud to be her class mates and humbled as she has demonstrated more than any of the others, what it is to live by the motto of our institution – 'not to be ministered unto but to minister' "

Another contemporary who made a pilgrimage to visit her in Dohnavur has described the experience thus. "One would expect to see a worn out old lady doctor, but what impressed me was to meet an energetic, enthusiastic, small made woman with lively bright eyes and always ready for more action. Patients, young and old, poured in constantly for her advice, her healing touch and her comforting presence. The respect that they had for her and the confidence in her was only too obvious."

Christian Medical College salutes this selfless and steadfast life of service appropriate to the community which mothered her at one time and to which she is a mother now. For a lifetime of deep Christian commitment and sincerity beyond the call of duty, and for being a living example of the motto of this institution, we are proud to present the Paul Harrison Award to

### Dr. Ponnalari Carunia

Director  
10.11.2008

Principal

As I have mentioned, each child's health was maintained very well. Missionary Nurse Atharavu Sittie (Alison Wiggins), who came to Dohnavur from Christchurch, New Zealand, in November 1938, was in charge of the babies' nursery. She knew every child and worked in the fellowship family clinic. She weighed every child once a month until they reached twelve years of age and kept records of them.

I grew up under her loving care. Hundreds of children passed through her care. She ensured that every child received the vaccines against smallpox, tetanus, diphtheria, and whooping cough. In 1955, the whole fellowship family was vaccinated for tuberculosis, for the epidemic was spreading in nearby villages.

The scar is still there on our left shoulder. When they gave the testing medicine, through injection, to about nine hundred of us on our arms, they said only two people came positive after seven days. Their arms were swollen like from a snakebite, so they did not have to go through what we all went through to get the vaccination. They were Anamal and Devarul.

In 1965, the polio vaccine was discovered. It was given orally, first to the children and then to the adults. There were about twenty missionary family members in Dohnavur Fellowship at that time. One missionary, Meleela Sittie (Silvia Crawley), got polio. In 1957, she used to go swimming in the irrigation well in the garden in the evenings after work.

Many years later, when I came to America and married Ben Michael Carter, I learned that his mother, Hilda Carter, contracted polio in 1952. They said this occurred after she was swimming at a public swimming pool in Texas. She slowly became paraplegic and spent six weeks in the iron lung in the hospital. She was never able to walk again.

Nonetheless, she raised two sons; at the time, one was two years old and the other nine months old. She did all this from a wheelchair while her husband went to work every day to earn the money needed to feed the family. But that is another story, to be told in part 2.

# CHRIST IS IN ME

## Tonsillectomy

On August 22, 1957, Atharavu Sittie, the nurse in charge of the children's well-being, told my house mother, Rajamacottie, that I must go to the hospital that evening after school. Why? Because the next morning, I and three other girls, Sahera, Samihara, and Annaselvam, were to have our tonsillectomies.

We four girls spent the night before our surgery in the hospital. At dawn, we were given only black coffee. As children, we did not get coffee every day. By 9:00 a.m., they started to take us, one by one, to the operation theater, and the sound of the trolley bed rolling on the tile floor made me apprehensive.

I was scheduled to be the last one to go into the surgery room. It must have been about 10:30 a.m. when they pushed me into the anesthesia room to administer chloroform. I closed my eyes tight, and Manosanthie Sittie, the anesthesiologist, started singing Psalm 117 in Tamil very loudly! She asked me to sing along with her, which I did, and then gradually, I went a little under and stopped singing.

Now came a horrible time! When I was taken into the surgery room, I had not yet gone deep into sleep! I hated that chloroform smell, so I did not breathe it deeply. When they started operating on me, I felt excruciating pain! I struggled and screamed as they tried to remove the left-side tonsil. I heard someone say, "More chloroform, please." At this point, I was very much afraid of the chloroform. I then went unconscious. Finally, they finished the surgery.

They later told me that I started singing songs about heaven in the recovery room. My singing was perhaps because my subconscious knew that my house mother, Lola, had passed away on this very day the previous year. It was the first anniversary of Lola's Glory Day. Lola made her children memorize many hymns and songs in the summertime, so I knew them by heart.

Then I kept on singing other songs! The nurses around me were trying to stop me from singing, for my mouth was bleeding.

The only thing I was aware of was that I was very thirsty. I tried communicating with the nurse by singing the song we learned at school on Good Friday. It was how Jesus cried out from the cross that

He was thirsty! Then one of the nurses said, "Oh, she wants some water to drink."

She brought water in a cup and slowly poured it into my mouth. That gave me great pain trying to swallow the water, but I kept on humming and singing the heavenly hymns. It seemed to me that heaven's door was opened for me to peek in as I was still semiconscious. The Bible says that where your treasure is, there will your heart be also. My heart, mind, and soul had longed for the kingdom of God since I was five years old, and now, at age twelve, and even more than ever when I was unconscious.

Meleela Sittie, who was suffering from polio and was in the opposite ward in the hospital, told me later that she was greatly comforted by the songs I was singing. The bleeding stopped soon, and my wound healed within a week. After two weeks, I returned to school to catch up on my missed lessons. The good part was there were no bad marks for the two weeks I was in the hospital—haha!

A story in pictures: how Salma obtained her sponsors.

Left to right: Roland and Agnes Robbins with Salma Carunia-Carter at Cambridge University in England. The Robbins were Salma's sponsors (prayer friends).

Left and right: Rajarathine Carunia, chief nurse in Dohnavur Fellowship, who worked with Dr. Nancy Robbins and introduced little Salma to her in 1946.

Salma and Mike having dinner with the Robbins family (Agnes and Roland, along with their daughter Ruth) in 1985. Dr. Ben Michael Carter is not pictured, as he took the photo. Roland Robbins was Nancy Robbins's brother.

Place of Healing, Parama Suha Salai (Hospital).

Left: Salma's friend from school, Devashanti.
Back: Dr. Ponnalari Carunia.
Middle: Inbamani Carunia, lab technician. She worked with much dedication in Dohnavur Hospital for over fifty years!
Right: Naveena Carunia, who was a theater sister for fifty-six years! Behind the nurses is the operation theater, where surgeries were performed.

Left: Dr. Ponnalari Carunia.
Right: Jeyapackiam Carunia, RN and midwife, who worked as a staff nurse from 1981 to 2020. From 2018 until the present day, she teaches practical nursing. She was with Salma in Salma's house, age six to eight.

Center: Dayavallie Carunia, who worked in
hospital collections from 1975 to 2020.
Right: Sunithie Carunia, assistant to theater sister Naveena
Carunia, who Salma taught in seventh grade.

The entrance to the hospital. The hospital was built in 1936.

Dr. Ponnalari Carunia, 2005.  Nancy Robbins (Karunai Sittie) and Jackie Woolcock (Kiruba Sittie) and a young Dr. Ponnalari Carunia, 1979.

Between 1996 and 2005, while working at DFW Hospital Council, Dr. Carter wrote a poem to all of the nurses he worked with around the world.

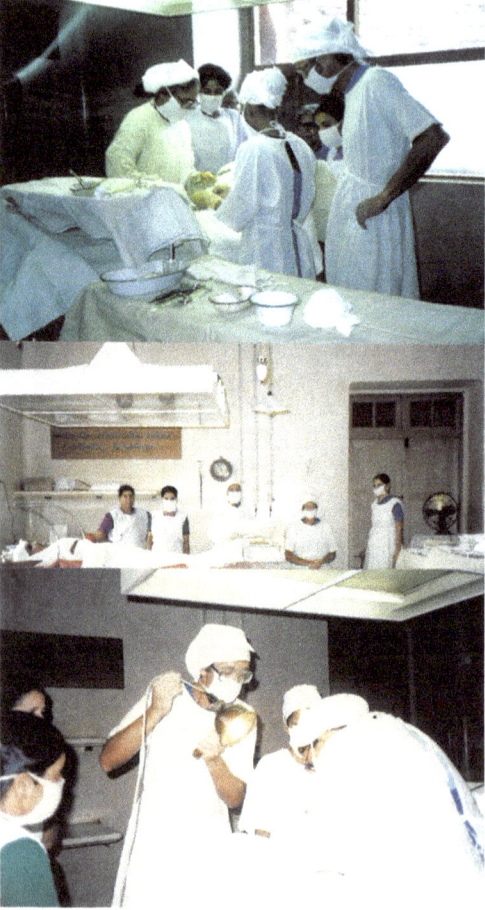

Dr. Carter holding a light in order to aid Dr. Ponnalari Carunia as she delivers twins via C-section at Dohnavur Fellowship Hospital. Dohnavur Fellowship is a Christian volunteer organization in Southern India. Dr. Carter was visiting his wife Salma's home at Dohnavur Fellowship, 1991.

I Am Your Guardian

I am your guardian.
I'm there for you every day.
You're my vocation and
I will provide care your way.
I'm here to minister.
I am hands sent from Heaven.
I give you care and support.
I hustle 24/7.

I am your guardian.
When your physician leaves,
I will remain by your side
For your concerns are mine.
I want your wants dignified.
And when your visitors go,
I am the person who stays.
I'm there to tend to your needs.
I am the one who obeys.

I am your guardian.
When Florence Nightingale
Went to the Crimean War
It was the wounded who
She made that hard journey for.
She brought compassion to
The ill, the limping, the lame.
It's the twenty-first century
but that's still the same.

I am your guardian.
I am there
Before we draw up your chart.
I am there
For every beat of your heart.
And in your darkest times
I will be your burning light.
I will shine through your pain.
I will shine through your night.

You are my first concern.
When I sign in on my shift.
I want you whole again.
I want your spirits to lift.
And when your spirits flag
I really do sympathize.
I feel your struggle for breath.
I see the ache in your eyes.

I am your guardian.
I'm there for you every day.
You're my vocation and
I will provide care your way.
I'm here to minister.
I am hands sent from Heaven.
I give you care and support. I hustle 24/7.
I am your guardian.
(Dr. Ben Michael Carter)

## All of the missionaries who played a part in Salma's life.

Top row, left: Mabel Wade (Preeya Sittie), 1907–1961.

Top row, middle: Beatrice Taylor (Kamala Sittie), 1928–1968. She was in charge of the children's compound. Salma played with toys at her house every day.

Top row, right: Jessie Walker (Seetha Sittie), 1927–1964.

Center left: Frances Beath (Premie Sittie), 1910–1960.

Bottom left: Godfrey Webb-Peploe (Devasamathanam Annachie), 1927–1949, who was in charge of the boys' compound in Vanacharbu.

Amy Carmichael, 1893–1951, near Victorian water fountain in Belfast, Northern Ireland, where she helped a poor old woman to cross the street. This began her missionary life helping others. In 1986, Salma and her husband Mike visited the fountain, which still stands today.

Top left: Vivien Tompkins (Vivillia Sittie), 1930–1971. She took care of disabled children in Muppandal.
Top, second: Silvia and Lilian Crawley (Meleela and Mevara Sitties), 1946–1981/1944–1977.
Top, third (above): Barbara Wavre (Rajeeva Sittie), 1940–1962, with her children Susanna and David. She was the arts and crafts teacher to Salma at the Jeevalia home school.
Top, third (below): Hilary Rogers (Vimala Sittie), 1955–1992. She was a dentist.
Top, fourth (top): Alice Roberts (Mellial Sittie), 1926–1970. She was the music and sewing teacher, choir director, organ player, and netball coach. She was very much involved in Salma's life.
Top, fourth (bottom): Andree Golay (Jaya Sittie), 1951–1959.
Bottom left: Nancy Robbins (Karunai Sittie), 1946–1977. She was the family doctor.
Bottom center: Salma Carunia-Carter. She is grateful to all those missionaries who helped her in her life.
Bottom right: Margaret Holland (Suganthie Sittie), 1965–1981. She worked in the office and later taught the office staff how to use computers.

# CHRIST IS IN ME

Top left: Jacky Woolcock (Kiruba Sittie), 1969–1987. She was a family doctor and was loved by all of the nurses that she worked with at the hospital in Dohnavur.
Top center: Margaret Wilkinson (Nura Sittie), 1944–1981. Mother to the second sixth generation Dohnavur family.
Top right: Anihala Carunia, PharmaD. She was a pharmacist and later vice president in Dohnavur Fellowship.
Middle, left to right: Jack Trehane (Thyahan Annachie), 1936–1978; Salma; Barbara Trehane (Sura Sittie), 1940–1978.
Lower left: Lilian Crawley (Mevara Sittie) 1944–1977, with Salma in Ottawa, Canada, 1979.
Lower right, left to right: Lilian Crawley with her sister Silvia (Meleela Sittie), 1946–1981. Lilian was the main secretary for Dohnavur Fellowship. Silvia taught secretarial courses to high school graduates.

Top left to right: In London, England, Margaret Holland, Salma Carter, and Alice Bell (Praba Sittie), 1965–1984. She was a radiographer.
Center left: Margaret Holland on her birthday.
Middle left: Ruth Dix (Dayali Sittie), 1949–1978. She was the superintendent of the Dohnavur Fellowship hospital.
Middle center: Anihala Carunia, PharmaD. She was a pharmacist in Dohnavur Hospital.
Middle right: Eleonor Backhouse (Vimba Sittie), 1946–1989. She was assistant to the headmistress of the school. She taught Salma English in first and second grade and continued to be involved in Salma's life until 1978.
Lower left: Evelyn Bowden (Evu Sittie), 1937–1959. She taught Salma English and nature study and was very involved with Salma's life up until seventh grade.
Lower right, left to right: Salma Carter with Olive Fuller (Pramila Sittie), 1945–1981. She worked in the village center.

Dohnavur Fellowship secretaries in the United Kingdom. Olive Gibson (Sisunesa Sittie), who Salma knew in her childhood, returned to England and started an office for Dohnavur Fellowship in her own home in Wimbledon, which was right next to the world-famous tennis court. Vera Owen (Memuthu Sittie) was a secretary with Olive Gibson in the Wimbledon office from 1948 to 1972.

Evelyn Bowden, who taught English to Salma from fifth to seventh grade. In 1959, she departed to Australia to take care of her parents, and then, after ten years, she returned to work as a secretary at the Wimbledon office in England.

Left to right: Jean Van der Flier (Dayavu Sittie) worked from 1990 to 2003, Salma, and Joan Kelland (Vera Sittie).

Left: Tahany Hanna (Nambikai Sittie), from Egypt, who worked from 2003 to 2018. She is dearly missed by all of us from Dohnavur Fellowship.

Left: Tahany Hanna (Nambikai Sittie). She loved the people at Dohnavur Fellowship dearly and sent birthday cards to everyone at the fellowship in India.

Evelyn Bowden (Evu Sittie) with Salma at the Bible seminary in 1970. After ten years, she returned to visit Dohnavur Fellowship. Upon her return, she began searching for Salma, whom she left behind as a detainee from the home school in 1959. She was told that Salma had gone to Bible seminary. In her surprise and disbelief, she went all the way to see Salma in the seminary. Rosie Hyler, who was going to be trained by her in the Wimbledon office in England, came with her. Salma and Rosie became friends. After many years apart, Salma and Rosie were reunited in 2018. Never lose hope! There is redemption for everyone!

Rosie Saunders (thank you, Rosie!)

Rosie has been closely associated with the Dohnavur Fellowship for fifty-three years! An amazing time span in which she initially served as secretary with Evu Sittie (Evelyn Bowden) in the Wimbledon office, which she joined in 1970. Rosie's interest in and love for the work of the Dohnavur Fellowship grew over the years. She became a DFC member in 2006 and, a few years later, joined the board of directors. Then finally, to complete the full circle, Rosie took on the challenge of becoming the DFC administrator at a time of transition. She has been in this position for the last five years (from 2018 to 2023).

Kamalavallie Carunia, MA, MEd.

Celebrating her third birthday.

Kamalavallie was the vice president of Dohnavur Fellowship from 2012 to 2018.

Kamalavallie Carunia was the English correspondent for the Dohnavur Fellowship newsletter (*Dust of Gold*) from 2017 to 2023. She worked with Rosie, coordinating the monthly letters for the orphanage. She joined the fellowship as a staff member in 1997, after she completed her university degrees when she was thirty years old. For many years, she helped in the main office and also taught in the home school. In 2012, she was appointed as vice president of Dohnavur Fellowship by the council due to her qualifications and ability to govern with knowledge and compassion. She is a God-fearing individual and had dedicated her life to serving in the Dohnavur Fellowship. Rosie takes her hat off to Kamalavallie as a faithful and very skilled coworker. In 2023, she was forced out of the council, where she officiated church services and helped with the youth group. In spite of this, she still feels that God has called her to work at Dohnavur Fellowship.

Salma with Margaret Wilkinson in Belfast, Northern Ireland, 1986.

# CHAPTER 6

# Nura Sittie

Nura Sittie (Margaret Wilkinson), the beloved mother to the second, third, fourth, fifth, and sixth generations of Dohnavur Fellowship.

Before I share with you about my life with this amazing and loving person, full of wisdom and grace, you should hear about how God bought her to us at Dohnavur. The following information comes from the book *At BBC Corner: I Remember Amy Carmichael*.

Margaret Wilkinson was born in Londonderry, Northern Ireland, in July 1917. When she was two years old and her brother was five years old, her father died. Her mother was without her husband's help through the troubled times in the immediate aftermath of the First World War. In her book "At BBC Corner: I remember Amy Carmichael" (1996), she says that her mother took the children to Castlerock, a small village on the north coast, for the whole summer every year till she finished her schooling.

She loved being near the Sea. At Castlerock, as a teenager, she shared in all activities of the CSSM beach mission held there each year. She did her Junior Certificate Examination on June 8th, 1933. When she was 16, she followed her brother to Cambridge University in England.

There she read a book, *Mother India*, by an American woman, which also makes mention of an *Irish woman, AMY CARMICHAEL, who was rescuing Children from Hindu temples* and making a home for vulnerable children. Her curiosity aroused, she read Amy's book "Gold Cord" and decided to become a missionary like Amy, to help her in Dohnavur Fellowship Children's Home, even though her Irish Presbyterian Mother thought that Dohnavur was a convent where Margaret would be dedicated for life.

In 1939 she graduated from Cambridge and came home to be with her mother, who was ill. In those days, women were not allowed to participate in the graduation ceremony. Yet, they received their degrees or certificates by mail. Her brother had passed the Bar exam, so she went to England to attend his graduation ceremony in London where he was called to the English Bar. She then returned home to see her mother, and shortly after that, her mother passed away.

The Second World War had started, and her brother joined the military service and was posted in 'the North Irish Horse,' a tank regiment training in Northern Ireland. Margaret still wanted to go to India as a missionary, so once the family matters were settled, she started to make her plans.

A few months after Margaret arrived in England, the Japanese bombed Pearl Harbor, the United States entered the war, Singapore fell, and even India was threatened. The possibility of her passage to India became more uncertain, so she did one-year teacher's training as they needed an educator to teach the older girls in Dohnavur. She was now classified as a *religious sister* in the Dohnavur Fellowship. She went to spend a weekend at Southampton University as she was working with the Christian Union. She needed a permit to enter the area around Southampton, for the Allied Forces were gathering along the south coast for what we remember as D-Day, that landing on the mainland of Europe, which took place on June 6th, 1944.

# CHRIST IS IN ME

This book, published in 1938 in Japan, offers a grim reminder of WWII. Salma found it in her late husband's library after his passing. It was given to Dr. Carter by his father, Benny Carter, who obtained it when stationed in Japan during WWII while serving in the US Army. He was later deployed to the Philippines.

So dramatically did the war situation changed in the months following D-Day that by the end of October, the Dohnavur Office in London phoned and told her she had been granted passage to India. In fact, she was told to be ready to leave in a week from an unnamed port, which turned out to be Liverpool, England.

The ship, initially a luxury liner, was converted during wartime for carrying troops. However, as not every bunk was occupied, about seventy missionaries were granted passage, and Margaret Wilkinson was one of them. Out of Liverpool, the ship sailed north to the River Clyde, then anchored off Greenock for a week till other convoy ships arrived. Then together, all the vessels moved off down the Irish Sea, landing for a short time at the entrance of Belfast Lough, and that was her last memory of the Irish Sea that she loved.

The ship traveled through the Bay of Biscay, as she watched the migrant birds heading to South Africa.

Perhaps this is where she picked up her love for birdwatching, for she took us children for bird walks in the evenings. She would teach us the name of the water birds at the reservoirs and the migrant birds. Sometimes, she would show us birds at a great distance through her binoculars. Her house in Dohnavur was next to mine, and she would often come to my backyard where the migrant birds like pita, paradise flycatcher, and woodpeckers could be seen at the Rangoon creeper under the large mango trees. These trees shade the swimming pool that I have told about in my story.

(Continuing from the book *At BBC Corner: I Remember Amy Carmichael.*)

Then the ship entered the Suez Canal. She saw the allied troops encamped thickly along both sides of the Canal, and the shipload of women and children traveling East gave the men strong hope that the end of the war was at hand.

She was on board the ship for well over a month, and of course, wartime security had meant no word was allowed to be sent ahead, saying when it might reach India. However, when the ship arrived at Bombay, India, some missionaries met her and sent a telegram to Dohnavur. They set her on a Train Journey of 400 miles southward to Madras, where she was put in another train going further down south almost to the tip of India to Tirunelveli Junction, where the Dohnavur Fellowship members met her.

She had a meal and had to let go of her western dress and put on a blue SARI that all Indians wear. Then on December 12$^{th}$, 1944, she reached the Dohnavur Fellowship. Her car was driven straight to the House of Prayer, set among the Children's Cottages and surrounded by beautiful trees and colorful flowers on its sides and as she walked into the church where old and young were gathered. A small band of blue-clad Children waving colored flags, and the crowd sang:

> O God of stars and flowers forgive our blindness,
> No dream of night had dared what thou hast wrought.
> New every morning is thy loving-kindness.
> Far, far above what we had asked or thought,
> So, under every sky our alleluia.
> With flowers of morning and with stars of night,
> Shall praise thee, O Lord Jesus, alleluia.
> Till thou shalt fold all shadows up in light.
>
> (Amy Carmichael, this is sung to the tune of "O Danny Boy.")

The Dohnavur Fellowship family welcomed her with an Irish tune she used to sing in the Londonderry air where she was born. I, Salma, was less than a month old and was in the babies' nursery with Kirubai, and little did I know that Nura Sittie was to play a major role in my life as I grew up. Here, I am reminded of the verse in Isaiah 64:4, "For since the beginning of the world men have not heard, nor perceived by the ear, neither hath the eye seen, O God, beside thee, what he hath prepared for him (her) that waiteth for him."

## SALMA CARUNIA CARTER

(Continuing from the book *At BBC Corner:
I Remember Amy Carmichael.*)

When she arrived in December 1944, the whole community in the Fellowship, from the youngest baby to the most aged senior, numbered around 800 people. Of these, about 50 were called fellowship members, inclusive of Indians and missionaries from overseas. They were the core group, leaders of different areas of work of the Fellowship. Lola was one of them, as were the first children of Amy Carmichael, such as Leela, Seela, Mala, Rukma, Rajarathinie, Paripu, Preena, Tara, Preethie, Saralee, Suseela, and Sella. They joined for their daily prayer meetings and the monthly prayer day in Amy's bungalow and shared about the work of the Fellowship and prayed for the Fellowship.

When I was older, someone from that group told me that missionary Premalu Sittie (Helen Bradshaw), who was in charge of the children's compound from 1925 to 1952, mentioned my name and prayed for me almost every day from the time I came to her compound. I wondered why. I can understand that now. She worried about my future, for I was a very lively girl: you get branded, and there is not much room for such a lively girl to advance in education.

This is why I told you in the previous chapter that she entrusted me to Lola, the leader of the school compound. Even though Lola already had twenty-four children to look after in her large family. In June 1952, I went to the school compound and joined Lola's family, as she could handle the lively little Salma, whom she came to love.

Nura Sittie says in her book, *At BBC Corner: I Remember Amy Carmichael*, that in England, in the mid-forties, there was considerable concern about children being brought up in institutions. *The Curtis Report* published in 1946 spoke of the difficulty of training children in an institution to live a healthy, independent life. Hard as that was in England, it was harder in the Indian countryside where I grew up, and it was not the custom for girls to be free and independent. We Dohnavur Fellowship children were sheltered from babyhood. We were trained to obey the fellowship/Amy's rules and regulations and did not have enough opportunities to make choices or decide anything for ourselves—no questions asked! Nura Sittie changed this attitude, allowing us to choose what we wanted to be when we grew up.

On August 15, 1947, India became independent from British rule. The whole fellowship family gathered around the flagstaff in the field of our clock tower and raised the new Indian flag and sang the new national anthem, "Janna Ganna Manna" ((People) One who decides the fortune of India instead of "God, Save Our king). This is a new chapter of India's history, and within a few years, most of the British left India.

Terrible riots and massacres accompanied partition in the north and the setting up of Pakistan, but the extreme south where we lived escaped that. India became a republic on January 26, 1950.

Nura Sittie wrote that she felt a tremendous sense of responsibility to help the very sheltered women and the girls growing up to play their part in this new chapter of their country's history

The government of Madras was able to press on with plans for development in education. Primary education was extended to achieve literacy throughout Madras State, now renamed Tamil Nadu. Higher education was to be more available, not only for boys but also for girls. The government required that schools must be staffed with teachers holding certificates recognized by the government.

This was a huge blow to the private homeschooling of the Dohnavur Fellowship, as their teachers did not possess these credentials. The government recognized degrees or diplomas which were not available to Dohnavur girls because the British missionaries taught Dohnavur children, and no credentials were given to them.

Amy herself was the teacher till 1913. Due to the growing work of the fellowship, she handed over the responsibility of education to Nesa Sittie (Agnes Nash). Agnes had offered to help with the school as she had fifteen years of experience teaching at Sarah Tucker College in Palayamkottai. When she took over the fellowship home school in 1913, she received a note from Amy Carmichael, saying, "Need for us to train our children for eternity and not just to enjoy the lost world." This became the motto of the school.

Nesa Sittie retired long before I was born but stayed in Dohnavur Fellowship. She never returned to England, as she could not travel anymore. I knew her in person, for we children went to her house on Sundays, as we liked to hear the old English woman talk in English, which we did not understand. If we touched anything in her home, she came running after us, and we used to scream and run away, playing cat and mouse with her. Nesa Sittie passed away in 1961.

In 1938, Margaret Wilkinson had written to Amy expressing her desire to come and work in Dohnavur Orphanage. Amy asked her to do teacher's training while waiting in London for her passage to India. With this, she could teach the older girls. Amy also asked Nesa Sittie to write to her about the motto of the mission school. This was important, so she and all the teachers would share this vision.

Amy said it might become a government-recognized mission school one day. But she insisted that they appoint only Christian teachers.

Rukma and Paripu, who Amy trusted, helped Nesa Sittie from the beginning. In later years, Rukma moved to other responsibilities. Paripu, teaching math to seventh grade, moved out of school just before I reached the seventh grade. Paripu became the leader of the school's Round compound, as well as a council member.

After joining Dohnavur, Nura Sittie remembered one of her fellow students she had met at the Christian Unions. She prayed for her to join the work in Dohnavur Fellowship. That is how Vimba Sittie (Eleanor Backhouse) came to teach in the fellowship on October 9, 1946. She retired in 1989. She arrived just before I turned two years old, and I knew her all my time at the Dohnavur Fellowship.

She was put in charge of the primary home school and taught us English in first and second grade. She never liked me, for I was a lively child, and I still remember that I hardly stayed in her class as she always sent me out of the class to sweep around the school compound.

When I went to elementary school in third grade, Muthara Sittie (Peggy Craig) taught English and created the black mark register.

She had a strong Scottish accent, and she rolled the R very well. Next year, she married Dr. Ben Walkey and went to live in the hospital compound.

In the fourth grade, Nura Sittie taught us English. She dramatically read the lesson books to us, especially poetry, and she made us understand with her actions. She made individual scorecards with our names and made a red or blue mark if we answered her questions correctly, encouraging us to learn more. But she was given more responsibilities of the fellowship and left the Jeevalia home school.

Evu Sittie (Evelyn Bowden) taught English from fifth to seventh grade in home school Jeevalia. She came from Australia in July 1937 and returned home to care for her parents in 1959. Then she went to England and worked in the Dohnavur Fellowship office at Wimbledon, England, from 1970 to 1980. She was an excellent teacher, and I spent hours with her learning to spell. She also taught us nature studies, where we learned about snakes, other insects, and the different plants and wildflowers. I liked her class very much.

Just as I was beginning to enjoy school, Vimba Sittie was transferred to home school Jeevalia. My troubles started over again, for I was a marked troublemaker in her sight, and my punishments were severe.

One day, Christina, the school principal, told all the classes to assemble inside the courtyard, so about one hundred of us sat in lines waiting to hear what she had to say. It was unusual for us to sit in the courtyard. Soon, she came with a large box of chocolates. We all were so excited because we had never seen real chocolates before! She said someone from England or Switzerland had sent these for the children in this school.

Then she started to call out the names individually and gave each a piece of chocolate. I was waiting and waiting for my name to be called and was afraid that the chocolates would be finished before my name was called. The courtyard was beginning to become empty! Perhaps eighty students had already gone home with the chocolates, and only twenty were left.

Vimba Sittie was assisting Christina in handing out the chocolates. *Oh no,* I thought, *with her there, I would be the last one to be called if any was left.*

Then, my name was finally called. I was the ninety-ninth student to receive a piece of chocolate! I went forward to accept it and was so sad. I immediately threw it down on the floor to show my disgust. However, I quickly became happy that I got one, and so I picked it up immediately and shoved it in my mouth! I was afraid they might take it away from me.

Then the last person's name was called, Asala. She was also furious but glad that she had one. I had never seen such chocolates till I came to America, and now I can't even eat them, thinking of the orphan girls like me who don't have such delights. See picture on page 155.

## Mellial Sittie

Mellial Sittie (Alice Roberts) came from Scotland to Dohnavur in October 1926. She conducted music (singing classes) at the school for all age groups. She was also a sewing teacher and in charge of the sewing room. We did not know how to read music that was not taught to us. All the songs were written and compiled into songbooks.

She taught us the lyrics Amy Carmichael wrote, set to music by her coworkers. I still remember the song about the tamarind tree: "O tamarind tree. I am nine years old, and you are a hundred and one. Did the angels plant you long ago to shadow us from the sun? O shadowy beautiful tamarind tree, how kind of the angels to think of me." Yes, we had many huge trees in our compounds, and many of them were tamarind trees. The fruits are used by Indians to add a little tartness to their food, especially in their curry. It also gave us shade from the hot sun where, at times, the temperature goes up to 120 degrees during the summer months.

Mellial Sittie was known as a kind teacher, and I never got bad marks in her class. Sometimes, she let us choose the songs to sing, which we liked, and I always chose song number 10 from the paper book, which goes like this: "When the golden sun goes down, and the hills grows dim and gray…The blessed shepherd let me sleep."

Even though we children did not understand every word of English, I somehow understood this line as I saw the sun going down behind the western mountain every evening when we played from 5:30 to 6:30 p.m. in the large playground where the clock tower stood. I also understood that Jesus was my Shepherd, who would watch over me and keep me safe at night.

Mellial Sittie also taught us English songs according to the seasons as she played a small organ. The first thing we learned from her in third grade was to take a deep breath and let it out slowly. She made us do that exercise for the first five minutes. In the beginning, we all kept repeating after her as she said, "Breathe in, breathe out." We did not understand those English words! She couldn't say them in Tamil, so we all had a good laugh at our limited knowledge of English. She spoke very softly, and sometimes, it was hard to hear her, especially when girls were talking among themselves. But she never shouted or raised her voice.

She taught us from the church hymnary that appeared in 1898. The revised edition was published in 1922 by the General Assemblies of the Churches. She also taught us songs for every season, and we learned many Christmas songs. The one I liked is "When the morning stars sang together and all the sons of God shouted for joy" (Job 38:7). Among the Easter songs, I liked the song "Now the green blade rises from the buried grain."

Mellial Sittie also took the whole schoolchildren to the games field, which is between the boys' and girls' compounds. We always went in a long line to and from there. It is where the clock tower stands in the middle. See the clock tower picture on page 159.

In fifth grade, we played roundus with a flat bat and tennis ball. It is like baseball, but one must go around, touch all the bases, and reach the home base to score a point. It was a lot of fun, and I hit the ball out of the park to run through the first, second, and third bases and reach the fourth base. You do not get to score if you stop on one of those bases. One must go or run around all the bases, which is why the game is called roundus.

When I reached sixth and seventh grade, I was able to join the netball team. Mellial Sittie was the umpire, and she taught us how to play netball, as it is called in England. No net is tied around the hoop at the goalpost, and we shoot the ball through the hoop to score.

When playing netball, we had to stand still when we caught the ball in our hands and pass it without moving. Any little movement will result in a penalty.

That was hard, but I got the hang of the game well and became the goalkeeper, the only player who could shoot the ball inside the hoop to score. The big surprise was watching basketball played in America, where all players can move around the court. All players can run around the court and score, which is much easier than our netball rules.

When I was in the third, fourth, and fifth grades, whenever I passed the empty netball court, and as the ball was always placed on the ground, I picked up the ball, took aim to shoot, and ensured it went through the hoop. Since I was short, it took a lot of effort to shoot the ball through the hoop. I went home satisfied with making one goal/score I accomplished every evening. Three years of practice came in handy when I reached sixth grade and was allowed to play on the netball court.

In sixth grade, we had to choose our future profession, either to be a teacher or a nurse. Then one would wear a blue or purple band. The blue for teachers and purple for nurses. Devashanthie and I were good team players, but not on the same team, as I chose to become a teacher and always wore a blue band, and Desh wore Team Nightingale's purple. She became a volunteer nurse, working at the Dohnavur Fellowship hospital, and retired in 2006. See the picture of the nurses on page 107 (Desh is on the left side of the front row).

Playing netball and scoring points for my Slessor team gave me confidence. This sense of accomplishment helped me face the struggles of my future life with fortitude.

My life appeared set for a bright future and dreamlike, and the playground seemed to reflect it perfectly. As the game ended at about 6:15 p.m., I saw the golden sun setting behind the blue mountains. It was a beautiful sight as the darkness came quite suddenly once the sun went down in the southern tip of India. In my mind, I could picture the song, "When the golden sun goes down, and the hills grow dim and gray, Blessed Shepherd, let me sleep."

Evening games became my favorite time to advance my skills. Mellial Sittie contributed to it with her gentleness and kindness. Little did I expect that my world was suddenly about to turn upside down at the end of the seventh grade!

Mellial Sittie was the choir director as she played the organ in the church. She was responsible for teaching the hymnals to the schoolchildren, and we learned hundreds of songs and hymnals by the time we were ready to go to the boarding schools. At Christmastime, she took the choir, about forty men and women, and went around the compounds caroling, and the children of fifth, sixth, and seventh grades walked in front of them with red Christmas lanterns.

The lamps are called Japanese lanterns because of the red-colored shades around the hurricane lantern that each child carried. Amy spent her early missionary days in Japan and saw their beautiful red lanterns. The idea of the Christmas lanterns' red shades came from it. The southern part of India gets pitch-black after 7:00 p.m. during Christmas, and the red lanterns look very pretty as each child holds a lantern up as they go around the compound till the choir ends the caroling at 9:30 p.m.

It was a joy for us children to get up early to go caroling again, in the morning, around the campus with the lovely red Japanese lanterns. The teachers from the home school made a list of children who would carry the Japanese red lanterns, and I waited and waited for my turn.

For years, I saw my name only once to go with the choir in the evening but not in the morning. However, I got sick that Christmas Eve and spent that week in the hospital. Then the next year, I was hoping to be chosen, but my name never came on the list again, so I never got a chance to carry the red lanterns, for once you graduate from the seventh grade, that childhood joy comes to an end. I used to think if only Mellial Sittie could choose which child could carry the Japanese lanterns, I would have had a chance to go caroling with the choir, for she was kind and fair.

Mellial Sittie also taught us the songs that Amy wrote for her children. In the winter, the migrant birds come to South India, and I grew up enjoying seeing them year by year. They are golden oriole, pitta, paradise fly catcher, red-headed woodpecker, hoopoe, and blue-colored kingfisher. They would often be seen near the irrigation well just behind my house.

I still remember the song about the golden oriole, which goes like this:

> Once we had a Golden Oriole very tame was he,
> and he ate red juicy berries from the Banyan tree,
> a fat green caterpillar, liked him, and ate three.
>
> Ah, our lovely Golden Oriole, very ill was he
> for the third green caterpillar, of the luscious three,
> with his private little inside, much did disagree.
>
> So, he died, poor Golden Oriole, what a tragedy!
> But it is foolish to be greedy who so ever you may be,
> whether you're a Golden Oriole or a thing like me.
>
> Now he's stuffed, our Golden Oriole, dull as dull can be.
> Is he doing sums forever, counting 1, 2, 3?
> Luscious fat green caterpillars made me what you see.
>
> (Amy Carmichael)

Amy Carmichael was a good poet. She wrote many poems about birds, nature, and flowers for her children and many spiritual songs for everyone. I grew up learning them, and many of them come to my mind, especially as I am in a faraway country now and still sing them joyfully.

Mellial Sittie lived near the home school, and her house was surrounded by jasmine flower creepers. When it was in bloom, the pure white flowers looked like a million stars from a distance. Its sweet-smelling aroma floats in the air for miles. We could smell it even from the school.

At the home school, Mellial Sittie taught us how to darn the various shapes of tears in our clothes and stitch buttonholes and hemming. We all know the cross-stitch from A to Z, as we learned them in our sewing classes. I still do my darning and mending, for we learned to do everything by hand as there was no sewing machine for the children. Mellial Sittie retired, returned to England in 1970, and passed away in June 1987.

I now see how dear Mellial Sittie impacted my early childhood. She trained my voice to sing hymnals and songs. This helped me to become the song leader for the daily school assemblies in St. John's Girls' High School, Nazareth, Tamil Nadu, India. This is where I did my schooling from eighth grade to twelfth grade, which you will learn more about later.

Eight hundred students and about twenty teachers gathered in front of the school podium every morning at the school. We would start the day with a song and prayer. As the song leader, I led the hymn that was chosen for the day. I knew the tune of each and every hymn in the hymnal. St. John's Girls' High School is a Christian school built by the British to educate Hindu, Muslim, and Christian girls, and we all studied at the boarding school together in harmony.

I became the top player in netball in high school. We went to other high schools to play in matches or tournaments. In a way, I think this confidence on the netball court also helped prepare me for life.[1]

The sewing room.

Left: Packiavanie, who was the head seamstress of the sewing room. Second from left: Sarala, who helped as a seamstress in the sewing room. Third and fourth from left (on either side of Salma): Ramani and Jeyathai, who went to home school with Salma.

Inbageetha, dressmaker at the Singer sewing machine.

## Aesop's Fables

While I was in Jeevalia, we were allowed to go to the library on Saturday evenings to choose some books to take home and read for the week. They were divided into Sunday library and Weekday library, for we were *not* allowed to read any books on Sunday except the religious texts and the Bible.

I liked reading *Aesop's Fables* on the weekdays, for I enjoyed the moral teachings of the stories. Here I quote from the special edition, which is copyright 1947 by Grosset and Dunlap Publishers:

> Sometime, between the years 620 and 560 B.C. there came to the court of Croesus, last of the Kings of Lydia in Asia Minor, a freedman known as Aesop. While still a slave of Ladmon on the island of Samos, he had gained some local fame

for himself and considerable prestige for his master as a narrator of tales about animals. Once he became ex-slave, he arrived at Sardis to match wits with such exiled pundits as Solon of Athens and Thales of Miletus and the other sages and philosophers who gathered at the court of the outstanding patron of learning of that time. Aesop quickly grew in favor with King Croesus as a result of his shrewd intelligence and native wit, plus a certain amount of well-directed flattery. King Croesus probably learned more home truths from Aesop's fables than from all the serious disquisitions of the royal stable of Philosophers. Later on, Aesop was sent as an ambassador to the various capitals that the King acquired, what amounted to practically a hegemony over the other small Greek states. At Corinth, he warned people against mob law in a fable, later used by Socrates. At Athens, by the recital of "*The frogs desiring a king*," he warned the citizens of known tyranny.

It reminds me of Acts chapter 17 where the Apostle Paul was in the same territory preaching, as he stood against the political opposition with the biblical truth to the philosophers, Epicureans, and the stoics about the unknown God they worshipped. He gave them the doctrine of a true living God of the biblical worldview of Christ's bodily physical resurrection and explained from Mars Hill in Athens that Jesus was Christ. He died on the cross for our transgressions and rose again from the dead.

## Jesus Christ Is Alive Today!

One of my favorite stories was "Androcles and the Lion." It taught me to be kind and to be grateful for the help that I received. I liked the stories of the crow, crane, stork, beetle, mouse, wolf, fox, shepherd boy, hen, eagle, frog, goat, donkey, ant, and dove. The hare and the tortoise taught me to go slow and steady to win the race. "The Lion and the Three Bulls" story: "United we stand, divided we fall."

I could visualize these stories well, and they started having a special meaning for me. I could see these animals, except the lion. Seeing crows and the cranes, vultures, kites, lizards, frogs, bandicoots, rats and mice, snakes, and creepy crawlies was an everyday experience for me. We watched their behaviors as they crossed our paths every day. It seemed natural to me that the animals of the forest and barnyard should be endowed with human passions and feelings and even with human speech. I lived surrounded by birds that could be taught to talk, such as myna, parakeet, or parrots mimic speech, and I have heard them do that, too.

One more story, "The Race and the Three Golden Fruit/Apples," that I read in the Sunday library gave me much hope to run toward the goal. The story was about three amateur men participating in the Olympic games in Greece. As the three of them were racing, a spectator rolled a fruit made of pure gold out onto the racetrack when they were about halfway. One of the runners bent down to pick up the golden apple, which allowed the other two men to take the lead. After the two in the lead ran a few more miles, another golden fruit rolled onto their path. Then the second runner bent and picked up the fruit. Now there is only one runner in the clear lead. However, before he reached the finish line, another golden apple was rolled before him! But he did not bend down to pick it up; instead, he kept his eyes on the winning line and won the race. He was crowned with a wreath from an olive branch.

I was ten years old when I read that story. To this day, it stays with me and helps me remember not to be distracted by worldly allurements but keep my eyes on the winner's prize. As the Bible says, "Run that you may obtain" (Philippians 3:13–14). Also, Philippians 1:11, "Be filled with the fruits of righteousness which are by Jesus Christ…This one thing I do, forgetting those things which are behind, and reaching forth unto those things which are before, I press towards the goal for the prize of the high calling of God in Christ Jesus, who is the author and the finisher of my faith."

## CHRIST IS IN ME

Amy Carmichael wrote lyrics that seemed to embody the very spirit of the story for her children.

> God of the Heights, austere, inspiring, thy word hath come to me.
> O let no selfish aims, conspiring, distract my soul from Thee.
> Loosen me from Things of Time; Strengthen me for steadfast climb.
> The Temporal would bind my spirit, Father, be Thou my stay,
> Show me what flesh cannot inherit, Stored for another day.
> Be transparent, Things of Time;
> Looking through you, I will climb.
>
> (Amy Carmichael)

At this point in my life, it is 2023, and I am now seventy-nine years old and continually running the race that is set before me on this earth as it says in 2 Timothy 4:7–8, "I have fought a good fight, I have finished the race and kept the faith. Henceforth there is laid up a crown of righteousness which the Lord, the righteous Judge, shall give me on that *day*."

> When peace, like a river, attendeth my way;
> When sorrow, like sea, billows roll;
> Whatever my lot, Thou hast taught me to say,
> It is well, it is well with my soul.
>
> For me be it Christ, be it Christ hence to live,
> If Jordan above me shall roll,
> No pang shall be mine, for in death as in life,
> Thou wilt whisper, Thy peace to my soul.

But, Lord, 'tis for Thee, for Thy coming, we wait;
The sky, not the grave, is our goal;
Oh, trump of the angel! Oh, voice of the Lord!
Blessed Hope! Blessed rest of my soul!

(Scripture Union London)

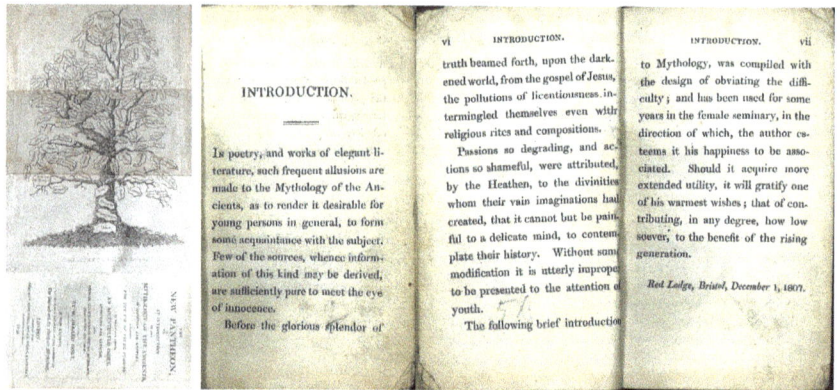

*The New Pantheon* (1815).
Salma found this book among her husband's possessions in his library after he passed away. It was published over two hundred years ago in 1815. The introduction was written at the Red Lodge, Bristol, United Kingdom in 1807.

## Girl Guides

In the early 1950s, the great educator of the Dohnavur Fellowship, Nura Sittie (Margaret Wilkinson), became one of the council members and Rajapan Annachie, nephew of Arulai. Arulai was Amy's first convert from Pannaivilai, who Amy wanted to train as a leader and her successor to run the fellowship after her. Tragically, much to Amy's grief, Arulai died in 1939.

Besides Nura Sittie and Rajapan Annachie, the other council members were Tholan Annachie and Ubaharie Sittie. Nura Sittie now taught less and less in the prep school as she became more involved in the general administration of the fellowship.

Britain introduced Scouts and Girl Guides, founded by Lord Baden Powell, in the Christian schools in India. The different Indian provinces had their associations for Scouts and Guides. What was to be their position after independence? The new Indian government clarified that they valued Scout and Guide training and wanted it to continue. There should have been one movement in which both traditions could be combined. After much deliberations, the Bharat Scouts and Guides were formed on November 7, 1950. Finally, all India Girl Guides Association merged with the Bharat Scouts and Guides in August 1951.

The Dohnavur Fellowship schoolgirls were happy to join the Guides, and Nura Sittie was the leader. She took some students to the training camps held in our district. A Guide was a sister to every other Guide, and the spirit of the community grew. The songs that they sang at the campfires greatly helped them see the uniting movements with North and South by singing camp songs in the languages of both North and South India.

However, the merger was not without its hiccups. It was noticed at the first training camp that the state commissioner appointed for training for Madras State was a Hindu Brahmin, the highest caste in Hinduism. And being a Hindu Brahmin, she did not want to break the caste barrier and eat with everyone. As a strict Brahmin, her caste did not permit her to eat food prepared by anyone except another Brahmin or to sit and eat alongside people of another caste.

In her book, *At the BBC Corner: I Remember Amy Carmichael*, Margaret Wilkinson said that some of the campers felt there was no reality in a Guide movement whose law held that a Guide was a sister to every other Guide and yet we could not eat together. When the high commissioner confronted her, she started eating at different times but came and sat with the campers and communicated with them. They were happy and respected her for it.

In middle school, the children had a club called Blue Birds. Tarahai Carunia was in charge of it, and she selected the girls who could be enrolled and attend it every Thursday evening. I hardly remember attending the Blue Birds, for Tarahai did not invite me to join. So I always stood outside the camp to see the club members playing games and singing jolly camp songs. I also watched the Girl Guides, who held their training simultaneously at the playground where the clock tower stood.

One day when I was sitting outside my house, watching from a distance, as I could not join them, Lola came along and saw me sitting on a stone seat, watching them playing, and said, "Don't hurt yourself watching them. Just come home and play." Lola knew that some of the teachers, like Tarahai, kept me away from what children of my age enjoyed.

When I reached sixth grade, Nura Sittie asked me to join the Girl Guides. I jumped at the chance and got enrolled. She told me she would award me with a Girl Guide badge if I passed Tenderfoot tests.

I was excited and immediately learned the motto of the Scout and Guide, "Be Prepared," and the Guide law. I then went to her house on Wednesday afternoon during the school recess and stood at attention. I raised my first three fingers in half salutation. I said, "I promise on my honor to do my best and to do my duty to God and country and always to help others and obey the Guide law," then stood at ease. After passing the Tenderfoot test, she was pleased and gave me a Guides badge to pin on the blue sari I got as a Girl Guide uniform.

The Girl Guides training started, and Nura Sittie made clay ovens in her backyard for us to boil water in the clay pots.

She gave us only two matchsticks from the matchbox to make fire with twigs we had to collect. We passed the test if we could light the fire with one matchstick. At the same time, she timed us to make sure that we brought the water to boil within the stipulated ten minutes. That required a blazing fire, for which we had to collect a lot of twigs or firewood, and that was very hard for us to find in the immaculately clean campus where we lived. Also, no paper was allowed to light the fire, so starting the fire with the twigs required a lot of skill.

The Girl Guides activities required us to learn many things, like the flags of various countries, the names of the wildflowers and animals and the migrant birds. We had to memorize the Morse code and the use of semaphore flags. She would test us with a large white flag or hand signal. I still know the Morse code for most of the alphabet.

Every Thursday evening, she played team games with us, and on school holidays, she taught us tracking, which everybody enjoyed. The teams competed to find the treasure (prize) by following the tracking signs she concealed around and outside the campus. We enjoyed that day of running around inside and outside of the campus. We were rarely allowed to go outside of the campus.

Nura Sittie also taught us general knowledge that helped our early age development. This was important because we had no contact with the outside world. Remember, we lived in the convent-like fellowship, surrounded by the ten-foot red brick wall.

We enjoyed singing campfire songs in the evenings, and I still remember some of them as I learned them when I was twelve. Someone from Canada came and taught some camp songs, one of which goes like this:

> Our paddles keen and bright,
> Flashing like silver;
> Swift as the wild goose flight,
> Dip, dip, and swing.
> Dip, dip, and swing them back,
> Flashing like silver;
> Swift as the wild goose flight,
> Dip, dip, and swing.

(Margaret E. McGee (1889–1975) in 1918)

The hundredth birthday of Lord Baden Powell was celebrated in 1957. Nura Sittie organized a big rally at the end of the week-long celebrations. We learned much about the Scouts and Guides movement and its activities. We had to memorize many things to present to the spectators who came to see the celebration. At the end of the ceremony, all the Girl Guides had a flag of each country. I still remember the flag I was to hold was Haiti, a republic in the West Indies.

I liked its color, and it looked pretty, although at that time, I did not know about the West Indies, but learned that there is a small country/island called Haiti. Little did I know or dream that one day I would go to the Caribbean Islands to do missionary work in San Juan, Puerto Rico (1980–81).

Sellammal Carunia drew all the flags of the different countries. She then pasted them onto a cardboard backing and attached them to bamboo sticks so we could wave them. However, after the practice of long weeks, my flag could not be waved high, for it fell off the bamboo stick.

I was given another white flag with a large red circle in the middle. It said Japan on it. But I was not very happy. It was not very colorful as the one I was waving at the camp! But with this, I learned about the flags of two countries I had never known. I only knew of the Indian and British flags at that time, which we often saw.

All the Girl Guides had to memorize the song that we were to sing at the closing ceremony, and it went like this:

> Who opens the gates that leads to the pathway
> over the hills,
> Who whistles the tune that teaches our feet to go
> with a will,
> Who hoisted the sail that carries the boat across
> the bay, and
> Who lighted the fire to give us a song at the close
> of day.
> The Chief, The Chief,
> Who goes across the bay
> T'was he lighted the fire to give us the hope at
> close of day.

Then we sang the song's chorus hailing the chief and raised and waved our flags. It was a very grand ceremony which I can never forget.

In the evening, we went into the church with colorful lanterns and recited the things that we learned about the life and history of Lord and Lady Baden Powell and Scouts and Guides.

Above: Girl Guides in their uniforms. Salma is fourth from left with the double braids.

Margaret Wilkinson's (Nura Sittie) house next to Salma's house in the school compound.

Right: Sellammal, who was very skilled in arts and crafts. She wrote text from Bible verses on wooden plaques with imperial letters, which went on sale among the Christian community.
Salma has brought three of these text plaques with her to America, and they are displayed on the walls in her home here in Irving, Texas.

To Sellammal's right is Salma's friend, Chinammal Carunia, who you will read about in the final chapter. She became a pharmacist with Salma's help from America.

Men, left to right: Jeyaraj Anantha, Thurandran Anantha, Peranantham Anantha (his wife, Niha, is a nurse; their daughter, Sashikantha, became a member of the staff), Sahaja Anantha (who married Christina's sister, Jeyacottie), Raja Anantha.

Christina holding Danaseelie.

Christina opening the playschool. Tarapu (right) was in charge of the children at the playschool.

# CHAPTER 7

# Christina

I passed sixth grade and went to seventh grade in Jeevalia (home school). The Indian government required teachers to hold a Secondary School Leaving Certificate (SSLC) to teach. Christina Jeyaventhan, the principal of Jeevalia school, was encouraged to sit for the matriculation government exam. When the result came that summer, Christina passed the SSLC exam, and everyone went to congratulate her. It was a big achievement, for she studied privately in her own time and without any official tutors while continuing to teach in the fellowship secondary home school.

Christina was the daughter of Mr. Jeyaventhan and Vineetha Carunia, born on Christmas Day. Her parents were members of the fellowship and had three other children. They lived in the Dohnavur campus, and Christina grew up in the fellowship under her parents' care until she was eighteen. Once she became a teacher at the fellowship's school, she lived in the school compound with us. She became the principal of the Jeevalia school in 1951 when I started third grade.

Pyarie Sittie (Frances Nosworthy) was the headmistress of Jeevalia from the time she came to help Amy in October 1914 till she retired and returned to England in June 1952.

She taught nature studies class and took the students outside to interpret nature, showing them the real natural world. Pyarie Sittie chose Christina to replace her and made her the principal of Jeevalia home school.

Christina was always fair and kind. I remember holding her hand when walking on Sunday evenings outside the campus. She would tell us about the English stories she read when she was outside the campus. These stories interested me.

When I started the seventh grade, for some reason, Christina was removed from the headmistress position and became my class teacher. Later in my life, I learned the reason for her demotion. When preparing for the Secondary School Leaving Certificate to take the government exam, Christina needed some help in math. Her parents arranged for a young man, Sathyajeevan Anantha, from the boys' compound to help her with mathematics. He tutored Christina in her own parents' house and in their presence. This occurred when she visited her parents on Thursday evenings from 5:30 to 6:30 p.m. His visit violated the Dohnavur Fellowship regulations, which said unmarried men could not communicate with young single ladies!

The fellowship leader, Ubaharie Sittie (May Powell), was known to be a stern disciplinarian. She handed out punishments left and right. I had some personal knowledge of how strict she could be. Since I lived close to Ubaharie Sittie's house, I often saw many women come out of her house crying after meeting with her.

When the matter of Christina came up before Ubaharie Sittie (May Powell), the whole family was very severely punished. Christina lost her position as principal at the school, and her parents were expelled from the fellowship. This was done even though Christina's father had a long history of working with the fellowship. He was working in our workshop at the time and had been a goldsmith at the nearby village.

He had come to the fellowship to help Amy Carmichael. He later married one of Amy's children, Vineetha Carunia, a nursing supervisor in the fellowship hospital. See picture on page 38.

They had four children, all born in the fellowship. However, they had to go. They moved to a faraway village where Christina could go only once a year when she got two weeks' vacation.

Christina had two sisters. Nasamithiri lived in the fellowship and helped raise the orphan children for many years. She passed away in 2021. She was a very kind mother to many of the Dohnavur children. The other sister, Jeyacottie, a lovely tall and very fair woman, who was a nurse, worked in the government hospital in the district of Tirunelveli. Later, she married Sahajah Anantha, a Dohnavur boy and a friend of Christina's tutor.

Christina also had a brother of my age, but he was born very weak and needed much medical care. He lived with his parents and passed away in his late twenties. Christina once told me he was doing evangelistic work in the village and lived with his family until his death.

I was thirteen years old when I started seventh grade. Tarahai became the headmistress of the home school. Christina was my class teacher and taught almost all subjects except English and nature science.

I never understood math and was failing all the time. The main reason was that we Dohnavur children never handled money and never saw even one rupee. In those years of my education, we tried to figure out problems using combinations like one paisa, four paisa in one anna, and sixteen annas in one rupee. We also had to know about the British pound sterling for twelve pence in one shilling and twenty shillings in one pound. It was so confusing!

In the third grade, we had to memorize multiplication tables, the numbers from 2 to 16. Though it caused a lot of grief then, today, I am glad we learned by memorizing them. Now this fortunate generation can use the calculator for math!

November 23, 1958, I turned fourteen years old. Sadly, at the end of the summer, I was not promoted and had to repeat the seventh grade. Tarahai, the headmistress, and Vimba Sittie (Eleanor Backhouse), the assistant headmistress, never liked me ever since I was in first grade. Tarahai taught scripture class, and I liked the Bible class very much because I was good at that subject and did well in the exams. Yet she developed a dislike for me. I did not know why.

It could have been that she didn't like that I was a friend of Reva, one of Tarahai's children. Or maybe because Reva liked Christina and always stayed back after school on Saturday to help Christina clean our classroom. However, often, I had to do the cleaning after school as punishment, for I usually still had twelve bad marks for the week. (That count was lower than the previous years. I was improving!) Reva helped me with this cleaning.

Sadly, Asala was no longer in the school with me, for she had been sent to repeat fifth grade at a boarding school. Reva and I worked together, and our friendship grew.

Tarahai, the headmistress, did not beat us anymore but punished me differently. For example, she would send me out of school to cut grass in the field for a week. That area was full of thorny plants called tribulus, which shed many of their thorns. I had a hard time avoiding stepping on them with my bare feet, for we did not have shoes. One step on a hidden bunch of thorns gives you unbearable pain. I would try to push the thorns on the plants aside with one hand and use the sickle with the other.

Years later in 1991, when I was teaching English in Nanchang, China, some white patches appeared around my face. I went to see the Chinese doctor, who prescribed medicine for this condition. The pharmacy filled it with fourteen brown bags! They told me to boil them only in clay pots which were on sale at the hospital. When I came back to our apartment, I showed my husband and emptied one package into the mud pot. There were many different roots and leaves from plants, but to my great surprise, I saw a lot of thorns from the tribulus plant! I was very familiar with those thorns from my teenage years working in the fields. Now I needed to boil and drink a package, one in the morning and one at evening. Well, when I swallowed this herb cocktail, it tasted ever so bitter. But I wanted to get cured, so I followed the prescription. It did cure the white patches week by week for the next three months. Each weekend, I would get the medicine of this bitter herb cocktail. My husband always tells me not to worry about my appearance because he loves me as I am. Now I realize what a lucky woman I am to have had his love. I was glad to have my beautiful brown face back. This caused me to remember one of the Christmas songs that Isaac Watts wrote, music by Handel, I sing, "Joy to the World!"

No more let sin and sorrow grow
Nor thorns infest the ground
He comes to make his blessings flow
Far as the curse is found…Garden of Eden!

My house mother, Rajamacottie Accal, came back from her job at 10:30 a.m. every day to the field to bring me some water and showed that she cared about me and still loved me as her child.

This punishment, working in the fields and cutting weeds, took place about three or four times during the year I was in the seventh grade. Each time, I was forced out of school. Since I was nine years old, the sickle had become my constant companion. I could do it whenever help was needed to clean up the fields and gardens. My education suffered, but I had mastered cutting the grass with my hand while squatting. For the next fifteen years of my life, whenever the fields needed to be cleaned, I was always there. When I came to America, I was amazed to see that they were using machines to do the work I had done with my hands and squatting on my legs for years! Today, I hear that they do not cut grass (many snakes are now multiplying) because their mission is now to sustain the livelihood of the environment. Oh, how the world has changed from my time, as the government stepped in!

We went back to school in the evenings from 7:00 p.m. to 8:00 p.m. We did our homework in the study hall, for we were not allowed to take our books out of the school. One teacher on duty oversaw the students' self-study, so Tarahai devised another punishment for me at nighttime. While doing my homework, I had to sit away from the study hall. This was a desk in a dark corner. It was lit by a mere ten-watt bulb fixed high on the ceiling. Only the school had electricity in those days. Luckily, I had perfect 20/20 eyesight! Praise God!

I still remember my time with Christina whenever it was her turn for supervision duty. After homework, we stood outside the school and watched the stars and planets. I learned from her about the stars. Even today, when I am out in the late evenings, I try to find Orion the Hunter, a constellation lying on the celestial equator between Canis Major the big dog and Taurus the bull.

My home was not very far from the equator. In my childhood, we only had the dim light of hurricane lanterns, as there was no electricity. This kept the night sky darker, so the stars shone brighter and were visible. Christina pointed out the Pleiades, a conspicuous cluster of stars in the constellation Taurus, commonly spoken of as seven, though I could see only six. She, too, called it a group of six in Tamil. Sometimes, we could see the planets Venus, Mars, and Jupiter. My favorite cluster of stars is Southern Cross, very bright stars forming a large cross, a constellation between Centaurus and Musca. Since I lived in India, the Southern Cross was visible throughout the year.

In 2016, I visited my Dohnavur sister Atharavu who lives in Auckland, New Zealand. I told her that, as a child, I had learned that the Southern Cross constellation was visible from there, and it is featured on their country's flag, so I am keen to see the Southern Cross at night. Fortunately, I was sleeping in an upstairs bedroom with a window, which gave a wide and panoramic view of the utmost part of the world.

Every night, I got up to see the Southern Cross, but it was not visible until very late. Finally, one night at about 2:00 a.m., I got up and peeked through the window. A very large cross of bright stars spread through the night sky. And the Milky Way, with its millions of stars spread across like a path I wanted to stroll upon. I remember my hard childhood in South India. However, I thanked the Lord Jesus Christ, who was crucified on the wooden cross to save me from my sin and allowed me to see these beautiful stars from the utmost part of the world, as it is called down under.

## I Have to Repeat the Seventh Grade
## I Am Thirteen Years Old

In the rigorous standards of the home school, a student had to score 50 percent marks on average in all subjects combined with being promoted to the next grade. At the end of May, the scores were put on a board in the center of the school compound for everyone to go and see. Hundreds of us ran to see our results, as everyone was looking forward to going to the next grade.

I also ran to see my result as I was in seventh grade, and it said next to my name: Average 49 percent, Not Promoted. I was despondent and crying as I had to repeat the same grade.

I was small and slightly built, only four feet tall and sixty-five pounds. I did not look very big compared to my younger classmates. I guess this helped me fit in sometimes.

On June 6, school started. There were twenty-five students in seventh grade, including myself and Devarul, who was my age. She also failed seventh grade and was a repeater and lived in the same house with our dear Rajamacottie Accal.

Arul was a very easygoing child and a good companion for me. Arul came to the Dohnavur Fellowship at eight years old and had a lot to learn about the way of life in the orphanage. We were now only seven girls who lived in the house called Sardonyx.

There was a large mango tree right behind my house, and in its season, it produced a lot of mangoes, and we children were delighted to pick them up from under the trees and eat them. We could also hear them falling on the roof at night. As soon as we got up, at 5:30 a.m., we had to all kneel in a circle, and one girl prayed and thanked the Lord for keeping us safe and giving us sound sleep during the night. Then we all said the Lord's Prayer together every day. I still remember saying it in a rush to be the first to get out of the house to gather the mangoes that fell from the tree on a windy night in our backyard.

I put them in my sewing bag, as everyone had a large sewing bag to keep our sewing kits. Then I hid it from Rajamacootie Accal, fearing she would not allow me to take them to the school. Many students came to my locker during break time, where I kept all the mangoes. I distributed the big and small mangoes I had gathered from my backyard that morning. There were three varieties of mango trees in my backyard, which yielded lots of fruits I enjoyed giving to the other students in my class. As of 2000, those trees are all gone!

In the Dohnavur Fellowship school, many teachers had no teacher's training or certificates because they grew up and were educated in the Dohnavur Fellowship. Initially, Amy did not want to send her children to outside boarding schools. Under the new government of

India, things began to change after 1947. New laws required that only qualified and well-trained teachers and nurses were allowed to work in schools and hospitals.

Fortunately, Nura Sittie, a trained teacher from Ireland, came to Amy's aid and explained the need to modernize the children's education. Nura Sittie convinced Amy about the future of her children's education. She got Amy Carmichael's consent to inquire about boarding schools for girls.

It so happened that there was a headmistress of a large high school in Trichy, who Amy knew from her early days at Pannivillai, South India. This lady was the daughter of a Brahmin who had come to faith in Christ. Being a high caste Brahmin, she was privileged, got a good education, and became the principal of a large high school.

Nura Sittie took Shanthie Aruldasan, a teacher at home school Jeevalia, with her to Trichy, a two-day's train journey from Dohnavur to see the headmistress of the school. The school principal at Trichy was happy to admit about nine Dohnavur girls from June of 1949, when the new school year began. At the same time, some of the boys were sent to the Dohnavur village CSI (Church of South India) school as day scholars.

The first Timothys, girls who went out to boarding school (1949).
Top row: Ubahari, Sulochana, Balaleela Carunia, Renuha, Premananthie.
Bottom row: Jeyacottie Jeyaventhan (Christina's younger sister),
Suhinie Carunia, Nesarathina Carunia, Preethapu Carunia.

Christina and Nishka, two Dohnavur Fellowship girls, were allowed to study privately in their own time for a Government (Secondary) School Leaving Certificate (SSLC) as they were already working as teachers at the fellowship school. Later, one more girl Tarahai joined them in the College of CSI (Church of South India) and returned with the government certificate to teach in the fellowship private school.

All three, in later years, joined the fellowship and became council members and helped in the general administrative work of the Dohnavur Fellowship for the rest of their lives. They were the first ones who got higher education under Nura Sittie's leadership as she continued to help educate those from second through sixth generations. I am part of the end of the second generation.

Teacher Amirtha Davairakkam, BA, BEd, supervising her students in the same classroom where Salma studied in fifth grade. The table she was using, which Salma remembers also using, is one hundred years old. Now, Amirtha is taking computer classes, which are being taught by Kamalavallie Carunia, MA, MEd., who is the most knowledgeable and equipped with excellent English proficiency and computer skills.

The courtyard in Jeevalia home school, where Salma studied from third grade to seventh grade. Once, someone sent chocolates from England to the one hundred home school students, Salma waited a long time until her turn; she was number ninety-nine. She was glad they didn't run out!

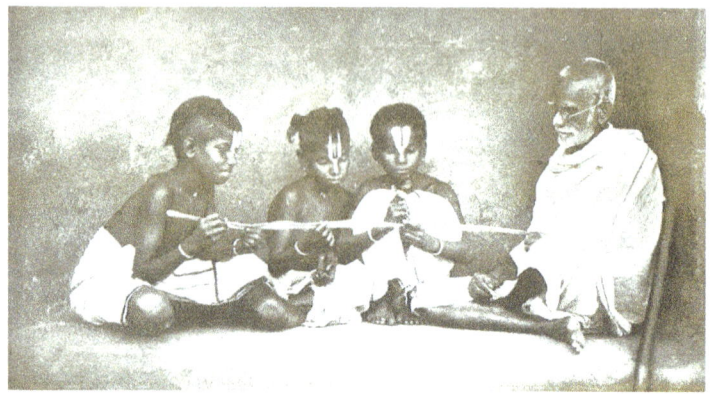

Before the British rule in India, only the Brahmins
(high caste) were allowed to have an education.
Above: a Brahmin village teacher teaching Brahmin boys to read
and write on a palm leaf, which was used as parchment.

Above: Gideons (boys), 1948, and Timothys (girls),
1949. Went out to boarding school.

Nesamithiri (Christina's sister).

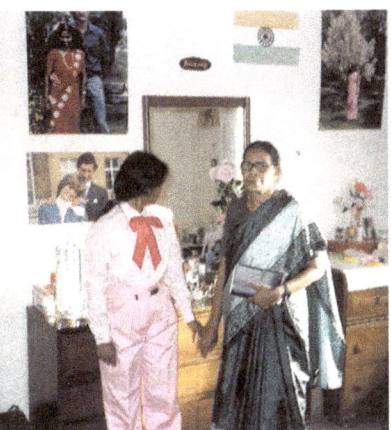
Christina visiting Salma and Mike's home in Wheaton College, Illinois, USA, 1985.

Right: Porupu Carunia, who lost one of her eyes at birth. She took care of Christina in her old age.

Christina proudly showing Salma's home, Dohnavur Fellowship, to her husband from USA, Dr. Ben Michael Carter in August of 1991.

Years later, my husband, Dr. Ben Michael Carter, visited my home in August of 1991. He was so in awe of our beautiful home, he wrote the following poem:

Salma

Where the Monkey leaped to Jaffna
from the Western Ghats
And Naraikadu rustled among its pools and rocks,
My wife in her blue sari paused,
Knuckled her toes to orange dust.
Tangled by shadows the air was too tired to pant.
The well with its frogs lurked
deeper than a child's plunge.
She wears a flannel shirt now,
Talks of Lushan, Dallas, Skye,
With the opinions of one who knows.
Her smile is quick through its mingle of languages.
The desert she loves has turned small,
So small she can tuck it away each morning
And step refined into the strong world.

Vanacharbu (open field of wood).
Men's compound, 1924. The tower was built in 1942.

Jeevalia schoolgirls playing in the playground. The girls played in the evenings when the boys were away playing in their playground faraway. Salma remembers watching the sunset and singing "When the golden sun goes down, and the hills grow dim and gray" while playing. The clock tower in the background was built during WWII in 1942, originally to house a siren. As Big Ben struck every hour, the family was reminded to pray for the many casualties of war. As time went on, they prayed for the fellowship's work.

Arul, the first boy to be brought to Amy Carmichael as a baby in 1918.

The boys' compound, which operated from 1918 to 1984. Almost eight hundred boys were raised here. Today, it is used for the Santhosha Education Society.

Mimosa's fourth son, Devavaran, father of Annaselvam. He is an excellent musician.

Annaselvam and Salma Carunia.

Mimosa's grandson, Rajamanian, and great-grandson Albert, who became a medical doctor in 2023.

Salma with Jack Trehane in London, 1996.

Tyriyam Annantha, who was a mechanic.

Kaniharan playing the joy bells.

Santhosha Vidhalaya (Santhosha boarding school for Indian missionary children) main entrance.

Nesarathina Carunia, who became a member of the staff in 1959. God called her home on July 29, 2023. Her loyalty and contribution to Dohnavur Fellowship and Santhosha Vidhalaya was commendable. Later on, she became more loving and willing to adapt to change. She was a vibrant and charismatic leader.

Kamaneri Ricelands (1938).

Amy Carmichael purchased eighty acres of paddy field in 1938 to feed her large family.

Paddy seedlings.   Paddy field.   Paddy ready for harvest.

In recent times, modern technology is used to harvest the rice.

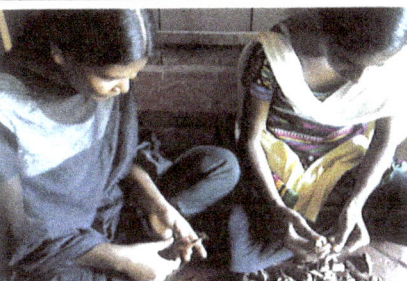

Upper left: irrigation pond.

Upper right: millet planting. Millet is a highly nutritious grain which is resistant to pests and drought.

Left: women cleaning tamarind fruit. The tamarind is used for Indian cooking, used notably in curry dishes.

# CHAPTER 8

## Life in Dohnavur

I enjoyed growing up in the Dohnavur Fellowship Children's Home. We knew the names of the flowers, birds, and insects surrounding us. We also learned to be careful when treading on creepy crawlies like scorpions, centipedes, and snakes. India has many venomous snakes such as cobra, saw-scaled viper, krait, and Russel's viper.

After the rain, the oleander plants in front of every house would crawl with gray and green caterpillars. We knew the habits of the different caterpillars. We waited till we saw the silver chrysalis pinned to the pointed leaves of the oleander plant. We children then plucked the leaves that had the chrysalis and tied the leaves with thread and hung them on our windowsill from one end to the other end.

At sunrise, we would gather at the windowsill every morning to witness the metamorphosis. I had watched the miracle slowly evolving as a butterfly unpacked itself and sunned its speckled, crumpled wings till the crumples smoothed and the wings dried. The butterfly fluttered away as we used to sing the song we learned in kindergarten: "O kind wind come and fan my wings, O sunshine makes it dry…I'd fly away…"

When I was in the school compound (Round), my house was surrounded by trellises with a green plant called porana, which produced small white flowers that hung over and flowed down. This has the appearance of a waterfall. The sweet smell overwhelmed the house and the surroundings. After Christmas, once the flowers faded away, it was the season for black caterpillars, and they had spikes, which I did not like. If they came inside the house, I swept them out of the house. See the picture on page 169.

Then in February and March, there were lots of large black red-spotted butterflies which came from nowhere. Hundreds came to drink nectar from the nearby bush called duranta, which bloomed in a bouquet of lovely purple-colored flowers in the backyard.

At the break time from school, I would go there to see the beauty of those butterflies as they came in a bunch, and I tried to catch them and play with them, for they had enormous wings. I put them on my shoulders but could not take them to school, for they flew away as I ran back to school.

Butterflies live short lives, so I could not have them as a pet, but I had rescued a baby squirrel once from the rooftop inside our veranda, making me a charming pet. It needed some milk and a small peck of plantain to feed it when I ate. I kept it in a small bag that was used for Christmas presents every year and hung it on the hook of the windowsill to keep it from predators. We were only allowed small pets like squirrels and birds; no cats, dogs, or other animals.

I liked the tailorbirds and sunbirds, and we watched them nesting in the bush around the house. If any of them got hurt or needed a home, we could have them as pets, for a birdcage was provided for us to raise them.

Once, we had a tailorbird that needed care for its broken leg. I remember we took it to the clinic to bandage it up and kept it until it was ready to fly. Then it became attached to us and rested on the creeper that grew up to the front roof. We brought grasshoppers for it in the matchboxes, and it would fly to our hands to feed it. I enjoyed this kind of interaction with nature very much. One day, the bird flew away, never returning, and I was very sad to lose the bird that we had nursed to good health.

Amy wrote a song for her children for a situation just like this:

> Flowers and ferns and trees and skies, singing birds and butterflies, these praise the Lord; Alleluia, Amen.
> Silver Stars and Silver Moon, Sunrise, Sunset, Sunny Noon,
> These praise the Lord; Alleluia, Amen.
> Let us all with one accord, Sing and magnify the Lord,
> O, Praise the Lord; Alleluia, Amen.
>
> Once I heard a little bird singing very clearly;
> And the bird that I heard, Sang, God loves me dearly.
> Please stay now and tell me how little bird you know it.
> Every day come what may, many kind things show it.
> Sun and rain, ripening grain, food and water given;
> leafy trees, all one sees under the blue heaven.
> Then the bird that I heard sang it very clearly,
> God loves you-off it flew—Loves you very dearly.

## Girl Guide Patrol Leader

One good thing happened to me when I repeated the seventh grade. One evening, when we returned from Jeevalia, we were surprised to see Nura Sittie (Margaret Wilkinson) sitting on the front windowsill, talking with my house mother, Rajamacottie. It was very unusual for her to come and speak to the house mother at their house. Normally, Nura Sittie, now the leader/president, would send a message to the house mothers to come to her house.

We changed our school dresses and put on our working dresses to water the plants. I kept running to fill my buckets from a large cistern as I was watering the plants around the house and watching Nura Sittie talking to our mother, Cottie Accal, as we called her. At 5:00 p.m., Nura Sittie left for tea, which was served to the missionaries in the bungalow. I immediately ran to Cottie Accal to ask her why Nura Sittie had come to our house, but she did not spill the beans.

After a week, Nura Sittie called me to her house and told me she had decided to make me a Guide patrol leader. This was very good news, and I ran home to share the good news with my beloved house mother, Cottie Accal. I told her, "Nura Sittie has confidence in me and has made me a patrol leader and also given me the patrol leader's haversack."

She only smiled as she already knew. It seemed that Nura Sittie didn't want to judge me by the school report but wanted to learn what my house mother would tell her.

The haversack, worn over one shoulder by the petrol leader, carries provisions such as a notepad and pencils. It also has the team badge stitched on it. My team was called the Allamanda, which had the yellow flower badge.

Allamanda is a yellow-and-purple-colored flower plant. I had eight to ten girls on my team and enjoyed leading them to many victories in our sports/games. It was the first time I was given responsibility. I remembered when my teacher Navarathinie tried to make me a class leader in fifth grade and how it was foiled, for other teachers were against it. Now, no one dared stand in Nura Sittie's way when she made me a Guide patrol leader. I enjoyed being in the Guide camp under Nura Sittie's leadership.

These men and women took on the new role of leadership at Dohnavur Fellowship.

Left to right: Davapiriam Devairakkam (Mimosa's second son), Thyaharaj, David Aruldasan, and Rajapan Devairakkam (Mimosa's eldest son).

Thyaharaj married Veera Carunia (photo on page 38; she is on the right in the top middle photo), and had four children, Ambujah, Susibai, Pasantha, and Vijayakumari.

David Aruldasan married Kirubaipu Carunia, and they had two children: Mehara and Punthura.

Rajapan married Nurani Carunia, and they had four children: Rajamanian, Arulananthie, Rajaventhie, and Rajan.

Back, left to right: Nesarathina Carunia, Christina Jeyaventhan.

Front, left to right: Nishka Carunia, Shanthie Caruniapu Aruldasan.

Margaret Wilkinson (Nura Sittie) took us schoolchildren to see the migrating waterbirds, such as flamingos, spoonbills, painted storks, kestrels, red-napped ibis, horned ducks, coots, black-tailed wits, moorhens, bar-headed geese, and amor falcons. Sometimes, we saw the birds nesting on the nearby trees. She also brought her field glass to better see the birds at a distance.

Salma lived in this house from fifth grade until seventh grade, plus two more years, with her dear house mother Rajamacottie Accal. Little did Salma expect that hers and Ponnalari's time with Rajamacottie would soon come to an end. The house was closed due to all of the girls being away at boarding school in 1959.

Salma with her dear house mother, Rajamacottie, reunited in 1972. The porana flowers still grow there today.

Salma remembers coming home from her school break and chasing and playing with butterflies every day in her backyard.

This is how Salma sat, ate, and prayed while being taken care of by her beloved house mother Rajamacottie Carunia in Dohnavur Fellowship.

This is the gazebo in the middle of the school compound where the results of the final exams were displayed. When Salma went to see her result, she saw that she did not pass seventh grade. This began the darkest and saddest time of her life. A few months later, she lost her beloved house mother, Rajamacottie Carunia, who was sent away to the youth hostel in Bangalore.

Entrance to God's Garden (graveyard). Amy Carmichael's tomb is in the middle, with the fellowship members buried all around her.

# CHAPTER 9

# The Adolescent Years 1959 to 1965

In June 1959, the school year started as usual. About eighty girls and sixty boys from Dohnavur Fellowship were sent to boarding schools in four different provinces/districts in Madras. Everyone gets a steel trunk in which they pack their different colored clothes.[5] In those days at Dohnavur, the girls wore blue uniforms and boys were in red.

The hostel-going girls were called Timothys, and the boys were called Gideons. When they came home for holidays/vacations, they were known as Timothys and Gideons to the Dohnavur family.

Preparations for going to schools outside Dohnavur were made in April and May during the summer holidays. Most children would leave home for the first time and step into a world they knew nothing about. They were only twelve or thirteen years old. Each child was not allowed to go anywhere alone and, therefore, were accompanied by an adult escort/chaperone.

---

[5] I don't know if these were really made of steel, but it was metal of some kind and durable and heavy. So I will refer to them as we thought they were steel trunks.

Many leaving home for the first time would cry while going out to the bus stand, which was half a mile from home. Some were excited to go to the railway station for their first train journey once the bus arrived at Tirunelveli Junction.

To attend schools in the three districts of Trichy, Tuticorin, and Ramanathapuram, one needed to travel by Train. Trichy and Ramanathapuram were overnight journeys by train. Only hard wooden seats were booked and no sleeping berths. They always traveled in a third-class compartment. One had to sit for many hours on the hard bench-like seats and sleep on each other's shoulders as the trains were packed with people in India.

The trains were so full of passengers that there was sometimes no place to walk, even to the toilet, as people would sit on the floor with their goods, such as large pots, pans, and various bundles. But that was not for me to see or experience in 1959.

I call this year from June 1959 to June 1960 the hardest year of my life, as I shed lots of tears in the beginning! At the same time on my coming day, November 29, 1959, a great mystery was revealed and made known to me!

The results of the Jeevalia school exams came out in the middle of April. They were always posted in the gazebo/pavilion in the middle of the school compound. I ran to see the result of the seventh grade and found that it said Not Promoted next to my name. *I was devastated!* I started to cry as this was the second time, I had failed in the seventh grade!

I came home to my kind mother, R. Cottie, sobbing and told her my result. Her face showed that she was very sad and worried about my future. Then I saw that Devarul, who, like me, was repeating the seventh grade, had also failed, so I had company, facing the same uncertain future, as we both failed seventh grade twice. However, Devarul would be sent to a boarding school to repeat seventh grade for a third time, but I would not.

Our fates were different. In Matthew 24:40–41, I felt like what it says, "Then shall two be in the…One shall be taken, and the other left."

## I Was Left Behind!

That was how I felt! But nothing could dampen my spirits. I was way up in the big tamarind tree, which I often climbed, reaching for the skies, for I enjoyed watching birds and squirrels nesting in the trees. That was when I was called to go and see Nura Sittie at her house on May 15, 1959. I came down through the large branch that I climbed up.

Nura Sittie (Margaret Wilkinson) was appointed as the leader/president of the fellowship after Amy Carmichael and Ubaharie Sittie (May Powel). She had to decide my future, and I stood beside her large writing desk in the middle of her house. She told me in a kindly manner, "Salma, you are not going to school this year; instead, you will work in our vegetable garden and in God's Garden." (God's Garden was the name of the graveyard!) This announcement would mean a whole year of very hard work or will become my fate for the rest of my life!

I was sobbing and asking, "What have I done? Lord, help me, Jesus…I know I am…now that I need you…so help me, Jesus…" It was the darkest hour of my life; I was only fourteen years old! I was still a child trying to figure out this unexpected fate of my life. Moreover, I was never given the reason for my detention.

Dear Nura Sittie comforted me by saying she would take care of me and promised to send me to boarding school next year. On that hope, I swallowed my tears and looked up to God, who is my refuge and strength, a very present help in times of trouble. Yes, I am in big trouble, but He can deliver me if I only learn to trust Him (Psalm 46:1).

We were taught and trained to accept the elders' decisions and those who rule over us. The next day, another girl in my class named Thilasa Carunia came to me and said she would work in the garden with me, for she was also detained from school and would not attend boarding school.

Nura Sittie (Margaret Wilkinson) told me that she was taking me out of the authority of Vimba Sittie (Eleanor Backhouse), who I knew had taken a disliking to me. I was, anyway, missing so many classes because of these punishments. However, at this moment, I did not understand at all! I had just been kicked out of the home school and felt sad that I would not attend the boarding school with Davarul.

I began working in the garden, tilling and hoeing the hard ground for planting the seedlings and carrying buckets of water to water the plants daily in God's Garden. And every day, we must clean the birdbath that stood above Amy Carmichael's grave. I liked that, as we could see different birds come to drink water from it, and I knew Lola, who died when I was in fifth grade, was buried right next to Amy so that I could visit both graves simultaneously.

On June 1, 1959, all the girls in my house were gone to boarding school. They went with their steel trunks packed with six sets of new colored clothes, whereas I was still wearing the old blue uniform of the fellowship. It used to excite us to get colored garments, for we wore the same old blue suit all our lives in Dohnavur. On the first day of work, no one was in the house except me and my dear house mother, Rajamacootie Accal.

They had put a label on me. I was the black sheep of the school. Mostly it's a snap judgment, a prejudice, based on the picture they hold in their minds. Labels help with food or other consumer goods, but not with people. Tags are attached to people with little thought but play havoc with the lives of people so labeled. Everyone is classified.

It's neat and reassuring. You know where you stand, and Christians do it too, evangelical or liberal, so says Eddie Askew, the international director of the Leprosy Mission, in her book *Disguises of Love.*[2]

Eddie Askew also says in her book "that they, who label people, must understand that people are not stereotypes as we do not fall off the end of an assembly line, all neatly programmed to react in the same way. People are different and similar only in their diversity—in the mixture of good and bad in the richness of experience we are continually adding from birth. We realize that we are made up that way, and we hope that others will allow us the freedom to be what we are and try to accept people unlabeled. The Only label that matters is Love." Jesus said, "I am the Good Shepherd. I must bring the other sheep I have which are not of this fold, and they shall hear my voice, and there shall be one-fold, and One Shepherd" (John 10:14–16).

Left to right:
Salma Carunia, Usila Carunia Navenaseelan, Thilasa Carunia, who was also detained from school with Salma. Deepa Navenaseelan, Usila's daughter

June 6, 1959, all the children in the Round compound went to school. It was the start of the new academic year. I went to work in the vegetable garden. From 8:00 a.m. to 6:00 p.m., with a lunch break from noon to 2:30. Working in the garden was not a new experience for me. There was a vegetable garden right behind my house. As Lola's children, we always worked in this garden on Saturday evenings as part of our extracurricular activities.

I went to the garden at 8:00 a.m. with Thilasa. I reported to Sellacottie and Samathana, the two ladies caring for God's Garden.

They knew me well because they told me Lola, who was in charge of all the green gardens, talked about her beloved Salma when they gathered for a short meeting every morning.

On my first day at work, we were assigned to weed the tomato patches. This was done by squatting on the ground and using the large spade that Sellacottie handed to us. My mind was in turmoil. All I could think of was all the girls of my age had gone to boarding schools, and I was left behind!

I was facing the morning sun, and the beautiful yellow rays of the sun were shining on me through the large mango tree near the irrigation well. However, my *body, mind, and soul* were groaning, travailing together. The whole creation around me seemed to groaneth and travaileth in pain together (Romans 8:22).

At the same time, something was happening to my *body* when my *mind* was processing the fate of my life throughout this whole year. My *spirit* was crying, "Abba, Father, the only father I came to know, the heavenly Father, for I am an orphan!" It says in Romans 8:23 that not only the creation, even we groan within ourselves waiting for the adoption—the redemption of our body.

In the garden, I felt that my body, mind, and soul were working together. Even though God had made us in three parts that function differently. Our body is mortal (man is subject to death), and the mind, the part of man that thinks, feels, wills, reasons, understands, perceives, and experiences emotions, will also die with the body. But there is another part of me, the spirit, which is immortal and will live forever, eternally!

"God breathed the breath of life (Spirit/Soul) into the body that He created, and man became a living soul" (Genesis 2:7; Psalm 139:14).

Hardly had I worked for an hour when I began to feel very sick and started to vomit. The ladies in charge sent me to the clinic, where Rachania Carunia, the nurse, gave me some medicine and told me to go home and rest.

At this time, my house mother, Cootie Accal, was home, busy packing her things, which was unusual. I wondered what was happening but thought maybe she was closing down the cottage since all the girls in that house had gone to boarding school, except me.

I started to cry and held her feet every time she walked past me as she moved in and out of the house. I felt very insecure. My heart was heavy, for I was going to lose my gentle, beloved house mother Rajamacottie.

I was weeping and felt *so lonely*!

Miss Shanthie Aruldasan, the first Indian who was now a coleader to Nura Sittie, came to my house and saw me resting. She told my house mother, Cottie Accal, that I had to return to work in the garden in the afternoon. It was agreed.

I rested till 2:00 p.m. and went back to work in the garden, and Thilasa was waiting for me, so we started to work together. April, May, and June are the hottest months in India. The temperature sometimes goes up to 120 degrees in the afternoons. It is very hot to till the ground, so we then went to God's Garden to water the plants in the graveyard.

October 23, 1959, was Devanesan Annachie's (John Risk) birthday. The custom of the Dohnavur Fellowship was that everyone goes to the leader's house to wish him well. However, I had a problem. I was fourteen years old and could not go alone to his house, as it was in the boys' compound. I could not go with the students of my age because I was no longer in the school, so I had to go with a group of working women. As I was the only one left at home, Lola's garden was left to me. I took a lovely red rose that bloomed in my garden, but did not dare give it to him in person, so I laid it on his desk.

Being detained from school and sent to work in the garden had its own social consequences. I was separated from the schoolgirls but was not an adult, so I now had to take the walk of shame wherever I go. This became painfully apparent every Sunday while going to church (House of Prayer). I would now go in a procession with adult odd girls/women, for I could no longer go in the line or sit with the schoolgirls. My privilege of moving with girls of my age and going to places was suspended for the entire year, and now I have a label: "detained from school." I kept saying to myself, "Salma, don't lose hope. Have faith in God, and He will never forsake you." Later in my life, I always cared for those girls who trod the same path as me.

Salma sitting with Chandravathy, who she helped raise. They are sitting on the edge of a water cistern, where she carried many buckets of water to water the gardens. There was also a papaya tree, from which they enjoyed eating fruit. Over to the right is where Lola's potted flower garden was.

Girls who grew up alongside Salma: Atharavu Row, Rathana Carunia, Saroruha Richard.

It gets a little cooler in November and December, and the lilies start coming up from the bulbs, especially the red and white ones like I saw at Amy's grave. Thilasa and I would fill buckets and go around the graveyard/God's Garden to water the plants. All of the following flowers and plants could be found there: zinnias, many-colored cosmos, chrysanthemum, begonia, coreopsis, convolvulus, aster, cowslip, daisy, white tuberose, trumpet lily snapdragon, marigolds of many colors, hibiscus, and yellow sunflowers.

A large almond tree stood at one end of the garden, and its ripe fruits fell on the ground. We picked them up and hid them until it was time to go home at 6:00 p.m. We dare not eat them immediately for fear the ladies in charge of us will find out that we were eating almond fruit while watering God's Garden.

To get the almond nuts, we had to pound the fruit with a stone, and its dark red fleshy part would stain our mouth and lips very red, which is hard to hide, for we did not have any lipsticks. However, today, I do not wear lipstick as I find that they have chemicals in it, as I like to keep my lips natural. I am seventy-nine years old now, and people mistake my age for thirties, and I am proud to declare that I am an old woman who is looked upon in India as a wise woman!

There were also five large mango trees on the boundary of the garden and one near the irrigation well. In the mango season, ripe yellow mangoes would fall from the tree, which we would try to eat. However, Sellacottie, who oversaw us, demanded that we bring them to her, and she would eat them without sharing them with us. Thilasa and I could not eat any garden product, even though we worked hard day in and day out, because we were detained from the middle school in 1959.

I still remember one day when we were weeding the beans patch, Samathana called us by name and said, "Salma and Thilasa, I am going to teach you a song," and we asked which one. She said:

> There were ninety-and-nine that safely lay,
> In the shelter of the fold;
> But one was out on the hills away,
> Far off from the gates of gold.
> Away on the mountains wild and bare,
> Away from the tender Shepherd's care.
> But all through the mountain, thunder-riven,
> And up from the rocky steep,
> There arose a cry to the gate of heaven,
> Rejoice! I have found My sheep!
> And the angels echoed around the throne,
> Rejoice, for the Lord brings back his own!
>
> (Church Evangelical services,
> Scripture Union, London, 1939)

I learned the song's tune and was always determined to remain in the fold. Especially when I was out of the fold, it felt like I was missing something.

At that time, I did not know much English, but I somehow understood, and it became meaningful whenever we sang it in the House of Prayer.

Every day when we went to work in God's Garden, we would pass by the six-foot stone cross at the entrance of God's Garden in front of a big tamarind tree.

I remember my childhood, when I was six or seven years old, on a Good Friday, two older sisters brought us children to God's Garden. We were all seated at the foot of the cross as they told us the story of the crucifixion. Then we sang a Good Friday song, and the ladies prayed for each of us to understand what had happened on that day when Jesus Christ was crucified and died for our sins.

The Path of Quietness leading to God's Garden on Easter Sunday.

Jesus paid it all. All to Him I owe
Sin had left the crimson stain,
He washed me white as snow.

My verdict, not guilty!

On Easter Sunday, in the bright moonlight at five o'clock in the morning, the fellowship family gathers (even today) at the corner of the path to God's Garden. Men and boys come from the north, the women and children join them from the south, and all wait quietly until an Easter hymn is played on the tubular bells up in the House of Prayer tower.

Then the leader gives the Easter greetings (like the early church fathers/disciples did), "The Lord has risen," and all reply, "The Lord is risen, indeed! Alleluia." After that, the choir begins the Easter hymn. We all follow them, going around the garden, singing Easter songs (Christ the Lord is risen today, Hallelujah) in English and Tamil and, in the end, standing in a circle under the beautiful big old tamarind tree near the entrance.

The story of our risen Lord is read on the first Easter morning story, and the service closes with the final hymn. About 350 to 400 of us, everyone continues to stand on the ground until we hear the song played on the tubular bells from up in the church tower:

> Hallelujah! Hallelujah! Hallelujah!
> The strife is o'er, the battle done;
> The victory of life is won;
> The song of triumph has begun. Hallelujah!

(*Golden Bells*, published 1923)

At the Cross, where I first saw the light
It was there by faith I received my sight!

Communion was served in God's Garden at the gold of dawn on Easter morning.

## My Verdict: Not Guilty!

This experience of the dawn service was the highlight of Easter Sunday. Once I was baptized and confirmed, I had the knowledge and joy of Easter communion. The mats are spread under the hundred-year-old tree at the entrance to God's Garden (this is the fellowship's graveyard). That is where the communion table was prepared, and I was kneeling during the service, facing toward the east. During the service, dawn breaks, and the sun rises in all its beauty above the palm trees beyond our garden. Its light shines over the ten-foot-high red wall protecting our garden from thieves and stray animals.

It is springtime, and I see the different kinds of butterflies coming out of chrysalis. They were beautiful tiger swallowtails, black swallowtails, monarch, lovely cabbage white, and eastern tail blue. I enjoyed chasing them as they flew higher and higher, away from my outstretched hands with which I wanted to pet them.

Let me tell you about some joy I got working in the garden and smelling the flowers that bloomed daily. One day, a sweet smell hit my nose while walking by the cowslip creeper. I remembered the song that I learned in kindergarten and sang as it goes like this:

> Oh, what a sweet smell fills all the air,
> Where does it come from? Where? Where?
> From the Cowslip Creeper there, there, there.
> Yellow Bell Cowslip Creeper, there, there,
>   there.

> (Amy Carmichael)

As the months passed, while working in the garden, I began observing how the plants and vegetables grew and progressed from the seedlings. The plantain patch was easy to look after, for they came out of stemlike roots and start growing up in a bunch, and one must separate them, as they each became one plantain tree. In time, a large red budlike flower will pop out at the top of the tree. However, the leaves were very dense and long, so sometimes, you cannot see the flower till it came out and started to open in the sun, and as it peeled the red rubberlike petals one by one, the circle of flowers can be seen. The pod of plantain is called circumscissile, which means opening along a transverse circular line as a seed vessel. It takes time as it grows very slowly.

Once the flowers mature into plantain, there are about twenty in each stem. Several stems on a branch so they weigh thirty to fifty kilos, causing the tree to lean outward. Sellacottie, who took care of it, put a strong log to support it and prevent it from falling as each tree yields 150 to 300 plantains.

Sometimes, there were not enough vegetables to send to the kitchen. In that case, they cut and shipped the red buds to make a delicious flower curry for lunch. They also sent unripe green plantains, which made a tasty curry. Since each tree produces only one flower, they must cut the whole tree to harvest one big bunch of plantains in one stalk. It is said that every bunch of plantains has an even number of plantains, and each row decreases by one so that one row has an even number and the next row an odd number. This also made me think that "The lives of each one of us is ordered by the Lord" (Psalm 37:23).

A wide irrigation well in the middle of the garden had a low wall surrounding the well. I learned to swim in that well. A manservant employed by the fellowship came with two bulls every morning. He would yoke them and drive them around and around in a circle to operate the Persian wheel, which seemed like it had hundreds of little buckets. These went down into the well to bring water and poured it into the upper concrete cistern. From there, it flowed to the whole garden through the water spout.

One day, Sellacottie told me at the plantain grove that she had called for me many times. I told her I did not hear her calling my name, for the garden was so wide and I was working on the other side, watering the large blue plumbago bush. So she jokingly told me there should be a book written about me, that every page should be called Salma. Haha!

When I was only fourteen, there was no hope for that kind of proposal or prophecy. So I just laughed. And now, after sixty-five years, I remember her saying that to me in the garden at the low point of my life in 1959. And here I am today in 2019, writing a book and the stories of my life as she predicted.

Pastor Harry Smith.

Pastor Harry Smith of Our Redeemer Lutheran Church (Salma's church)
2505 W Northgate Dr, Irving, Texas 75062, USA - prharry@orlc.org

When I went to the Our Redeemer Lutheran Church on a Sunday in August of 2022, which was the third Sunday of the month, I was assigned to read the scriptures for the morning service from John 2:1–11 and knew that it was the first miracle Jesus performed at the wedding in Cana.

In his sermon, Pastor Harry Smith pointed out that when they ran out of wine, it was a matter of shame for the master of the feast, according to the custom of that part of the world. When Mary, Jesus's mother, alerted him about the lack of wine, Jesus said, "My hour has not yet come," then he commanded the servants to fill the six stone pots with plain water. These pots were set for rites of purification according to Jewish custom. There the miracle happened, and they drew out not water but now wine and took it to the master of the feast. Jesus manifested His glory, and his disciples believed in Him and no walk of shame for the master of the feast.

I now look back on my time in 1959, when I was carrying a lot of buckets of water in the garden and walking the walk of shame as a way of purifying my body, mind, and soul.

## The Righteous Call to the Lord and He Listens
## Psalm 34:17

The month of August 1959 brought several changes in my life. My house mother, Rajamacootie, was taken away from me, and I started residing with Sellathai's family. I was not happy there.

Nura Sittie, knowing that I had failed in the seventh grade twice because I was weak in math, assigned Sittara Carunia to teach me and Thilasa. Sittara Carunia had graduated from high school with Ponnalari Carunia. They both were given a one-year internship, as was the practice of Dohnavur Fellowship, before starting pre-university.

From 10:30 to 11:30 a.m., we went to the school office veranda, and Teacher Sittara taught us math. It was a double blessing as we escaped working in the garden during the hottest hours!

One day in August, I went to Nura Sittie's house in the evening just before 7:30 p.m. She was getting ready to go to the bungalow for dinner where all of the missionaries ate. I went to show the result of my math test, but the real purpose was to ask her about my house mother, Rajamacootie. Even though I was now living with the family of Sellathai, I asked her when I would be able to return to my house mother, Rajamacootie.

She told me Rajamacootie was going to go to the new hostel in Bangalore to help with young adults. I started to cry softly, thinking that I would never go back to my dear house mother, Rajamacottie, as she had now been taken away from me.

To my surprise, Nura Sittie came near me, hugged me, and comforted me by saying that she would see to it and arrange a place where I could be happy. It was her dinnertime, but she prioritized a child needing a comfortable home. This was unheard of and unexpected. A leader was comforting a person like me with a hug, wiping my tears with her handkerchief, and sending me with the hope of a new home. Until then, I had never experienced this kind of loving-kindness and care from the leadership, as we always did what we were told, *no questions asked.*

Then Nura Sittie even told me that she would see that I am sent to boarding school next year! At that moment, I didn't understand what a great favor Nura Sittie was doing for me. It was only much later I learned that when I failed in seventh grade class the second time, Vimba Sittie had proposed that Thilasa and I be sent to work in the laundry as a punishment! Years later, in the 1970s, Margaret Wilkinson liberated them from this place.

The laundry was a terrible workplace where all the misbehaving adults were sent. There they remained for several years! But Nura Sittie had not only sent me to the garden in the first place but also decided to send me to a boarding school after only one year of punishment. Nura Sittie arranged for me to live in Shanthie Aruldasan's house. She would be my new house mother. I knew Shanthie Accal from before, as I would spend two weeks every year in her house with her children. This came about when my house mother, Rajamacottie Accal, went for her vacation to our holiday home, Joppa, in Cape Comorin. I was very happy with the news that I was going to live with Shanthie, as she would be my house mother from now on.

The next day, I told Thilasa as soon as she came to work with me in the garden. She said, "Sal, let us take your locker to Shanthie Accal's house now." Thilasa is much stronger and bolder than me. We went immediately as Sellathai's house, which was next to God's Garden. Both started to drag the locker, which kept all my clothes, to Shanthie Accal's house.

This was located at the other end of the school compound. Finally, we made it to Shanthie Accal's house. We discovered that Shanthie Accal had already prepared a place for my locker in her house! I was filled with joy and settled down at the new cottage. It was called Jasper, the first precious stone of the foundation of the city wall in Revelation 21:19.

I was happy at Shanthie Aruldasan's, the Jasper house family. She reminded me a lot of my dear mother, Rajamacottie; indeed, they were cousins! Shanthie (Aruldasan) was then the coleader, so she had a lot of authority from then onward. Therefore, it was very good for me when I became one of Shanthie's children since she protected me throughout my teenage years, as Lola had done before.

Shanthie had eight children: Arulkanthie, Kanaha, Sahera, Premala, Jeevanthie, Anihala, Inba, Arina. They were close to my age, and I enjoyed living with them. Each house has its customs and practices. One was how the food was served after it came from the community kitchen. Shanthie's helper, Pottamari Carunia, helped with serving the food to the children in this house.

She was a polio victim, so the missionaries treated her kindly. At breakfast, Pottamari mixed the spicy curry and milk with leftover rice from the previous day. We had no refrigerator to keep the food cool in those days. Then it was all mixed in with the red ragi porridge. It tasted horrible! In my previous home, R. Cottie gave us a red porridge with milk in our brass bowl. But she kept the rice and curry on our brass plates. This tasted much better.

One day, Shanthie noticed my face at breakfast and asked me what was wrong. I told her that at R. Cottie Accal's house, she did not mix everything in one large serving bowl. Instead, we got it separately, which tasted better. She then told Pottamari to serve rice with curry and porridge with milk separately from now on. All the children were happy and said to me that it was a good thing that I came to their house, and now they'll never have to eat porridge mixed with rice and curry ever again.

They were glad that I became their mouthpiece, for I was unafraid to speak up. (But sometimes only because I didn't know I shouldn't!) Because of my questions, there were many improvements from how they were before. They all became my best friends even after separating and going out into our own worlds.

Later Pottamari became a very good dressmaker and started working in the sewing room. Shanthie had to let her go to live in a house near the sewing room. Then Dayavathie came to live in our home and helped Shanthie. Dayavathie Carunia, six years older than me, was preparing to go to the sewing/dressmaking school while working in our sewing room. In the evenings, when we were the only ones left at home, we played snap (a card game), snakes and ladders, halma, and checkers together and enjoyed each other's company.

In June, when I was detained from school, Nura Sittie gave me a marble solitaire board to play in the evenings. I was alone as the other girls had gone to the Jeevalia to do their homework. My mother, R. Cottie Accal, taught me how to play it, and I soon mastered it. I played with it for a whole year and returned it to Nura Sittie when I was ready to attend boarding school in June 1960.

On my Coming Day, Dayavathie gave me a lovely colored silk ribbon. I was on cloud nine, as I had never before owned a colored ribbon, for we all have the same blue ribbon we tied to hold the braid. By then, I had nice, long, curly hair falling below my hip. One

Saturday evening, after washing my hair, I proudly tied my hair with the new colored ribbon.

Now, it was then after 6:00 p.m. and very dark. I used this ribbon only at night when no one could see its glamour.

I knew Shanthie would not spoil my joy of having the new silk ribbon, but others might. One evening, when I was sitting on the veranda after dinner, Pottamari came to see Shanthie and saw me wearing a colored ribbon! Suddenly she leaped, took the ribbon from my hair, and said this was not allowed as one must always wear a blue ribbon only. I was heartbroken but accepted that she had the right to correct anything against Amy's or the fellowship's rules.

However, Shanthie noticed the drama on her veranda and told Potamari to bring the ribbon to her office. After a week, dear Shanthie gave it right back to me to enjoy more Saturdays with it.

As I have already explained, at Dohnavur Fellowship, we do not celebrate birthdays. Most of us do not even know our actual birth date. Instead, what was observed was the day we were accepted at Dohnavur. Eight of us shared the same Coming Day, November 29. We were Mala and Seela, who were sisters (Mala was the older one), Sathyavathi, Naveenaseelan, Uthaveseeli, Salma, Sunderavulli, and Dayaleela. Our names were called out during the Sunday worship service on a Sunday nearest our Coming Day, and special prayers are offered. The Coming Day child's house is decorated with lots of flowers from the garden, and they wear differently colored saris on that day. Everyone comes and greets them after church.

All who have the same Coming Day share a special relationship even though they may have a large age difference. I came to the fellowship forty years after Mala and Seela. Since that day, Seela always sent me lovely pink cabbage roses from her garden on my Coming Day. I had her roses made in braids and tied around my head and a large bouquet pinned on my shoulder. I smelled roses for the whole day, for this type of roses are very sweet-smelling. See photo on page 38.

I always remember her kindness and visiting her in the hospital when I went to India in 1991 with my husband. She had the joy of meeting my husband as I told him that Seela gave me lots of love when I grew up in the fellowship. On November 29, I have a basket of silk pink cabbage roses on my mantelpiece at my home in America. They remind me of those lovely cabbage roses I had on me for my Coming Day at Dohnavur Fellowship.

## A Mystery Is Revealed to Me

November 29, 1959, my Coming Day, was on a Sunday. My house mother, Shanthie, gathered lots of Jasmine and some pink cabbage roses from her garden and asked me how many flower bunches I wanted to put on my long hair. I told her eight, and she smiled; she normally made four to five bunches for children.

However, at eight o'clock in the morning, she made eight with flowers from other gardens. She also made one long corsage for me to pin on my shoulders. Normally, only small girls are allowed flowers on their shoulders, but I was still a child even though I turned fifteen on that very day, for I had not yet come of age.

That day, I wore a colored sari and Shanthie combed my hair, tied eight bunches on my long hair, and pinned one long corsage of flowers on my shoulder. They smelled better than any perfume! I felt happy. I remember seeming to fly around like a beautiful butterfly. It helped me bury my sadness at being punished and detained from school for a whole year.

The Coming Day girl gets hard candies and a gift on such a Sunday, and Shanthie told me to go to Priya Sittie's (Frances Nosworthy, see picture on page 36) house to get mine. I told her the only present I longed to have was a new Bible.

The reason goes back to when I was in seventh grade. Tarahai, the acting headmistress, told everyone to bring their Bibles to the staff room to send to the bookbinders to bind. I put my Bible in there along with others. Mine was tattered, and the back binding was coming off because I used it too much by reading it every day. I could see that the Bible is one of the great works of classical literature.

However, Tarahai did not send mine to the bookbinders, and Thilasa told me her Bible was also not sent, but she did not care about it. But I was crying and said, "Oh! I care about it, for that is the source of my life, and I get counsel from it." So finally, on this

Coming Day in 1959, when Shanthie asked me what gift I wanted for my fifteenth birthday, I showed my old Bible to her- and asked her for a new Bible. She looked at it and said she would write a note for the person in charge of the books in Amy's bungalow to get a new Bible to replace my old one. I was ever so happy about getting a new Bible!

After the English service, everyone came to see me at Shanthie's house, decorated with lovely seasonal flowers, white trumpet lilies, blue plumbago, and lovely ferns and creepers. Sirappan Annachie (Philip England, Tari's father) came to wish me well on my Coming Day. I was a bit ashamed of myself for I had not gone to boarding school.

He understood my discomfiture and was very reassuring. I still remember his words. He said, "In quietness and confidence shall be your strength" (Isaiah 30:15). It seemed he was trying to pinpoint my inner strength.

I asked about his daughter, my friend Tarie, who had gone to England six years previously to study in boarding school, as she celebrated her fifteenth birthday ten days earlier on the nineteenth. I wondered when I would get to see her. He knew this was impossible then, so he asked me to write to her. (Tarie didn't read Tamil, and I didn't know how to write a letter in English yet.)

Shanthie allowed me to visit my beloved mother, Kirubai (Grace), at lunchtime. Her friend Rajarathinie and others gathered at Manohara Accal's house and waited for me to have lunch with them. I had a feast eating with all those who loved me dearly; it was almost like a reunion with old folks who still loved me and were praying for me. I was proud of their love because these were the elders and the first generation of Amy Carmichael's children, who knew Lola, and were like pillars of moral support to me, and I cherish their love even to this day!

After lunch, I went to see Seela, who sent roses every year on my Coming Day, for it was her Coming Day too, and I gave her my best wishes.

In the evening, I went for a walk with a few other girls and, by 6:30 p.m., came home to get ready to go to church for the singsong service. Shanthie tied some new bunches of jasmine and rose at my long braid, and I wore a pale pink voile sari. In this service, the leader, John Risk, would call out names written in the Coming Day book and pray for them (we called it the Book of Life). In it, the names of all the children of Amy have been written according to the date they were brought to the Dohnavur Fellowship.

 Amy Carmichael called her children "lotus buds."

Every fourth Sunday, they took an offering at the evening singsong service. I told Shanthie that my house mother, R. Cottie, had given me three pennies. I kept it for Harvest Festival to buy ice cream, but now I have decided to give it to the Lord to put in the offering plate at the singsong service. During the service, John Risk, who was conducting the singing service, stood in the front with the wooden offertory plate. The people discharged from the hospital went to put their thanksgiving offerings. I also got up from where I was sitting in the middle of the church and went in front to put my three pennies, which was all I had. I felt happy that I gave everything I had to God.

After dinner, Shanthie took me to the school office, and we sat on the veranda. She talked to me about spiritual things and encouraged me to trust only God. She said she could see I have a bright future, and only time will tell. Then she prayed with me, gently kissed me, and wished me well for the coming year. Then we walked back home and went to bed.

Before I lay down on my grass mat, I knelt and said my evening prayer, mulling over what Shanthie had shared with me half an hour ago. I asked God to reveal His will for me and to grant me forgiveness for my sins. At that moment, our clock tower struck 9:00 p.m., and the church tower tubular bells began pealing. Piratha, who was up in the tower, started to play the song (Amy designated three songs for each day, to be played at different times): "Jesus, lover of my soul, let me to thy bosom fly…hide me, O my Savior hide, Till the storm of life be past! Thou of life the fountain art, freely let me take of Thee, Spring Thou up within my heart, Rise to all eternity."

## CHRIST IS IN ME

At this very moment, while I was kneeling on the floor praying, I felt something like lightning went through me! I came to know God, Lord Jesus Christ as my personal Savior. I felt God's omnipresence and came to know Him. At that time, I had no particular sin to confess. Since I was three years old, I always asked him to come and cleanse my heart. But this night, something very different happened. I tell you that knowing Jesus Christ as my Lord, Redeemer, and Savior who had revealed the mystery to me. At that moment, I flew into His bosom, for I knew I was safe there till the end/death. The lightning that went through my body was the power washed with the blood of Christ and cleansing. I am now free and happy in the Lord. "At the cross where I first saw the light and the burden of my heart rolled away, it was there *by faith* I received my sight, and now I am happy all the way."

I felt free, like his burden rolled away in the story of Christian when he came to the cross. The angels put a cross on his forehead, clothed him with a change of clothing, and gave him a sealed scroll to show at the Celestial Gate. I felt what went through me is explained in Ephesians 1:13, "In Him the message of truth, the gospel of your salvation—having also believed, you were sealed in Him with the Holy Spirit of promise."

This day, the eyes of my heart were opened. I was enlightened and knew the hope of my calling now, for He gives me the spirit of wisdom and knowledge through the spiritual meaning of His words and revelations. I say age matters because in 1 Corinthians 13:11, it says: "When I was a child, I reasoned like a child, but now when I became a man (woman), gave up childish ways." I had begun to understand the Word of God and its spiritual meanings.

Sunday, November 29, 1959, on my fifteenth coming day, the mystery was revealed to me, which is the title of this book/story.

Colossians 1:27 says, "Christ is in you the hope of glory."

I went to bed a very different person! I had peace! And I knew that this Lord and Savior of mine would see me through all my troubles, and *joy* came into my heart. I could have leaped and praised God as the lame man did on the streets of Jerusalem or Damascus. Oh, it is such a joy to know that someone will be with you always, who is a Divine Presence. I have now learned to put my *trust* in Him only, and my *faith* in Jesus Christ increases as I pass through the troubled waters. The Bible says justification by *faith alone*. I now know that God is still on the throne. He never forgets His own. Though trials may press us and burdens distress us, He never will leave us alone. Praise God! Now I belong to Jesus Christ, my Savior, Redeemer, and Paraclete (Comforter).

The next morning, I woke up and went to Shanthie, my house mother, and told her what happened to me on Sunday night. I proclaimed I came to know Jesus Christ as my personal Savior/Redeemer. Knowing Him as He reveals the truth, especially my understanding of His Word, and I am now safe with Him. All she could say to me was "Salma, go and show it in your life." I knew that Shanthie was a wise woman who did not speak much.

Monday! Life is back to normal. I put on my blue sari and went back to work in the garden, for I must work there till the end of summer, but I now have hope and am looking forward to going to boarding school in June 1960 when the next school year starts.

On my way to work, the blue, violet, white, and red morning glory, which crept over the walls and trellis along the way, greeted me along with the extremely large trumpet-shaped flowers, which are lovely and reveal the glory of the Lord and his handiwork. Each flower blooms in the morning and withers away in the evening—living only a single day. But the next day, masses of new flowers will again open out, and the plant will continue blooming till winter, for the morning glory needs plenty of light and thrives in the sun.

I am no longer ashamed of myself and have new strength and courage to face the day because of what had happened to me last night. I am a new person now with faith in God. It gives me new *joy* to live, as there is peace in my heart. I knew in my heart the lightning that went through me last night was the beginning of something I did not know before; as it says in the Bible: "I will light your heart," so my faith started growing strong. I was ready to face life with new strength and courage. The Lord sent me Paraclete, a person called in to aid.

# CHRIST IS IN ME

*Be still, sad heart! And cease repining:*
*Behind the cloud is the sun still shining*

—"The Rainy Day" by Henry Wadsworth Longfellow

As I was watering the plants at Amy's grave, I noticed that the tuberoses had started to sprout as they bloom in late winter or early spring, sometimes between October and January, depending on planting time. The stem with flowers can be over three feet tall; normally, there will be only one stem from each tuber. The flowers are waxy white and grow in clusters at the end of the stem. They are long-lasting and have a cool, sweet fragrance. In India, they are used for making garlands for weddings and special occasions.

Then I went to the far side of God's Garden to water the periwinkle and oleanders across the lawn, where I squat and cut grass with the scythe. Periwinkle flowers are either pink or white, and white ones have a faint scent. The leaves are shiny green, and it is a low and compact flowering plant that grows to a height of six to eight inches. The oleanders are beautiful but poisonous flowering plants that grow ten feet tall and need water daily.

They have narrow dark-green leaves four to twelve inches long and are attractive in all seasons. The flowers appear in white, pink, and crimson colored terminal clusters in summer.

There were other flower beds, such as globe amaranth, which I had growing up when Lola gave us children a small plot to have our own little garden. It has rounded papery flowers that look like clover blossoms. This plant has narrow dark-green leaves two to four inches long and is covered with whitish fuzz. Purple is the most common color of globe amaranth, but there are some pink and white colored plants too. It generally grows about one to three feet tall, and when cut and dried, they make excellent long-lasting indoor ornamental arrangements.

Then there is the ubiquitous hibiscus, which bloomed nearly all year round and needed water daily. The large colorful flowers come in countless varieties and every shade of the red/yellow part of the spectrum. It is a shrubby plant with glossy green oval saw-toothed leaves. The flowers are large, three to five inches across. Hibiscus cannot thrive in the cold, for it is a tropical plant. However, one variety can stand up to frost: *Hibiscus syriacus*, also called Rose of Sharon. I marveled at seeing the tropical hibiscus plant when I visited Israel with my husband in 1995 and even took a picture of me standing underneath the beautiful red blossom of the blooming tree. I also saw the oleanders were in bloom beside the Sea of Galilee. There I sat on a rock near the sea and sang this song which I learned growing up in Dohnavur:

Oleander

We grow beside the shining Sea set round
    with hills in Galilee;
We often saw our Lord and knew; He saw us
    and He loved us too.

For He loved all the little flowers that smiled at
    Him through sunny hours
And, when the sky was dark and gray, Still smiled
    and did not go away.

We tried to make the world sweeter for Him who
    walked with holy feet,
Along its way and by its sea set round with hills
    in Galilee.

(Amy Carmichael)

I like to sing this hymn of promise and praise as I look back upon my life:

### Hymn of Promise

In the bulb there is a flower, in a seed, an apple tree,
In cocoons, a hidden promise, butterflies will soon be free.
In the cold and snow of winter, there's a spring that waits to be,
Unrevealed until its season, something God alone can see.

There's a song in every silence, seeking word and melody,
There's a dawn in every darkness, bringing hope to you and me.
From the past will come the future, what it holds, a mystery,
Unrevealed until its season, something God alone can see.

In our end is our beginning, in our time, infinity,
In our doubt, there is believing, in our life, eternity.
In our death, a resurrection, at last, victory.
Unrevealed until its season, something God alone can see.

(Words: Natalie Sleeth; Music: Natalie Sleeth; ©1986 Hope Publishing Co.)

I finished work at 6:00 p.m. and was heading home, still exuberant. The bougainvillea leaning from the other side of the wall, a quarter of a mile long, appeared to be saying or singing, "Day is done, gone the sun from the hills, from the sky. All is well, safely rest, God is nigh," bidding me good night, through their shades of purple to dark pink, salmon, and orange petals glowing from the rays of the setting sun. The petals make this lovely plant so eye-catching. However, come Saturday, I had a back-breaking job sweeping up the dry petals, shedding on the road by thousands, and taking them to the rubbish pit.

When I was a child, we played on that heap of dry petals that came up to our hips. They had soft orange papery petals. Bougainvillea was named after the world traveler Louis de Bougainville, who discovered it in Brazil in 1790 and brought it to Europe, where it became widespread and popular. However, it came from a warm and sunny climate and is not of European origin.

On my way to work the next morning, I was thinking about my future. I came upon the verse from Jeremiah 29:11, "For I know the plans that I have for you declares the Lord, thoughts of peace and not of evil, to give you a future and a hope."

As I walked past the trees and plants on my way to the garden, I came upon the honeysuckle, which means the sweetness of disposition. I inhaled their sweet-smelling fragrance. Then I walked past my old house and saw the yellow allamanda, which I had watered for years, was in full bloom. They looked as if they were ringing their yellow bells silently, for they were glad to see me passing by. Suddenly, I noticed the purple passion flower, which signifies *faith*. These flowers have held traditional meanings for centuries and can be found in mythology.

The Victorians codified these meanings into an elegant language without words, says the illustrator Pierre-Joseph Redoute. I stopped to see the passion flowers on the trellis. I started to sing the song written by Amy Carmichael. Lola had made her children memorize when I lived in her house as a nine-year-old child:

"Dear Flower, you tell a story of suffering and
    glory: I softly, softly sing to you,
O purple Passion Flower.
A little child am I and often wonder why your
    story is so sorrowful,
O purple Passion Flower.
Three nails, five wounds you show, and I can
    never know the pain you try to tell me of,
O purple Passion Flower.

> A crown of thorns you show and I can never
>     know the pain you try to tell me of,
> O purple Passion Flower.
> And yet beyond the sadness, there is mysterious
>     gladness, and reverently I sing to you.
> O purple Passion-Flower.
>
>                    (Amy Carmichael)

I reached God's Garden, still singing the passion flower song to myself, and started watering the flower patches beginning with the petunia, which means "never despair." I needed that encouragement to keep on doing my work in the garden. At that moment, Shanthie came to the garden and told Thilasa and me that Nura Sittie decided that we both work in the garden till 10:00 a.m. and then go to Mala in the spinning room. We were to learn how to spin yarn.

Mala, who was Seela's elder sister, loved me dearly from childhood, for Mala, Seela, and I shared the same Coming Day. I was very glad to go and work with her, but more than that, it was nice and cool to work under a roof sheltered from the hot sun.

She taught us how to use the spinning frame, a machine for drawing, twisting, and winding yarn. One has to sit on the wooden board, hold it to the floor, and spin the wheel with the right hand while making a thread with the twisted yarn feeding at the needlepoint in the front of the wooden board. We quickly learned it and began to enjoy spinning every afternoon, sitting under the roof, away from the hot sun in the garden. See Mala's picture on page 38.

December 25, 1959: Christmas! Christmas Day is very special in the Dohnavur Fellowship family. Celebrations start at 4:30 in the morning, with the choir going around caroling through the compounds accompanied by a group of about fifty schoolgirls carrying colored lanterns. After the caroling, lots of good food and coffee follow for breakfast.

At eight o'clock, we all go in a procession to the cattle farm, led by the band and choir singing nativity songs, where worship service is held, and we are reminded that Jesus was born in a stable. When we returned from the farm, we children ran to where each person was given fifteen hard candies. Some ate them immediately, and those who had self-control kept them to last a little longer. I usually kept mine for two to three months! Then we attended church services which were given in English and Tamil and lasted till noon.

Later that afternoon, at 5:00 p.m., the whole family assembled again in the field near the clock tower, from babies in arms to seniors, women, girls, men, and boys. This was where they all got Christmas presents! Everyone in Dohnavur, from babies to the oldest person, received a gift on that day.

It took about two hours to distribute these as each person's name was called according to their house. The gifts wrapped in colored paper were all on a large bench covered with a blue cloth in front of the tower. No one knew what they were getting, and everyone waited anxiously to hear their name called.

I was living in a house called *Jasper*. When it was called, I got my Christmas present, a lovely wooden pencil box with a lid with a beautiful tulip flower painted on it, a pencil, and a small cake of sandalwood soap, all packed together in a colorful bag. I was very happy. It gave me the hope of going to boarding school in the following year.

I immediately planned to use my pencil box to keep the fountain pen when I got to the boarding school in June of 1960. My house mother Shanthie chose this Christmas gift for me. I brought this lovely pencil box to America in 1978 when I came to study at Bethany Missionary College in Minneapolis, Minnesota! I used it in the classrooms!

At 7:00 p.m., we all go to the singsong service in the House of Prayer. All the children sit on the tile floor around a beautifully decorated pine tree in the center of the church and sing carols in English and Tamil. The one you see below by Amy Carmichael is one we sang:

> The Lord of Love on a certain night said, "Lo,
>    the world's lamp grows dim,"
> And, He made a Song, and filled it with light,
>    And He called His angels to Him;
> And He said, to His kindness, "My poor people lie
>    all out in the dark; take this new Song and fly,
> Fly down to them, sing it to them or they die."
>
> In each angel's heart like a little bright sun was
>    the beautiful song, and new,
> And they wanted to sing it to everyone, as the
>    Lord had told them to do.
> "For now," said the angels, the one to the other,
> "whoever will sing it will know his great brother,
> And see in the light of it each man a brother."
>
> So, they flew past many a burning star, that sails
>    in the outermost deep,
> And they passed the white moon and they travelled far
> Till they came to a field of sheep;
> And the men that tended them woke as the light
> Of the wonderful Song broke forth in the night,
> And the world has been lighter since that night.

Num. 24:17; Rev. 22:16

The Christmas Day ended with dinner and bedtime at 9:00 p.m. Little did I realize that this was the last day of my childhood!

The next morning, a Saturday, I went back to work in the garden. I was cutting grass with a sickle (curved blade mounted in a short handle) near the waterspout, not far from the irrigation well. In contrast, all the Timothys, then home for vacation, were working on the other side of the garden. Because I was a detainee, I was separated from other school-going girls even while doing the same task, like cutting the grass.

Nesarathina, who was in charge of the Timothys, oversaw them while walking on the top of the concrete irrigation system around the garden. When she came near where I was working alone, she acted all high and mighty. She yelled at me, saying that I was below the level of everybody and had no future or hope of being educated. She was trying to crush my spirit, saying that I was a nobody and could not go anywhere from here. It was hurtful, for I knew she had the power to deprive me of higher education.

In 1959 Sura Sittie (Barbara Trehane), who was responsible for the girls who went to boarding schools, was given a new responsibility and put in charge of the hostel in Bangalore. This is where they made soft toys and marketed them. Management of the boarding-school girls was then transferred to Nesarathina, one of the first groups of Timothys (that is what the girls were called). She also finished high school at Trichy and graduated with a bachelor of arts (BA) and bachelor of education (BEd) from Women's College in Madras in three years. She also had work experience of one year outside Dohnavur, so Nesarathina became responsible for the Timothys. This made her feel she was above all of us. She ruled over us with unkindness on her way up to the leadership, was unjust and gave harsh punishments, and was especially cruel to some of us, like me.

However, I was comforted by John 14:1, "Let not your heart be troubled," and sang:

> Far in the Future lieth a fear like a long, low mist of gray
> Gathering to fall in dreary rain: thus, doth thy heart within thee complain;
> And even now thou art afraid, for round thy dwelling,
> The flying winds are ever telling of the fear that lieth gray,

Like a gloom of brooding mist upon the way.
But the Lord is always kind, Be not blind,
To the shining of His face, to the comfort of His grace,

Hath He ever failed thee yet?
Never, never; wherefore fret?
O fret not thyself, nor let thy heart be troubled,
Neither let it be afraid.

(Amy Carmichael)

Even after sixty years, I still remember the exact place where I was squatting and cutting the grass in the garden as Nesarathina was trying to break my spirit. But Nesa did not know that less than a month ago, on November 29, something happened to me on my Coming Day. I had come to know the divine presence of my Savior and Redeemer and, therefore, now had the inner strength! God gave me a promise through Jeremiah 29:11, "For I know the thoughts that I think towards you says the Lord, thoughts of peace and not of evil, to give you a future and a hope." I can stand on this promise now, and *my verdict is not guilty*. Then I sang as I remembered the verse in Isaiah 64:4,

No mortal ear has heard it, No mortal eye perceived,
No swift imagination has ever yet conceived
How singular the beauty, how bountiful the grace.
Prepared for him (her) who presses to Thy fair dwelling-place.
And I sing, yea, I sing in the ways of the Lord
That great is the glory of the Lord.

(Amy Carmichael)

I came of age. I felt very tired on that day but did not know the reason and did not find out till I went home for lunch from work. We girls gathered with our long skirts tied up to our shoulders to cover ourselves while bathing in the open at the borewell pump. We would sit under the spout while another girl would push the handle to get the water flowing. See picture on page 85.

That night, I started menstruating (Christmas night). However, I did not know till a girl, Sona Carunia, who was bathing with me, noticed blood on my clothes and pointed it out.

We were raised very innocently and did not know of such things until they happened. I was called inside the house where an adult privately explained it to me. She said I would go through this monthly, which was news to me! She also showed me how to prevent soiling my clothes. Today, I can tell you I am glad that they kept us innocent children as long as we were children. I was happy, running around climbing trees and frolicking in the wonderful clean world of my home, Dohnavur Fellowship.

Well, the day had finally arrived for me to get a bucket to soak the small cotton towels before sending them to the washerwoman. I wondered why everyone but me was getting an extra small bucket. Shanthie gave me a brand-new bucket, twelve new towels, and tape with two loops to tie around our hip to keep the towels in place.

I quickly cross-stitched my name on all of them, for we had never heard of marking pens.

On Monday morning, I went back to work in the garden for a few hours and found that we had a new supervisor named Kovalai, and she knew me as one of Lola's children. She introduced a new method of planting seedlings, which made our work easier. When the time came to uproot the dried eggplants, she told us to shout, "Oh my youthfulness," and pull out the plant in one smooth action. This was great fun for me and Thilasa, as we two worked together. Kovalai also allowed us to eat the ripe mangos when they fell from the mango trees around the garden.

One day, Kovalai told me to pick the tomatoes, and I picked about four buckets full, which were sent to the kitchen for cooking. While choosing the tomatoes, I heard a steady tapping noise from the tamarind tree. I saw a woodpecker trying to build its nest by making a hole in the tree. They look funny climbing up sideways to reach the safe spot to build their nest. Then while I was still watching it, it flew across the garden and landed on an almond tree.

We liked the almond fruit when ripe. The red, juicy, and mealy part can be eaten, but the thing we wanted most was the nut inside. I collected about ten to twenty of them and took them to a place where I could break them with a large stone to eat the nut, which is tasty and full of milk. I see a very different kind of almond seed in the West, and I can say that ours in India tasted better. I saw the same Indian almonds in Puerto Rico in 1980.

Then, the tapioca was to be pulled out when the tubers were ready to be harvested. (They boil the roots and make curry with them.) We trimmed many lawns around the fellowship as they always needed trimming. We sure had loads of work to keep us busy all the time.

Tapioca roots.

On January 26, to celebrate Republic Day in India, we went for a picnic to the foothills of the Western Ghats (mountains) to the rest river. We would put our things on a large flat rock and walk to a big pool called the Joy Pool. A waterfall of swift-flowing mountain river formed it. It was a great joy to jump into the bottomless pool from the high boulders surrounding it and swim in it before and after lunch.

We ate, sitting on the large flat rock surrounded by greenery, watching colorful flowers and butterflies flying in and out of the flower cups.

There I sat and sang the song:

"The butterflies said grace"
I sat in a green wood. A foaming torrent drummed,
"The Lord is great, and He is good,"
A tiny insect hummed.
The young leaves whispered, "Yes," a murmur by the mere

Of moss and fern, "His gentleness we love, and
 He is dear."
A little flower looked up, a smile upon her face,
Sweet food lay in her open cup; A butterfly said
 grace.
A shadow on the shore—The butterflies withdrew,
The wind shook leaves down on the floor, the sky
 hid all her blue.
Mist lay upon the hill, Sharp rain the river smote;
But on its glancing surface still I saw bright bubbles float.
They caught the fading light, that was so fain to go.

The water-way was as the white of moonbeams on the snow.
And as they shone and broke in simple gaiety,
I was aware of One who spoke by bubbles unto me.

(Amy Carmichael)

CHRIST IS IN ME

# The Agony of Waiting

I was counting the days as the summer approached. The school year of 1959–1960 will close at the end of March. The summer vacations will be in April and May. The schoolchildren will be returning home from the boarding schools. I knew I had two more months to wait for the next school year to start in June, waiting patiently for the hardest year of my life to end as it says in Proverbs 25:25, "Good news from a distant land, like cold water to a weary soul." I am also waiting to hear the good news from the fellowship regarding sending me to the boarding school in June of 1960.

To pass the time, I notice the trees and flowers surrounding us in Dohnavur. Each compound had beautiful trees that bloomed in their own seasons. Let me tell you about the beautiful trees in our Garden of Eden!

Banyan tree, an East Indian fig tree, whose branches send out adventitious roots to the ground, sometimes causing the tree to spread over a wide area. In kindergarten, I learned a story about this tree: On a stormy day, a little bird needed shelter, for he could no longer stay in the bush. The little bird went to a coconut tree, and asked for refuge, but was refused. Then the bird went to the neem tree, and was refused again. Finally, the bird found refuge in the Banyan tree. Later, the coconut tree and the neem tree were knocked down by the storm, but the Banyan tree still stood. Always help those in trouble, and God will help you in your times of trouble. (Ps. 46:1)

The laburnum, with its charming yellow drooping clusters, like a bell, was a joy to pass underneath while going from one compound to the other, for it stood at the end of the Square children's compound. The white hanging flowers of the cork tree had a lovely fragrance. When they fell on the ground, we children picked them up, for it has a long stem that we could weave like a braid to make garlands. Then there were the bright-orange cork flowers that bloom in clusters. They are bush plants, which often grew near the water pumps, where we took a bath in the open air, and they provided some privacy for us.

The fellowship compound was full of several very old tamarind, neem (margosa), and mango trees standing like sentinels of time. We gathered the dried margosa fruits in summer, for they made oil from their seeds. The tamarind fruit is used extensively in South Indian cooking.

The flame of the forest had spectacular bright-orange flowers. At the same time, you could see the tranquil beauty of the mauve coiled clusters of the queen of flowers in the Square at the children's compound. I used to climb this tree with my blue sleeveless dress to play and sometimes pick the large seed hanging from the tree because it tastes sweet.

The dry seeds make a noise when you shake the pod. We sometimes use them as musical instruments during the evening prayers accompanying songs in the children's cottage.

Near the garden where I worked, there were many acacia trees, and they made noise when the wind shook their pods high in the trees, and one knew that summer was approaching. It was also a lot of work to gather the pods when they fell and put them in the rubbish pit. The acacia trees provided quality firewood. All our cooking was done on firewood, as gas stoves were not even a thought. So you can see, many of those trees sheltered and fed us!

This is the swimming pool where Salma learned to swim from age five to seven.

I was told to clean the swimming pool to prepare for the children starting their summer holidays. It was three feet at the shallow end and eight feet at the deep end. I remembered my fear of going into that water when I was only five years old. But when I moved from the children's compound to the school compound, all had to learn to swim in the deep irrigation well without any floaters or other safety devices. Once we knew how to swim, it was a joy to jump into the deep well and enjoy swimming.

One summer morning, I checked the swimming pool and saw hundreds of dragonflies dancing and hovering over the water. They all appeared to have rainbow-colored wings, and they attracted me so much I wanted to catch one or two. This was tricky, for they hardly came to the water's edge where I stood. I could not get into the water for fear of wetting my clothes and not having another set of dry clothes to change into.

I waited and waited and went around the pool but could not catch even one, my playtime ran out, and I had to go. I began to wonder why all those years, I had never seen a dragonfly with rainbow-colored wings outside of that swimming pool. I had caught some from the bush, feeding on the flowers, but they were always black with colorless lacelike wings that had rough edges. Now I realize that when the sun shines through the water, the dragonflies' wings, in the reflected light of the sun, appear to be rainbow-colored! Then I just wanted to catch them to have a rainbow-colored insect to admire, as I loved the bright colors at that time of my life.

Every Saturday, I got off work at 4:00 p.m. to wash my clothes, including my heavy blue cotton sari (six yards of cloth) wrapped around me every day to go to work. We were issued half a cake of soap for bathing and washing clothes every month. Since I was working in the garden, hoeing and tilling the ground, cutting the grass, squatting on the ground, my saris and blouses got very dirty, so making the soap last a whole month wasn't easy. Somehow, I managed. To wash the clothes, I used to soak them in a bucket, then apply soap, raise the heavy clothes above my head, and bring them down with force on a large stone slab to take off the dust and dirt, and then rinse them with clean water in a large barrel under the water pump. Only certain clothes could be given to the washerman. He came from a nearby village every Saturday and used three to five donkeys to carry clothes to the nearby mountain stream for washing. However, the saris had to be hand-washed by us.

Sunday is the day of rest for all of us. But for me, even more fun as I eagerly waited for the clock to strike 4:30 p.m. when I could go to see my childhood mother, Kirubai. She raised me at the babies' nursery and would wait for my visit. She always had some snacks for me to eat and take home. She also shared her afternoon sweet tea with me, and this was a great treat, for we children do not get coffee or tea except on Amy's birthday, December 16, and Christmas Day.

After visiting her, I went to see Rajarathinie, who I called Achie'ka, who loved me dearly and kept me from getting sick. In later years, they both retired and stayed at the retirement home in one of the compounds in Dohnavur.

Dohnavur Fellowship had purchased a large piece of land in Muppandal and built homes for disabled children and adults. Muppandal in Tamil means "three pavilions." According to a legend, three kings lived in three pavilions in that region a long time ago. It is a beautiful place, with a panoramic view over a large tract of land, located in a hilly area, where wind from the Arabian Sea gusts through the mountain passes.

Many agave cactus plants grew on that land. They started a cottage industry and developed a process to extract sisal fiber. This was used to make placemats, coasters, hand dusting brushes, and various sizes of boxes, ropes, rugs, etc. In 1959, the fellowship started this cottage industry of extracting sisal fiber from the plants. Once again, Thilasa and I, being detainees, were the first ones to learn this messy, back-breaking, tedious, and not to mention very painful task as the cactus leaves had very sharp spines.

Getting this fiber out of a leaf requires working with your hands and toes. First, you bent down and used both hands to put the leaf on a wooden plank on the ground. Then you squat down and press it down with your large toe while holding a sharp flat chopper in both hands, putting it on the leaf! One must do this while carefully avoiding the sharp spikes on top of the cactus leaf. Once all are in position, you pull the leaf with both hands to scrape the fleshy green part from one side of the leaf. Then, you dip the fiber in a bucket of water and scrape it until it turns pure white. Then you turn the leaf and repeat the process with the other side.

It required a lot of body coordination and balance. Also, the right touch, as too much pressure on the knife blade will cut through the leaf fiber, too little pressure by the big toe stops all the fleshy parts from being removed.

Once the fleshy part was scraped away, the fiber still had to be pulled through several three-inch sharp spikes fixed on a wooden board to remove any flesh between the fibers!

Sellapu, who came from Muppandal, was our good teacher, and being young and supple, we quickly mastered the art. Soon, we were scraping one hundred leaves a day. We tried to finish our daily quota as soon as possible because squatting on one's haunches or heels for a long is not very comfortable! I never thought of it then, but now I wonder how I lived through it!

Muppanthal (Three Pavilions), built in 1925, "the place of fresh winds and wide views."
The cottages on a small hill, covered in thorn trees and bushes, was used to house the disabled women and girls. They produced useful items from the sisal fiber.

Top: women and girls collecting ground nuts (peanuts).
Bottom: Women and girls making items from sisal fiber.

Scraping sisal fiber.

Anburuha Carunia and Pakiavanie Carunia.

Home for disabled children.

Articles made of sisal fiber were sold to fund the home.

I lived through it and am sure God had a purpose in everything. He was preparing me for the life that was to come:

> God holds the key of all unknown, And I am glad;
> If other hands should hold the key, or if he trusted
>     it to me, I might be sad.
> The very dimness of my sight makes me secure;
> For groping in my misty way, I feel His hand; I
>     hear Him say, "My help is sure."
> I cannot read His future plans; But this I know:
> I have the smiling of His face and all the refuge of
>     His grace, While here below.
> Enough: this covers all my wants; and so, I rest!
> For what I cannot, He can see, And in His care, I
>     saved shall be, forever blest.
> (*Golden Bells*, published 1923, song 351)

Vivian Thomkin (Vivilia Sittie). When she retired, Tarahai Carunia took over her duties looking after the disabled children. Not pictured: Joan Stammers (Vasanthie Sittie), who took care of disabled children from 1942 to 1978.

Left to right: Visuvasie, Mathu (holding guitar), Preminithie (holding Jebaseela, who is unable to walk), Poovai, Nesamuthu, Tarahai Carunia (who was the headmistress of home school when Salma was in seventh grade), Senthamari, who passed away in August of 2024, to whom Tara told Salma's family history, learned from Evu, who brought Salma to Amy Carmichael at six days of age. Salma came to know of her family history in her twenties through Senthamari.

One day, while I was cleaning the birdbath, which stood on the top of Amy's grave in God's Garden, I saw John Risk, our fellowship leader, walking toward Amy's grave. There was a foreigner with him, and he showed him where Amy was buried.

Later, the visitor was shown around the compounds, and he stayed as a guest for two weeks to learn about Amy Carmichael's self-supporting way of managing the Dohnavur Fellowship. As I said in a few lines above, God holds the key to all unknowns. This incident was very interesting as I met this same man twenty years later in America! His name is Ted Hegre, principal of the Bethany Missionary College in Minneapolis, Minnesota, USA.

When working in the garden, the man I saw wanted to follow Amy Carmichael's model to establish the Missionary Training Center in Minneapolis, Minnesota, USA. He had read the books about the works of Amy Carmichael of Dohnavur Fellowship.

How could it be, other than part of God's plan, that twenty years after this incident, little Salma Carunia, one of the hundreds of Amy Carmichael's children, a detainee, would be accepted to *study* at Bethany College of Missions? To realize a dream to be trained as a missionary was *an unbelievable thing* that one could not see at that time. How did it happen that the detainee Salma of 1959, who was working in the garden and striving to spend the time waiting to go to boarding school to get a high school education, dreaming one day to go and study abroad? Yes! It happened! Yes, God was holding that key of all unknown doors for the bright future for me, which I could not see then, but I see that I have marked in my Bible October 21, 1978, next to Isaiah 64:4,

> For since the beginning of the world
> Men have not heard, nor perceived by the ear,
> neither hath the eye seen, O God,
> Beside thee, what he hath prepared for him that
> waiteth for Him.

I was eagerly waiting for April to end, as the names of girls going to hostels would be announced then. I very much wanted to attend school in order to become educated.

> Living, He loved me; dying, He saved me,
> Buried, He carried my sins far away.
> Rising, He justified freely forever.
> One day, He's coming—Oh glorious day!

(Scripture Union, London)

Salma standing beside Amy Carmichael's tombstone, which was built as a birdbath at Amy's request. AMMAI, which is inscribed on the side, means 'mother' in Tamil.

## CHRIST IS IN ME

# Nura Sittie Keeps Her Word

In the last week of May 1960, Shanthie came to the garden where I was working and told me to report to Nura Sittie at 10:30 a.m. My heart was leaping for joy. I was counting the days until this great moment! Good news at last! I thought God would get you through the Red Sea and get you over Jericho's wall where troubles will crumble at your feet. "Victory belongs to the Lord" (Proverbs 21:31).

When I reached Nura Sittie's house, I saw about twenty-five to thirty girls sitting on the floor, waiting quietly for Nura Sittie to read the school-wise names of the girls. Dohnavur girls were sent to ten different boarding schools in three separate districts. Finally, she called out the names of the girls going to the St. John's Girls' High School, Nazareth: Jeyaventhie and Jeevanthi, who were transferred from GBS Middle School, Palayamkottai, and they both started ninth grade, then Sahera, Urani, and me. Urani and I started eighth grade, and Sahera went into seventh grade.[3] Five new Timothys were added to the school in Nazareth, with two Timothys, Sarah and Arjeena, who were already in tenth and eleventh grade. I was very happy, for I knew the high school in Nazareth was one of the high standard schools. I went back to the garden to work till lunchtime. Here, I see my verdict is *not guilty*!

Hooray! I'm going to boarding school!

The next day, Shanthie took me to the sewing room, where they issued the school clothes. Colored clothes for the first time! Susi, who was issuing the school clothes, gave me some very old clothes. All the colors and prints have faded, passing from generation to generation as they outgrew them. At Dohnavur, the dresses were made of very sturdy cotton and used very carefully. Hence, they last long, even after color and patterns faded. Well, I only have a week to prepare and must stitch my name on all my clothes.

I continued working till the end of the week and prepared to go to the boarding school. I still remember that the last Saturday of my working year ended at lunchtime. I came home to wash my hair and the blue sari. I felt elated that my year of hardship and working days had come to an end after a whole year. I was hopping from one end of the drying room to the other, hanging my clothes on the clotheslines made of twisted coconut fiber. I was shouting, "Freedom, freedom, freedom!" I felt like a caged bird, and I very much wanted to go out and attend boarding school in order to become educated and be *free*!

Shanthie, my house mother, got me a nice green steel trunk for packing all my school clothes. Also, she provided me with a bottle of coconut oil, which we applied to our hair daily, and a bar and a half of coconut oil soap. One had to make it last the whole trimester from June to mid-September till our first vacation. Shanthie checked the school trunk to ensure everything was in it, including an aluminum plate for eating meals and a tumbler to drink water. We must leave the brass bowl, plate, and tumbler at home. We use our fingers to eat with, so there was no need for utensils.

I had to surrender the wooden locker I had been using till then and put all the home clothes and the other possessions, like the brass bowl, plate, and tumbler, in another steel trunk. The trunk with my name painted was put in a storeroom. It was given to us when we came home for the holidays (vacations); as at home, we wear blue saris. Our school clothes remained in the school trunk at the boarding school until the school closes for the summer.

When told I was going to and attend boarding school in Nazareth, I ran to my beloved elders Kirubai and Achie'ka to tell them the good news. They had been anxiously awaiting information about me going to the boarding school. Their hearts leaped with joy, and Achie'ka gave me a set of colored pencils and a pair of scissors. These were things I never had before and a padlock to lock my desk, where I will keep the fountain pen Shanthie issued me. Also, the Christmas gift I got that year was a nice pencil box, and now I am all set to go to boarding school!

Sunday evening is the visiting time. I ran to the babies' nursery compound to say goodbye to my beloved Kirubai, for on Monday morning, June 1, I am off to the boarding school. Then I went to the retirement home where Achie'ka was, and she prayed with me and sent me with good wishes for my studies. These two people are very significant in my life as they constantly checked on and loved me dearly. They shed tears with me and shared my joy with me. It was a little hard for me to leave them behind, but it was the price I had to pay if I wanted to go forward in my life, and I know it would make them happy to see me achieve greater things in life. I had already tasted life without education when I was detained from school for a year, working in the garden. Now I must forget those things which are behind and press toward the goal and run the race that is set before me.

June 1, 1960, was the greatest day of my life. Early in the morning, helpers came with hand carts and loaded the steel trunks of about eighty students, including ten of Shanthie's children, who were going to a boarding school on that day. Two helpers pulled each cart while other helpers walked alongside, holding up the trunks to prevent them from falling. It took half an hour to walk to the bus stand. The workers climbed the ladder at the back of the bus with our trunks while balancing them on their heads! They secured them on the roof's luggage rack. Our bus was going to Tirunelveli. At 7:00 a.m., my beloved house mother Shanthie kissed me goodbye. She told me to study hard to pass exams and get promoted to the next level. Shanthie had confidence in me, just like Lola did, that I, Salma, could do great things one day, but I needed to be educated!

Dohnavur is a small village with no railway station and only one bus stand. A few buses pass through Dohnavur, going to nearby villages. Therefore, mostly everyone has to travel twenty-seven miles by bus to the Tirunelveli Junction. That is where one can catch a train or another bus to destinations in the lands beyond.

Devarul, also in the eighth grade at Palayamkottai, traveled with me up to Tirunelveli. I went inside the bus and found a vacant seat near the window so the four of us to sit together. There were bars across the windows. I saw Tarahai and Vimba Sittie standing along with other fellowship members. Suddenly I feared they might try and stop me from going to boarding school! But then I realized that now, Nura Sittie was the leader. This thought calmed me. No one dared to cross her will, for she is the one who, along with Shanthie, is now sending me to boarding school! They both gave me the opportunity to be educated, and I thank God for them. Unfortunately, Thilasa was detained for another year.

My verdict, not guilty!

*May I run the race before me, strong and brave to face the foe,*
*Looking only unto Jesus as I onward go.*

—*Golden Bells*

Shanthie's family.

Kanmani and Aruldasan. See their story in notes & endnotes (p425).

Their children, Shanthie and David Aruldasan.

Teenage Shanthie with her mother, Kanmani.

David and his daughters, Punthura and Mehara.

Mani and Rajaseelie with Shanthie.

Salma and Anihala, Shanthie's children.

Shanthie's helpers and dear friends.

Salma came to say goodbye to Champu'ka, who took care of her in childhood, and Shanthie, her house mother.
Left: Rajaseelie, who was Salma's eighth grade student. She took care of Shanthie in her old age.
Right of Salma: Anihala Carunia, who became vice president of Dohnavur Fellowship.
Right of Anihala: Amaravathy, who was a right hand to Shanthie for many years.
Right of Amaravathy: Grace'ka, who was the head cook in the Round for over forty years. Rajaseelie (far left) was her helper in the kitchen since 1975 and still happily works there today at sixty-five years of age.

# CHAPTER 10

## My First Day Out of My Dohnavur Home!

I had never been in any vehicle before. I am now fifteen years old, and it is the first time I have stepped inside the very large bus that will take me to Tirunelveli, where I will see a train for the first time. Suddenly, the driver started the engine, and there was a strong smell of exhaust gases. I wondered what was happening, for I had never smelled petrol/diesel before. As the bus started moving, I felt homesick for my dearest Kirubai and Achie'ka. I would not see them for the next three months and began to cry. As the bus turned the corner, I saw my dear Shanthie waving goodbye to me.

Passing the trees as the bus moved by at first made me giddy. But the road was not paved and the ride was very bumpy. I then became sick, and I started to throw up. My feet had taken me everywhere for the past fifteen years, but this motion sickness was terrible! I was queasy all the way and wondered if I would survive to live in a different kind of world.

The bus took two hours to reach Tirunelveli, with ten to fifteen stops at some villages. At Tirunelveli, Balanie, our escort, hired two coolies to bring down our steel trunks from the top of the bus and carry them to the railway station, two trunks each, on their heads. We walked barefoot to the railway station, about half a mile, bringing the remaining three trunks, with two girls holding one chest between them. The coolies took us to the train going to Nazareth and placed our chests under the seats. Our chaperone paid the porters, but they haggled for more and created a scene. However, Balanie was firm and paid only the agreed amount. She had been given exact money for the expenses by the fellowship office and had no extra money to give them.

Once we were seated, Balanie gave us strict instructions not to speak to anyone, then she went to the ticket counter and purchased tickets for us. The train gave a long whistle and started moving. A ticket collector came and checked our tickets. The train stopped in many towns along the way, with people getting in and getting down, sometimes to get food or drink water from the taps on the station. However, we Dohnavur girls were not allowed to eat or drink food from outside, and in those days, we did not have water bottles, so we waited till we reached our destination. Those who traveled overnight were given food packets wrapped in plantain leaves, tamarind rice or lemon rice with boiled eggs.

## St. John's Girl's High School, Nazareth

After four hours, we arrived in the town called Nazareth. We quickly pulled all our trunks out of the train, for the train stops only for a few minutes at each station. Our chaperon Balanie hired a bullock cart to carry our luggage to St. John's Girls High School, about two miles from the railway station. The cart driver loaded five trunks onto the cart. Then we walked barefoot under the hot afternoon sun behind the cart. We carried the remaining trunks, taking turns, and tried to rest as many times as possible. Finally, we saw a gate with a signboard that said "St. John's Girls' High School, Nazareth." Inside was a large and tall two-storied stone school building. I was happy, for—in this beautiful school building—I would get a long-awaited education. My future starts right here!

The bullock cart went straight through to the school compound. It was near a large banyan tree next to the entrance of the boarding houses. One was for high school girls, and two were for those who take teachers' training. We left our trunks under the tree, awaiting the dean's permission to take them inside the boarding house.

In the meantime, the chaperone took us to the principal's office. She reported five new students and the two others who returned. The principal, Ms. Manuel, looked at each of us and suddenly, pointing her finger at me, said, "This girl looks very thin and feeble, and it doesn't look good to leave her in the boarding school." I began to think, *Oh, no, no!*

The principal hesitated to take a small, frail-looking girl due to an unexpected student death. During the previous year, a Dohnavur girl named Dayalauthavie had died suddenly after a short illness while staying in the school's hostel. This shocked the whole school. I was afraid and thought she would send me home with Balanie. Indeed, I did not look my age. I was fifteen and a half years old but looked like an eight-year-old!

I was shaken and started to pray hard. *Lord, not now, not after all the troubles I endured last year to come to the boarding school. Please do not let the principal send me back home!* Fortunately, the principal seemed to realize that it was late afternoon. We girls had been without food and water since leaving home, so she dismissed us to go to the hostel to eat lunch. I left as fast as I could. Balanie went to the school office and paid the fees for the first trimester. She bid us goodbye when her work was done and returned to Dohnavur.

In school, we got a new identity. At home, we were called Timothys, and we were known as Dons in school.

The boarding house was a huge stone building divided into three parts. The first section was a verandah enclosed with a wooden trellis. It had a small entrance door, which was never locked. Next was a huge middle hall with no furniture. It was our living room cum bedroom, and the third part of the hostel was the box room where we kept our steel boxes and clothes. It was also the changing room. We went behind the hostel to wash up. It had small compartments with concrete water cisterns.

One could only bathe every other day as there was not enough water for all students to take a bath every day. This was uncomfortable for the Dohnavur girls, as we bathed twice a day at home. The lavatory was far from the hostel and wasn't easy to use at night, as we did not have flashlights. The moonlight was a great help as it shone upon the path. Living outside our home at Dohnavur Fellowship was a different lifestyle, but we quickly learned to adjust.

Another change was that when we were at home, we were never given any money. However, when we came to the hostel, we were allowed a small amount of fifty pennies as pocket money every month, which came to one rupee and fifty pennies for the whole trimester. The dean gave the pocket money to us every Saturday, but I saved mine till the end of the semester. Then I would ask my day scholar friend Kasthuribai to get me something from the sweet shop outside the school compound to take home for the girls in the Dohnavur Fellowship.

Inbam Koilpillai, our dean, lived with us. She had a small room near the hostel entrance and slept outside her room on a cane bed. She was also the physical education teacher in the high school. She knew all her boarders very well, for she dealt with us in the boarding and PE at school.

There were ninety girls in the boarding house. We spread our straw mats on the floor and slept in a row on both sides of the hall. About twenty slept on the veranda. Ropes hung from the ceiling where we suspended our rolled-up sleeping grass mats in the air during the daytime. Those who had pillows kept them on the top of their steel box. We Dohnavur girls had no pillows, for we slept on the grass mat. We had a sheet to cover us, and sometimes, we used that as a pillow. The floor at the boarding hostel is not as soft as our home in Dohnavur.

The box room was opened at 6:00 a.m., the breakfast bell was rung at 7:00 a.m., and everyone had to be in the hostel veranda, which served as the dining room. We sat on the floor in rows of forty-five on one side and forty-five on the opposite, facing each other. The food is served from the middle by two students who serve rice from a large tub and then vegetable curry on top of the rice. No milk, fruits, or eggs were served in the boarding school, so I missed home food. Once everybody was served, the dean ordered us to give thanks. We stood next to our plates, and I always led the thanksgiving songs, and all joined in, then we sat down to eat. At 7:30, the dean ordered washup. Everyone went outside to clean their plates and place them on a stand at the end of the dining hall.

The school compound was very barren. There were two large banyan trees and some other trees on the playground. The path from the boarding house to the school, a five-minute walk, was very plain. I missed my home very much, where there were flowers everywhere. After the school assembly, we were asked to sit under a tree outside the building on the first day of school. There, a teacher called out the students' names according to the sections. There were 150 girls in eighth grade, divided into three sections, with fifty girls in each.

I was in eighth grade section A, and Urani was in section B. The school started at 9:00 a.m., but we boarders went to school at 8:00 a.m. to do homework. We had to take all necessary things, such as an ink bottle, pen, and books, out of the box room before breakfast, for it was locked from 7:30 a.m. to noon. Once at school, we cannot return to the hostel until lunch. Every evening at the end of the class, I put all my books and school things inside my desk and locked it with the padlock my beloved Achie'ka gave me. She also gave me a pair of scissors, which came in handy for the sewing class.

The medium of teaching was the state language, which was Tamil. My teacher, Mrs. Peter, was a widow and always wore a white sari, as was a custom for widows in India.

Our classroom had two windows at the back, facing the chapel. Some trees were near the chapel, and we got a nice breeze through the windows. Mrs. Peter was old and wise and taught all subjects except social studies. She always tried to teach us good morals.

Thanks to Mellial Sittie, who trained my voice in Jeevalia, I sang soprano well and was selected for the school choir. I got good marks in English, social studies, and Tamil and was not good at Hindi. Although it is the national language, it is never used in South India. However, studying Hindi under the three languages formula for education was mandatory. I continued to struggle in mathematics and will always remain grateful to my dear eighth-grade teacher for how she handled the quarterly examination. I did not do well in math; when the result came out, I got 20/100. I knew it was because of the good grace of my teacher Mrs. Peter, who added some points to my score. Knowing that she helped me also encouraged me to work harder. We were both anxious for me to pass the math exam next time!

In English class, we were taught prose and poetry. We learned the poem "The Miller of Dee." My teacher had made a tune for us to sing to make it easier for us to memorize it. Later in my life, I was at Aberdeen University in Scotland, UK, in 1985. That was where my husband was studying for his master's degree. We walked to see the River Dee flowing into the North Sea delta in the evenings. I remembered the tune for the poem and sang it for him as we stood on the bank of the River Dee.

Urani Carunia, who went to boarding school with Salma at St. John's Girls' High School in Nazareth.

Urani Borloz, feeding swans in Geneva Lake in Switzerland.

Urani Borloz at her home in Lyon, France. Her husband, Jean-Claude, passed away on March 10, 2024.

### The Miller of Dee

There dwelt a miller, hale and bold,
Beside the river Dee;
He worked and sang from morn till night
No lark more blithe than he;
And this the burden of his song

## CHRIST IS IN ME

Forever used to be:
"I envy nobody, no, not I
And nobody envies me!"

"Thou'rt wrong, my friend," said good King Hal,
"As wrong as wrong can be;
For could my heart be light as thine,
I'd gladly change with thee.
And tell me now, what makes thee sing,
With voice so loud and free,
While I am sad, though I am King,
Beside the river Dee?"

The miller smiled and doffed his cap,
"I earn my bread," quoth he;
"I love my wife, I love my friend,
I love my children three;
I owe no penny I cannot pay,
I thank the river Dee,
That turns the mill that grinds the corn
That feeds my babes and me."

"Good friend," said Hall, and sighed the while,
"Farewell, and happy be;
But say no more, if thou'dst be true,
That no one envies thee;
Thy mealy cap is worth my crown,
Thy mill my kingdom's fee;
Such men as thou are England's boast,
O miller of the Dee!

(Charles Mackay, 1814–1889)

On the other side of the sea, one can see the River Don. I saw many pink salmon jumping at the river delta as we enjoyed the North Sea breeze.

In September of 1960, the students had a two-week holiday, and we would go home. The Dohnavur girls kept an eye on the road from the second floor of the school building for a woman in a blue DF sari for Dohnavur children cannot step outside of the school gate without an escort. When she arrived, we picked up our bags we have packed and bid goodbye to Dean Inbam Koilpillai. The chaperone then went to the school office to close the accounts for the semester and collect our progress reports. We walked barefoot to the railway station to catch the two o'clock train to Tirunelveli Junction.

By 6:00 p.m., our train reaches Tirunelveli, and we walk to the bus stand, but this time, we do not have our steel trunks with us, so it is an easy walk with our school bags. At 6:30 p.m., the Dohnavur bus arrived at the bus stand, and I was very excited to go home for the first time from the boarding school. Girls from the other boarding schools also came to the bus stand from their schools. We all went home on the last bus, which one could not afford to miss, for there was no transportation from Tirunelveli till the next morning. The bus journey was very rough, but I did not notice it this time, and when we saw the Blue Mountains, we knew we were getting close to home. I knew that Shanthie was waiting to see how I had done in my first term, and above all, my beloved Kirubai and Achie'ka were waiting for me to come and see them the very next day. We reached home at 9:30 p.m.

Immediately, we sat down to eat dinner, waiting for us in our brass bowls, and drank milk in our brass tumblers. It was still rice and vegetable curry, but the home food tasted good! Oh, how I missed it. I was so happy to taste the milk again. Tired from the long journey, we went to bed. The next day, everyone noticed that I had put on some weight and looked like a happy teenager.

Girl Guides at St. John's Girls' High School in their uniforms.
Left to right: Kanthimathy, Selvamanie, Sundravallie, Salma Carunia, Sahera Carunia, Shenbahavallie Carunia, Anushia, Chandra, Hannah, Mary, Sounthara Carunia, Jemima.

Left photo, on right: Kasthuribai, who was Salma's high school friend from eighth to twelfth grade.

Right photo, on left: Kasthuribai, who gave me the graduation gift of a tailor-made orange blouse.

I talked to Kasthuribai on the phone on October 25, 2024. She told me her two daughters are working in America, California, and Washington, DC.

# CHAPTER 11

# Life as a Timothy at Boarding School

But vacation did not mean no work! There were many green meadows in the compounds around the fellowship. The Timothys had to go to work at 8:00 a.m. We would crouch with a sickle to cut the grass around the compounds till 10:00 a.m. Then at 10:30 a.m., we went swimming in the irrigation well and enjoyed swimming till noon. Then we had lunch, and I was glad to see the boiled eggs. We sat in a circle on the floor and ate with our fingers. In the afternoon, we can rest at home and catch up on sleep till 3:00 p.m., and those who want to go swimming again can do so. There was always the work of scrubbing the floors, sweeping the roads around the houses, and watering the plants. At 5:30 p.m., we Timothys went to the playground to play different sports. We also got to eat lots of plantains, papayas, tapioca, and boiled red sweet potatoes. Shanthie, my house mother, had a large custard apple tree, and I enjoyed eating the fruits from it before the squirrels could get to them.

Too soon, the vacation ended. I said goodbye to the two important people in my life, Kirubai and Achie'ka. They encouraged me to study hard and prayed with me as I took their blessings along with God's. On September 15, we packed our school bags with a bottle of coconut oil and sunlight soap, some homemade eatables, and a packet of peanut brittle to eat on the way.

We went to catch the 7:00 a.m. bus to Tirunelveli Junction. I made three bunches of orange crossandra flowers from Shanthie's garden to take to school. I told her I have three good friends: Kasturibai, Mangalavulli, and Jeyalashmi. The next morning at the school assembly, everyone noticed the distinctive orange flowers on the heads of us four friends. They knew that it came from Dohnavur, which was my home.

Monsoon rains relieved the heat, and the land became cool at 85 degrees. November 23 was my sixteenth birthday. Darmakani, my desk mate, brought me a small cupcake as a birthday gift. Oh, I had never seen such a cake in my life. In my excitement, I ate it all—including the paper wrapper, haha!

Now that I am writing this story in America, I have seen many cakes and varieties of baked goods. They never taste as good as the first cupcake I had on my sixteenth birthday in boarding school.

December came rolling along, and soon it would be Christmas. The school had a Christmas carol service and Christmas drama called "King's Messenger." All the Dohnavur girls were in the choir as Mellial Sittie trained our voices. However, Amy's rules strictly forbade us from participating in school dramas or any acting or dancing, so we lost our chance to develop in those areas. We had the half-yearly exam from December 15 to 20, and I spent time studying for the exam amid choir practices.

On December 21, we went home for two weeks' holiday to celebrate Christmas at home. I loved Dohnavur Christmas. I have already told you how we have a beautifully decorated pine tree in the center of the church. We gathered around the tree on Christmas Eve and Christmas Day and sang carols in English and Tamil. We sang about the stars and angels, a scene of the manger with the newborn baby Jesus, who became my Savior, and the story of the wise men who came to worship Him with gifts.

Like silver lamps in a distant shrine, the stars are sparkling bright!
The bells of the city of God ring out, for the Son of Mary was born tonight
The gloom is past, and the morn at last is coming with orient light.
Never fell melodies half so sweet as those which are filling the skies;
And never a palace shone half so fair as the manger bed where our Savior lies
No night in the year is half so dear as this which has ended our sighs.

Once a star rose in the sky, Silver star of <u>mystery,</u>
But the wisemen pondering knew what it said that they must do.
So, in that first Christmas-tide on their camels they did ride,
Rode to far Jerusalem, Rode to farther Bethlehem.
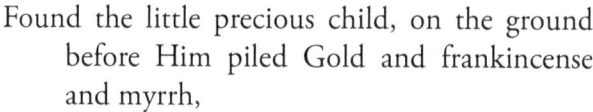
Found the little precious child, on the ground before Him piled Gold and frankincense and myrrh,
Hailed Him Royal Conqueror.

(W. Chatteron Dix)

When the morning stars sang together, and all the sons of God shouted for Joy (Job 38:7)
He was there who was laid in a rough manger stall, that Royal Baby Boy.
The King, the King of Eternity, laid by His glory for me.
Who hung the round world upon nothing, 'tis He, A babe on His mother's lap;

> Who made of the clouds swaddling bands for the sea,
> Her gentle hands did Him wrap.
> The King, the King of Eternity, laid by His glory for me.
>
> Whence is that goodly fragrance flowing stealing our senses all away?
> Never the like did come a-blowing shepherds from flowery fields in May
> Whence is that goodly fragrance flowing stealing our senses all away?
> What is that light so brilliant breaking here in the night across our eyes?
> Never so bright the day - star waking started to climb the morning skies!
> What is that light so brilliant breaking here in the night across our eyes?
> Bethlehem! there is in manger lying find your Redeemer, haste away,
> Worship the Savior born today as you find your Redeemer, haste away.
>
> (Amy Carmichael)

The Timothies worked hard to ensure all was neat and clean everywhere and swept all the roads around the fellowship. This important year of my life, in 1960, ended with going around the compounds, singing New Year songs, and eating good food at home.

On January 2, we went back to school for the last semester. I was glad to meet my three friends and gave them the orange crossandra bunches I had brought from home. They gladly pinned them onto their hair for the school assembly. I was glad to meet my teacher and knew this would be my last three months in her class. I studied hard that term. The annual exam was from March 20 to 25, which was always given on the last five days of school. I pretty much did well in all the subjects except mathematics. I was happy to finish the eighth grade and said goodbye to my teacher and three dear friends, and I hoped to see all of them in ninth grade in June 1961.

The school closed for a two-month-long summer vacation, and we were all in a hurry to reach home, but as usual, our chaperone had to settle all our dues with the school office and take receipts for it. As it was the end of the school year, we packed our steel trunks. We stuffed in all our notebooks, textbooks, and clothes, careful not to break the hinge of the chest. That would be a catastrophe, for we had nothing else to pack our things into.

We bid goodbye to the dean and walked to the train station with our steel trunks. It was a happy day as I successfully finished my first year in boarding school. My character report from the school was excellent, and I was eligible for baptism, which I was longing for!

We reached home at 9:30 p.m., ate dinner, and slept. As usual, the next morning, all Timothys went to work at 8:00 a.m. cleaning the compounds, cutting the grass, and tilling and hoeing in the garden. At about 10:00 a.m., the school office secretary, Meleela Sittie, called the boarding-school girls one by one to settle the accounts of the money spent on their education and pocket money. Everything was accounted for. The clothing items were issued at the beginning of the year, and the books were brought back—everything. There would be extra work and punishments for the lost items!

We enjoyed swimming, evening sports during the summer vacation, and the manual work we did every morning. There were scripture classes to attend every afternoon. Christina, the headmistress of Jeevalia school, announced the girls' names to be prepared for baptism, and I was one of them. Every day, I went to the class and memorized the verses that Christina gave us as homework.

The exam results from boarding schools started to be received in the third week of April; Nura Sittie announced them. On April 20, about 9:30 a.m., while we were working in the vegetable garden, someone called the students who went to Nazareth to Nura Sittie's house. It was a very important moment for me to hear what she had to say, as my fate was still in her hands. She said, "All of you have been promoted to the next grade." I was ever so glad and hoping to continue my education, but my life almost took an unexpected turn.

## God Holds the Key to All Unknown

The Dohnavur Fellowship School Council had four members. They were Nura Sittie (Margaret Wilkinson), the leader; Shanthie, the coleader; Christina, headmistress of Jeevalia home school; and Nesarathina, who was in charge of Timothys. They met in May 1961 to review the progress reports of about eighty to one hundred boarding-school students.

Before the meeting, Nesarathina had listed twenty students who should not continue their education. These were those who had performed poorly in school and would be too old when they finished high school. Later, I learned that my name was at the top of that list. It turned out that my school had not sent my marks for the annual exam. Instead, they just sent a card saying "Promoted to the next grade"!

The proposal to stop all twenty from returning to boarding school was accepted. As the meeting ended with a prayer, Shanthie, my house mother, was quietly crying. When the prayer ended, Nura Sittie asked Shanthie what was the cause of her sadness. Shanthie replied that she wanted me to return to boarding school to continue my education. Immediately, Nura Sittie told Nesarathina to cross Salma's name from her list. At that moment, I was allowed to return to school at Nazareth to continue my education. Here I claim Jeremiah 29:11, where God says, "I know the plans For I have for you...To give you hope and a future." I see that God holds the key of all unknown. I am glad and praise Him for it. Philippians 1:6 says, "For I am confident of this very thing, that he who began a good work in you will perfect it until the day of Christ Jesus."

This incident about the list of twenty was perhaps why Shanthie reminded me every year to study hard and ensure that I get promoted to the next grade. However, she never told me about the incident, as she didn't talk much. Nesarathina let it out one day when she was very angry with me! It happened in the early morning; we were at

God's Garden where she conducted morning devotion. She was my house mother that summer, as Shanthie had gone to summer school at the Bible college in Bangarapet. Knowing that Shanthie was crying for me kept me in school to be educated made me love my dear Shanthie even more.

During the last week of May, baptismal candidates have to give testimony about their Christian life before the leaders of the fellowship and all the missionaries. I was looking forward to this day, for I had a very meaningful testimony, and I did not shy away, like others, from telling what God had done in my life thus far!

When that time came, I saw everyone's eye was on me. They listened as my testimony was filled with supporting scripture, especially for the day of June 1959 when I found that I was detained from going to boarding school. That time when I felt that I was *left behind*! I told them the mystery was revealed to me on November 29, 1959. I was on my knees praying before bedtime, "Christ is in me, the hope of glory" (Colossians 2:27). This was the testimony I dared to profess in front of the congregation as they were gathered in the large classroom at Jeevalia. (Even in later years, some of the girls tell me they marveled at my *faith*. Sometimes, I wonder where I got that *strong faith* from that I boldly professed!)

On May 29, 1961, at eleven o'clock, I was baptized with the other girls. The pastor called my name for the ceremonial immersion in water and dunked me under the water. I stayed under for a while, praying that I was now dead to sin and would rise to the newness of life.

> 'Therefore, we have been buried with Him through baptism into death. We shall also be in the likeness of His resurrection and in order that as Christ was raised from the dead through the glory of the Father, so we too might walk in the newness of life" (Romans 6:3–4).

The pastor put a mark of the cross on my forehead with his thumb to show that I now belong to Christ and should consider myself a soldier for Christ. This mark of the cross that I had on my forehead on that day will never be exchanged for any other mark!

I remembered the story of Christian in *The Pilgrim's Progress*. He met the three angels at the foot of the cross, and they assured him that he had now gone through regeneration. Now the cross was a weapon to fight against evil as he proceeded toward the gates of heaven. To me, the cross is the seal of the righteousness of faith, and Ephesians 1:13 says that we are sealed with Holy Spirit. I now firmly believe that I can fight my battles with my faith in God by taking the full armor of God. Ephesians 6:13–17 says, "I must stand firm on God's ground and fight the evil days ahead of me by being raised with Christ"; Colossians 3:1 says, "Seek those things which are above where Christ is."

The whole Dohnavur family, about eight hundred, stood around the large cement cistern next to the House of Prayer during the baptism ceremonies. I was given a white Sari to wear after the baptism. Baptism symbolizes rebirth and is an outward sign of inward repentance.

The Bible requires that one must present themselves pure and blameless when washed with the blood of Christ. I stood before the congregation wearing the white sari as they witnessed my baptism, and singing, "Be faithful until death, and I will give you the crown of life" (Revelation 2:10).

Jesus paid it all. All to Him I owe.
Sin had left the crimson stain,
He washed me white as snow!

நீயோ எல்லாவற்றிலும் உன்னை நற்கிரியை களுக்கு மாதிரியாகக் காண்பி.

This is what I received on the day of my baptism, May 29, 1961. The text is Titus 2:7. I still keep it in my Bible sixty-two years later.

On June 1, 1961, I returned to St. John's Girls' High School in Nazareth. My baptism seemed to have made me more responsible about spiritual matters. I decided to stand firm like Daniel in the song: "Dare to be a Daniel, dare to stand alone, dare to be a purpose firm, and dare to make it known, as we are fighting against the powers of darkness!"

I entered ninth grade with Urani and Devarul, who finished eighth grade in Palayamkottai and joined us, so now we three were in the same school. Arul and I were in B Section, and Urani was in the C section. My class teacher, Panathie, who taught math and English, was very good, and I enjoyed learning from her. I started understanding math as she explained it well, but I still did not pass some tests. I was good in English, for British missionaries taught us English in Jeevalia. However, since they spoke English with a British accent, we sometimes had trouble understanding the English pronunciation of Indian teachers.

Christy Manuel was my social studies teacher in eighth and ninth grade. I did very well in that subject because she had a gentle and sweet voice and was also a very pretty woman, and I liked her method of teaching a lot.

We went home for the short Christmas holidays in the last week of December. After this, all the boarding-school girls and boys returned to school in January 1962 for their final semester. (The Dohnavur boys would be sent to the boys' schools and the girls to the girls' schools. This was per Dohnavur's policy of separating boys and girls even outside the fellowship.)

It was February 28, 1962. I was in the middle of an English literature class, and the teacher explained the story of Jason and the Argonauts. Suddenly, a school clerk came to my classroom and informed the teacher that all the Dohnavur girls were called to the principal's office. That was extremely unusual.

In the principal's office, I saw two fellowship members standing in the fellowship's distinctive blue uniform. One of them told us that this morning, our dear leader, Devanesan Annachie (John Risk), had passed away from a sudden heart attack. It was a great shock to all of us.

This news hit us children very hard, for we all knew him as our family's father. We Dohnavur girls were crying for the whole day. I especially remembered how I rode with him on his bicycle in my childhood on my birthdays. We missed him even more when we went home for the summer holiday at the end of March, as he was our pastor and the leader of the fellowship.

The final examination was over, and the results expected after three weeks, I packed my steel trunk. I headed home for the summer vacation with the other seven Dohnavur girls and the chaperone. After reaching home at 9:30 p.m., I had rice and curry for dinner, which tasted better than the boarding-school food. We had all the fruits to eat and enjoy while at home. Tired from the long journey, we slept on the floor on the straw mat, filled with a sense of harmony, oneness with nature, and the deep power of joy of being home from school. After three weeks, the school results came, and I was promoted to tenth grade, which made me very happy. I began to see a ray of hope, as in the poem of William Wordsworth, "Our cheerful faith, that all which we behold, is full of blessings."

Our summer vacation was a blessing for the fellowship staff, as the students from boarding school helped clean the compounds. Some of the students were sent to the children's nurseries to help. This allowed many fellowship staff to vacation and rest at Naraikadu. This was fellowship land with three houses at about three thousand feet in the Western Ghats mountains. Others went to Joppa, the fellowship's cottage at Cape Comorin, near the Bay of Bengal. Joppa was located at the southernmost tip of India, where the Arabian Sea, the Bay of Bengal, and the Indian Ocean meet.

Joppa (holiday house), built in 1925.
The house where Dohnavur family went for holidays by the sea.

Rajamacottie, who was sent to Joppa to oversee the holiday house after the youth hostel was closed in Bangalore.

Rajamacottie, the gentle house mother of Salma and Dr. Ponnalari, was in charge of Joppa (holiday house) at the southern tip of India for ten years. The holiday party enjoyed her joyful, tranquil company. In the pictures above, Salma and her husband, Dr. Ben M. Carter, along with Dr. Ponnalari are visiting her at the Joppa holiday house, as well as with other Dohnavur girls who were on holiday.

Upper left: Rajamacottie in her old age with the coffee cup Salma sent from America.
Upper right: Dr. Ponnalari and Salma visiting their house mother Rajamacottie.
Bottom: Rajamacottie (center seated in green) with the first couple from the 1960s, Enoch and Caruniapu with two of their children, Nancy and Rachel, from Bangalore with others from the youth hostel, in 1991. Sitting at the bottom, almost hidden, is Mularipu, who helped take care of Salma when she was six years old. Kovalipu (lower right, smiling), who worked with Salma in the hospital kitchen in 1965.

We were vaccinated during the summer holidays, before the start of the new school year in June. Shanthie, as usual, reminded me to study hard and pass tenth grade. I was excited to go back to school.

On the first day of school, the whole class was given new books for all the subjects. I noticed that the science and social study textbooks were pretty thick. But I know I am now in tenth grade and must learn more. It was the first time I studied about parliament. The teacher gave us the assignment to make a drawing/illustration from the textbook, and I got an A grade for it. This was my first hearing about the Lok Sabha (House of People) and Rajya Sabha (Council of States). However, I did not understand, for the teacher did not explain what occurred in those chambers.

Years later, in the summer of 1981, I was invited by an eighty-five-year-old lady named Zetta to come and stay with her in Virginia. At that time, her friend across the street, Ms. Elois Bible, went to Washington, DC, every day with her son, who was working there. One day, I got to go to Washington, DC, with her and saw Capitol Hill and the Chambers of the Congress and the Senate for the first time. I then understood what I had studied in tenth grade in 1963 and wished I could have seen the real parliament in my high school days to understand the lessons better.

In history, we studied the Indian history of the Mauryan Empire, the largest ever in the Indian subcontinent. Emperor Ashoka, 268–232 BC, was the third ruler of the Maurya Dynasty. The stone edicts put up by Ashoka reveal that the emperor was deeply moved by the massacre in the Kalinga War, in which more than 100,000 people died. He did not fight any more battles. The state emblem of India, the four lions back to back, and the wheel with twenty-four spokes on the Indian flag have both come from the Ashoka pillars.

The principal of the school taught English literature. Often, she was busy and came late to the class, so I used to go to her and ask about the day's lesson. She would tell me that there was an exercise book inside the teacher's drawer and ask me to write an essay from it on the blackboard, which I would do by climbing on the chair. Then

I sat down and copied it quickly. The principal came and explained the English essay, which we memorized, for we did not know much English as the medium of our instruction was in Tamil. This went on for a whole year, I enjoyed writing essays on the board, and it came in handy when I became a teacher.

Celebrating Christmas and New Year at home after the half-yearly exam was enjoyable. I was very happy that the last semester of tenth grade was approaching fast. I was encouraged by the song that we all sang at the New Year's evening singsong service

> He will never fail us; He will not forsake;
> His eternal covenant He will never break
> Resting on his promise, what have we to fear?
> God is all-sufficient for the coming year!
> Onward then and fear not, Children of the day!
> For His word shall never, never pass away!
>
> (*Golden Bells: For Church, Sunday School and Evangelistic Services*, published 1923, song 691)

On January 2, I went back to boarding school. I took some bright-orange crossandra flowers for my four good friends. A student named Wisy joined my class, and we became good friends. She came from a wealthy family.

The semester went on well, but I was still struggling with mathematics. My math teacher was Suganthie, the daughter of the Bishop Jebaraj in the Tirunelveli Diocese. She was a soft-spoken lady. I liked her and was not afraid to ask questions when she came near my desk to help me as she saw me struggling with the sums. Even then, I never passed the monthly tests of math. I was good in English, Tamil, and social studies but had trouble understanding science because the teacher read from the textbook without any further explanation.

## The Lord Is Near to Those Who Are Discouraged
## Psalm 34:18

As the year was coming to an end, it was time for tenth-grade students to give a farewell performance to the seniors in the eleventh grade. I was asked to recite an English poem which required some movements that required me to wear chappals (footwear). I told the teacher I did not have footwear, so she told me to go to the school shoe room and borrow someone's chappals. It was a custom in India that footwear must be left in a shoe room at the school entrance. Footwear was not allowed inside the school classrooms.

After the farewell, I returned the chappals from where I had taken them. However, the next day, one of the students, whose name was Ratha, came to me and said she saw me using her chappals for the drama the previous night, and now they were missing!

I told her that I had put them back in the shoe room. But she would not let me go and said I needed to pay her five rupees immediately. I told her that I had no money and had never seen even five rupees. My pocket money was only fifty pennies monthly. I lived a very simple life and had no shoes, no umbrella to protect me from rain, and no toothbrush, for I used my index finger to brush my teeth. And for this, I used the burnt-rice husk that I brought in a tin box to the boarding school from the orphanage. I had no money for toothpaste either!

But she got her teacher involved. Ratha's teacher kept coming to my classroom daily to ask about the money, even though they all knew I was an orphan and had no money. This depressed me, and I did not know what to do. All my classmates came to know about it. After a week had passed, I went to the school office to ask if they could let me have five rupees, but they told me that they were only allowed to spend the money on books and fees and not on anything else. So it will not be possible to give me five rupees out of Dohnavur Fellowship money.

For the first time, I thought it was better to die than return home and face intimidation daily! One evening, I sat on the top of the deep well in the school compound. I kept looking at the bottom. The water was black and didn't reveal the depth of the well. Even if I jumped in, I thought I would not drown, for I am a good swimmer. I was very hurt and sad. Then I remembered the story I learned in ninth grade about Dick Whittington, "Turn again, Whittington, thrice Lord Mayor of London," and I walked away from the well. As I was walking away, I began to recall words from several songs we used to sing: "Never say die and never give in, when life is difficult don't make it grim, look up and laugh and be determined to win." Then also I remembered the song that we sang at home on the New Year's Eve.

> For the year before us, oh what rich supplies! For the poor and needy Living streams shall rise; For the sad and sinful shall His grace abound;
> For the faint and feeble, perfect strength be found. Onward then and fear not, Children of the day! For His word shall never, never pass away.
>
> *Golden Bells*

So I knew that brooding on the top of the well was not the solution to my problem, and I realized that only God could deliver me from this grave situation. I must trust that same God who revealed himself to me on November 29, 1959, and I knew He is Lord and my Redeemer.

Unfortunately, my classroom was next to Ratha's, and she and her teacher kept coming to me for the money. I was now crying day and night, wondering where will I get this money. Will it fall from above? I knew that my faith was strong in the Lord and believed anything could fall from heaven as it had happened to Elijah, who was fed by the ravens.

I remembered another song we often sang on Sunday evening's singsong service.

> Courage brother (sister!) do not stumble,
> though thy path be dark as night;
> There's a star to guide the humble;
> Trust in God and do the right
> Let the road be rough and dreary,
> and its end far out of sight,

> Foot it bravely! Strong or weary
> Trust in God and do the right
>
> ("Courage, Brother, Do Not Stumble,"
> by Norman Macleod, 1857)

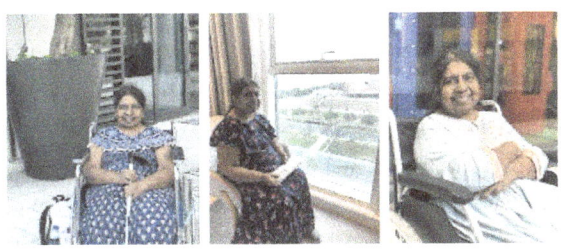

Wisy Glory in 2023, who was Salma's high school friend and helped her in her troubled times, when she had nothing. Her story is on the following pages.

Trusting God for a miracle, I went to my classroom on Monday morning and saw my classmate and best friend, Wisy, sitting at her desk in the front row. She always had rose flowers in her braids and almost daily brought some roses for me. Wisy saw me entering the classroom and beckoned me to come to her desk. I went to her desk, expecting a rose. She said, "Sal, show me your hand." She then counted ten 50 pennies and put them on my palm! I had never before held or even seen that much money in my life!

She told me that she saw Ratha sitting in the next classroom and asked me to go and give her this precious sum, which totaled the five rupees, which she was demanding from me.

I could not believe that I was holding five rupees. "Oh!" I shouted. "Is this for real?"

She said yes. When she told her mother about my predicament, her mother was upset.

"You should have told me before the past two weeks!"

That morning, she told Wisy, "Go give Salma these five rupees *today*!"

I immediately went to the next classroom and gave Ratha the five rupees that she demanded from me. She took it, and I was free from my burden. Yes, I knew God Almighty brought me out of that dark tunnel!

Wisy's father was a pharmacist and had his shop called Anbu Clinic next to the railway station in Nazareth. *Anbu* means kindness, and now whenever I go to India, I go to see my friend Wisy. She still lives in the same big house with her husband, who manages the Anbu Clinic. Fifty-five years after this incident, when I returned to India, I went to Nazareth and returned the five rupees she gave me when I was seventeen years old. I was especially happy to meet her very old mother and *thanked* her for her noble deed to a poor and needy orphan like me in 1963! My friend Wisy will never take anything from me, and I rejoice that we are still friends!

We, the Dohnavur girls in the boarding school, have very strict instructions not to take anything from anybody outside the fellowship. Breaking the rule will be met with heavy punishment. So I kept this incident to myself and did not tell anyone for fear that the other girls might tell tales when we went home for the summer holidays. My friend Wisy also never spoke to anyone about it, and I knew God had sent Paraclete (a person who came to aid) to set me free from this deep pit, and I thanked Him for it. Wisy passed away in March of 2024.

Then the end of the semester approached, and we all sat for the annual exams. On March 30, all the boarders went home for our summer vacation. I brought all my textbooks to return to the fellowship school office, as did all others. Summer vacation was hot and sticky, but we went swimming every day and enjoyed working around the compounds. I visited Kirubai and Rajarathinie, who had retired and resided in different homes.

I told them about my life at boarding school, which interested them, for they have not gone outside Dohnavur much. Most of all, they cared about me finishing high school and obtaining a Secondary School Leaving Certificate. These older ladies were my strong pillars and comfort. They supported me with their prayers. We all missed Lola, for she was not here on earth to see her Salma, who was now educated and advancing in life. I was glad that when the annual exam results came at the end of April, I was promoted to the eleventh grade. At last, I will sit for the government exams next year to get a high school certificate. It is called SSLC (Secondary School Leaving Certificate.)

## Last Year in School

In June 1963, I returned to the boarding school in Nazareth for my last year of high school. I was all prepared to work hard on my lessons, for I knew I would never be given another chance to finish high school if I failed the government exam.

Urani and I were in the A section, Arul was in the B section, three of my best friends were in the C section, and Wisy was in the B section. Nonetheless, we got together before the school assembly every day. My class teacher was Mrs. Catherine George. She was a very good math teacher and also very stern and strict. I was glad I was in her class, for I was very weak in math, but was very good at geometry and always scored high. A simple understanding of division and percentage was beyond me, but curved lines made sense. I was also good at graphs and could draw good diagrams.

This was important because I must pass the government exam's math section. Thus far, I have not passed math in the monthly tests, so I was studying hard. The math paper had three areas. One-third of the marks were for geometry and graphing. I knew that I could do that well and score full marks. But for the remaining parts, I must try hard.

In English, the teacher asked us to memorize the monologue of Puck, a mischievous sprite in Shakespeare's comedy *Midsummer Night's Dream*.

I did not understand what sprite, goblin, and goblet meant; it was too bewildering, and I could not memorize them. Therefore, I was instructed to write it down one hundred times! In our schoolwork in those days, there was no escaping the assignments by doing something else.

I enjoyed playing sports and was on the school netball, baseball, and volleyball teams for three years of high school and practiced regularly. We also played badminton. Only in the eleventh grade could one represent the school in tournaments and play against other high school teams. This allowed me to go out of the school with my team and see different places and their schools. Our school's physical instructor was also the dean of the boarding school. Urani and I were on the netball and volleyball teams and went to nearby schools for the tournaments. The most joyful thing was meeting other Dohnavur Fellowship girls studying in different schools. They gathered as spectators when we played and encouraged us on the court when the matches occurred. One of my best friends, Karunialeela Carunia, studied at a school where we played sports. I enjoyed our reunion for a few hours to see each other.

In the poetry class, we learned the poem of William Wordsworth (April 7, 1770–April 23, 1850):

### The Daffodils

> I wandered lonely as a cloud, that floats on high
>     o'er vales and hills,
> When all at once I saw a crowd, a host, of golden
>     daffodils,
> Beside the lake, beneath the trees, fluttering and
>     dancing in the breeze.
>
> Continuous as the stars that shine and twinkle on the milky way,
> They stretched in never-ending line along
>     the margin of the bay;
> Ten thousand saw I at a glance, tossing their
>     heads in sprightly dance.
>
> The waves beside them danced, but they outdid
>     the sparkling waves in glee;
> A poet could not but be gay in such a jocund
>     company.
> I gazed, and gazed, but little thought what wealth
>     the show to me had brought;
>
> For oft, when on my couch I lie in vacant or in
>     pensive mood,

## CHRIST IS IN ME

They flash upon that inward eye which is the bliss of solitude;
And then my heart with pleasure fills, and dances with the daffodils.

Our teacher told us to memorize this poem as she was certain it would come as one of the questions in the government exam. So I worked hard and learned it, although I didn't even know what a daffodil flower looked like!

I told you how in my childhood I used to borrow the same rainbow-covered book from the children's library from Premalu Sittie, who was in charge of the children's compound then. It showed yellow (daffodils) and red (tulips) flowers, but I did not know the names as I could not then read them. When I went to Scotland with my husband in my forties, I saw daffodils in the woodlands of Balmoral Castle and other places. Later, when we got to go to England and walked around Kensington Park, I saw the thousands of daffodils dancing in the wind in the meadows and woodlands! I remembered the poem that I learned when I was eighteen years old. Life has many surprises at every turn! And I was finally dancing with the daffodils in the wind in my early forties.

On Sunday afternoons, we had Sunday school for the boarders. Alexandra Samuel, our Sunday school teacher, read the book *The Robe*. She read it in English and explained it in Tamil. Later, when I came to America in my thirties, I saw the movie and understood the story better.

Miss Samuel was also the social studies teacher who taught geography, world history, and Indian history to the senior classes. She was very good at explaining the events. She taught us about Napoleon. Years later, in the summer of 2017, I visited Italy and went to Rome to give my husband's book to the Vatican for the Pope's library, which I was thanked for in September. From there, we went on to France and the island of Corsica. In Corsica, I toured the imperial city of Ajaccio, whose streets, monuments, and plazas all pay homage to the city's most renowned native, Napoleon Bonaparte. Near the one monument, I saw the rocks and caves where he played hide-and-seek in his childhood. They said he returned to visit his childhood playground when he was nineteen, a young man who would become the emperor of France. The conqueror's home island museum perfectly displays original furniture, memorabilia, and family portraits of his time and life.

For history and geography, the teacher used a large world map in the class. She brought it from the staff room where it was kept. This made it easy for us to visualize the lessons we were being taught. However, we had to pay attention and take notes, for we did not have an atlas to refer to outside of the classroom.

Tamil was taught in our high school by a Tamil pundit (a specialist in that language). I enjoyed learning from him. Tamil is one of the hardest languages in this world, for it has 220 letters in its alphabet.

As I was writing this part about my high school life, years later, in 2019, something interesting happened. That morning, July 10, I called my home, Dohnavur Fellowship, to talk to Memalar Carunia, one of my sisters. She told me that someone from a nearby town named Agnes had come to tour the fellowship with her family on *that day*. She had asked Memalar if she knew Salma Carunia, who went to St. John's Girls' High School in Nazareth from 1960 to 1964! Agnes said she knew Salma, for they were studying in the school at the same time. Memalar told me that Agnes remembered me as a very good and kind person. She said, "Salma was a happy teenager with two thick long braids, which sometimes held flowers. Salma often skipped joyfully around the school with a happy smile and led the singing at the school assemblies." I was amazed to learn this happened on the day I was writing about my school days then fifty-eight years ago. A classmate among the seven hundred students at St. John's Girls' High School, Nazareth, would even remember and ask about me! Memalar told Agnes that Salma had married an American and settled in the United States of America.

How amazing the way of the Spirit will stir our memories and lives! Second Corinthians 2:14–16 says, "Now thanks are unto God, which always causeth us to triumph in Christ and maketh manifest the sweet savor of his knowledge by us in every place…as of sincerity,

## CHRIST IS IN ME

but as of God, in the sight of God speak we in Christ." I was glad to know that I was acting as a witness for Christ fifty-nine years ago in my teenage life.

My last school year was ending, and I was studying hard. Finally, the great day of March 10, 1964, arrived, and I was in the exam hall with 149 other students. I located the desk with my roll number 74703 and sat down for the government public examination. Students could bring one or two fountain pens to the exam hall. At ten minutes to 10:00 a.m., the bell rang, and the proctors, who were teachers from other schools, handed out the answer sheets. We were instructed to write only our roll numbers and not our names on these. Once this was done, the exam papers were given out at 10:00 a.m. The examiner announced in a loud voice, "Start now."

If we ran out of paper, we had to raise our hands, and a proctor came to our desk and issued a supplementary answer sheet. After two hours, the bell rang, and a loud voice echoed across the exam hall, "Stop. Put your pens down." No one was allowed to add a dot or a dash after that, which was intimidating! We had no stapler; instead, we were given strings to tie the sheets together and hand them over to a proctor who came by our desks to collect them.

These exams were conducted over five days for eight papers in six subjects: English, Tamil, science, social studies (history and geography), mathematics, and Hindi. Tamil and English had two forms each, Paper-I and Paper-II. The Paper-II exams and the third language Hindi exam took place afternoons from 2:00 p.m. to 4:00 p.m. Remember, Tamil is one of the hardest languages in this world because it has 220 characters! Tamil grammar and poems are very difficult, and many students failed in Tamil and had to take the exams a second time to pass them. Tamil grammar is also very hard because some word sounds require particular annunciation of the characters to have the correct meaning. I am glad that I am done with that in high school and passed this subject with flying colors. I had my highest marks in Tamil, more than in any other subject in those final exams.

As I mentioned earlier, I had never passed math and was very much afraid when the day arrived for me to sit for the final math exam. After that exam, I was sure I had done well in geometry. I used a very good set of geometry instruments during that part: a divider, compass, set squares, and a protractor. These enabled me to draw very good diagrams. When I left, I felt that I could pass if I scored full marks for geometry; besides that, I thought I answered the sums questions correctly. However, I wasn't sure I had the correct answers for the other math questions.

Since I was unsure of passing, I did something I had never told anyone before. At the bottom of the math answer paper, I wrote, "Please, whoever corrects my math paper, have mercy on me, for I am an orphan girl and will not have any future without passing this exam!" Now that I have let the cat out of the bag, you know this secret too!

Hindi was another paper in which I was doubtful of scoring passing marks. I wrote two pages of an essay in Hindi and hoped to score passing marks. However, it did not matter, as these marks were not included in the final percentage determining a passing result. At that time, Hindi was spoken mostly in the north of India, but not in the south. The two major languages spoken in my province were Tamil and English.

March 16, 1964, was the last day of our boarding school life. I sadly bid goodbye to my four good friends: Kasthuri, Wisy, Mangalavalli, and Jeyalashmi. It was unlikely that I would ever see them again, for we were not allowed to write letters or visit our friends.

Kasthuri gave me a nice parting gift, an orange-colored tailor-stitched blouse. I did not tell anyone for fear, as we Dohnavur girls cannot accept gifts from any person, even our student friends. The gift was wrapped in a newspaper, and I did not open it until Christmas. I got a beautiful sari on that Christmas to wear with that blouse. When people asked me where I got the very good quality and tailor-made blouse, I was no longer afraid to say I got it from my friend Kasthuri at the boarding school—enough time had passed. This shows the very strict rules and regulations that we Dohnavur children lived under in those days.

I saved my pocket money to get the class 1964 graduation picture that semester. This cost me one rupee and fifty pennies. Urani and Devarul did not get one; they used their pocket money during the semester on other things. When the graduation photo came to the school, I looked very nice among two hundred students, teachers, staff, and employees. My double braid with a bunch of flowers stood like a tiara on top of my head, and I was standing by my best friend, Kasthuri.

My class teacher, Mrs. George, was very upset with me for having flowers in my hair! It was the season of Lent, and she scolded me, saying that I stood out in the crowd and this was haughty. Mind you, I didn't even have a mirror to see myself in those days. I never had the money to buy a mirror. Also, we were forbidden to show our teeth, which meant one could not smile at the photo shoot, so I was not even smiling.

Oddly, Mrs. George wore a broad-border silk sari for the year-end class pictures all those years. That stood out, and everyone complimented her. In the 1964 school graduation picture, I wore an old torn sari that many other Dohnavur students had worn before me. We all had hand-me-downs from previous generations, and there were holes in the sari in many places that I tried to hide under the folds on that day!

I couldn't help it if my face lit up and stood out. At that time, I was a poor orphan girl who did not have any earthly possessions. I did not mind my state of poverty but always had a very good cheerful disposition, as my heart was filled with *joy*, except when troubles and trials came. I knew I would never be able to buy a silk sari like my teacher, as I had no money and could not even dare to dream like Dick Whittington!

On March 16, the chaperone arrived at the school to escort us back to our home, and we three were ready with our steel trunks packed with our books, clothes, and school uniforms. It was an exciting moment to think we had finished our high school life. We could now look forward to becoming a teacher or a nurse, for only those two professions were available to Dohnavur girls in those days. I had always wanted to be a secondary school teacher. But first, one must pass high school.

Top row, third from left: Salma's friend, Mangalavalli.
Top row, Salma Carunia (with flowers in her hair) and her friend Kasthuribai.
Third row, far left: DevaArul Carunia.
Third row, eighth from right: Dharmakani, who brought Salma her first cupcake on her sixteenth birthday on November 23, 1960.
Second row, fourth from left: Alexandra Samuel (see story on p356).
Second row, sixth from left: Inbam Koilpillai, dean of boarding school and PE teacher.
Second row, seventh from left: Catherine George, Salma's twelfth-grade class teacher.
First row, fourth from left: Urani Carunia.
First row, sixth from right: Salma's friend Wisy Glory.

S. S. L. C. (XI Std.) Pupils & Staff — 1963-'64.

Top row, with flowers in hair: Salma Carunia and her friend Kasthuribai.
Third row, far left: DevaArul Carunia.
First row, fourth from left: Urani Carunia.
First row, eighth from left: Salma's friend, Wisy Glory.

Salma Carunia on her
graduation day.

# Period of Uncertainty

I was a candidate for confirmation, attended the classes, and became a member of the church on May 29, 1964. I was given a white sari with a green border to keep and wear for monthly communion services. Shanthie, my house mother, took me to the first communion service with Davarul, as we were both together in her house. It was a very special evening for me as God is active in the tensions of a *faith not yet mature.* A passage from John Bunyan's (1628–88) "To Be a Pilgrim" came to my mind:

> Who would true valor see, let him come hither
> one here will constantly be, come wind, come
> weather there's no discouragement shall make
> him relent his avowed intent To Be a Pilgrim.

Throughout the summer, I worked in the garden. The fellowship applied for a seat in three different teachers' training schools. However, before that, the government exam result had to come in June. So I waited!

I had time to reflect on how life had changed for me. At this stage of life, we cannot keep our hair loose or hang it in long braids. Now I am required to make a bun with my braids at the level of my neck. But not on the top of my head as I had seen my teachers do in the school, which I thought looked lovely. This is the final stage of my upbringing from babyhood to adulthood. At each stage, we wear different clothes: from blue cotton-strap knickers to blue cotton sleeveless knee-high dresses to cotton blue long skirts covering the legs. The final changes were sari: first, a half sari, and then a full six-yard blue cotton sari, which wrapped around us. That showed you were a full grown-up and expected to act like an adult. At that point, I must go and labor wherever the leader of the fellowship asked me to work.

Preparing to issue the exam results was in full swing at the board office. The SSLC marks were shown in a booklet in which all the marks for the four years of high school, VIII, IX, X, and XI, were entered. It also had a declaration that must be signed by the parent/guardian. It must list all particulars, like Name, Nationality, Religion, Sex, Date of Birth, Father's Name, and Personal Identification Marks. This must be correct, and no change will be made in the future. All the parents/guardians of the SSLC students had to come to the school office to sign the declaration. The Dohnavur Fellowship sent Christina Jeyaventhan to Nazareth High School to sign the certificate for the three of us. However, for some reason, the board did not accept her signature!

This caused the board to return the booklets to the school. Then the school forwarded them to the fellowship to be signed again! All this considerably delayed their final submission to the board. On June 6, 1964, the results were declared. The local and state newspapers published only the roll numbers of the successful students, but no names. Seven girls and six boys from the Dohnavur Fellowship had appeared for the board examination, out of which roll numbers of six boys and one girl was published. They had passed the board exam. *Six remaining girls, including mine, were missing.* That was a terribly sad day, especially for me!

All eight hundred in the Dohnavur family who knew me from childhood looked at me now as a failure. My future looked so dim, for I was told there would not be a second chance, and I did not know the reason why. Some others were comforted and told they could try for a second attempt in September. These results were also finally published in the *Fort St. George Gazette*. That listing still had my roll number and five other girls missing. But I did not give up my *faith*. This surprised the others, and they started to question my strong faith. Faith does not change your life. What changes your life is *He in whom you have faith* (1 Corinthians 15:1–2).

I was on my knees day and night while working in the vegetable garden, hoeing and tilling the hard patches, preparing them for new seedlings. Encouraged by the song of "To Be a Pilgrim" by John Bunyan:

> Whoso beset him round with dismal stories do,
>     but themselves confound,
> His strength the more is, no lion can him fright,
>     He'll with a giant fight,
> But he will have a right to be a Pilgrim.
>
> Hobgoblin nor foul friend can daunt his
>     spirit
> He knows he at the end shall life inherit,
> Then fancies fly away, he'll fear not what
>     men say,
> He labors night and day, to be a Pilgrim.

At that time, my house mother Shanthie had gone to Happy Valley in the Himalayas with another missionary to bring six adult Tibetan girls to the Dohnavur Fellowship. They had come to India after China invaded Tibet and needed a home.

On July 6, 1964, my prayers were answered! The exam's mark sheets of 150 students' booklets signed by the secretary, Board of Secondary Education, were received through post by St. John's Girls' High School, Nazareth. It was then discovered that Urani and I had passed the SSLC exam. The school quickly sent a postcard with the message that we had passed the SSLC, delivered by the postman at Dohnavur on Monday, July 6 at 9:00 a.m.

Neela Carunia, who was in charge of the mail room, immediately took the postcard bearing the good news to Nura Sittie. Unaware of all these developments, I came home from working in the garden to drink water. I was sitting on the veranda of the house, crying. My admission to the teacher's training college had already been canceled. I was being comforted by a two-year-old child, Chandravathie. She was sitting next to me saying, "Chamma, don't cry, don't cry," as she tried to wipe my tears away.

Suddenly, I saw Meleela Sittie (Sylvia Crawley) come to my house on her tricycle. (She had polio and could not ride a bicycle.) She quickly jumped down from it and said, "Salma, look into the Bible, John 16:20, 'Your sorrow shall be turned into joy.'" She added, "You have passed the government exam!"

My heart leaped with joy, and I must have jumped as high as the roof!

At that moment, Nura Sittie (Margaret Wilkerson) also came, parked her bicycle, and kissed me, saying, "You have passed SSLC."

That evening, I felt so peaceful that I could hear the children in the next cottage sing a song during their evening prayer. The song written by Amy for her children reminded me of God's care for his children.

Fear thou not the cloudy evening,
By dim waters fireflies glisten, 'Mid the dark
  leaves of the tree
Starry hosts are moving; Listen, listen for they
  speak to thee;
My Lord will take care of me.

(Amy Carmichael)

Salma's Tibetan friend, Randhal, in Dohnavur Fellowship, 1964–1966.

Chandravathy with her house mother, Amaravathy.

Chandra, who comforted Salma with the song of "Fear Thou Not the Cloudy Evening."

Shanthie, my house mother, returned from North India with the Tibetan girls. They were assigned to live in three cottages, two in each children's cottage. They spoke only Tibetan and could not understand Tamil, but they spoke some English so that we could communicate with them. One of them, Randhal, made friends with me, and we went for walks around the campus in the evening and enjoyed talking and getting to know each other. They only wore their own Tibetan dress, and the fellowship sewing room was able to get the pattern and make it for them. It is called *Chuppa*. This was an education for everyone who had never seen how other races dressed, according to their cultures and climate.

Unfortunately, I learned that the slot for teachers' training was filled. Therefore, I was sent to work at the fellowship's hospital kitchen. I worked hard, grinding the grains such as rice and black gram in a large stone mortar. The giant mortar is fixed to the floor with the ground-level top opening. The pestle is a heavy elliptical-shaped stone. To operate it, one sits on the floor, folding one leg and stretching the other out. This brings your arms close enough to hold the pestle and rotate it. The sitting position takes the strain off the back and transfers it to the folded leg and shoulders. Another girl sits on the opposite side, pushing the batter inside to prevent it from spilling. The partners switch positions often, as it is very tiring work. I would work grinding every morning till 11:00 a.m. Oh, but you are not finished then!

After grinding, you helped wash lots of large pots and pans. There was no running water, so one must do much pumping to fill the buckets and clean the pots and pans and scrub the kitchen floor. All of this must be finished before the nurses come to eat at noon! After lunch, we could go to the nurses' quarters for a little rest, but report for duty at 2:30 p.m.! After I left the fellowship, no hard work could ever frighten me!

The Indian food is made with many spices, such as roasted red chili, turmeric, roasted coriander, cardamom, asafetida, fresh ginger rhizome, fresh garlic, tamarind fruit, coconut, cloves, cinnamon, black pepper, cumin, mustard, onion, and curry leaves. Every day, new paste of spices is made on a flat grinding stone. This is manually done, as there was no electricity and no electric mixer grinders to perform our hard work in those days!

All the hard work was well rewarded as it resulted in a tasty spicy curry, the aroma of which spread throughout the compound. It was *very hard labor*!

One Saturday, I was given fresh coconut and green chilies to grind. The work was beyond me. My friend Usila sat next to me and helped me finish the portion that I was given. Nowadays, it is so easy, as all these spices, crushed by machines, are available in bottles and packets. I still remember the hard days I spent working in the community kitchen, grinding them with heavy stones. I worked in the kitchen for six months and then could go into nursing. So for the remainder of the year, I worked in the hospital.

Preena, grinding Indian spices on a grinding stone at her home before she was sold to the temple by her mother. She ran away to Amy.

Left: Preena, who escaped from the temple and ran to Amy Carmichael. She became the first child taken in by Amy at Dohnavur Fellowship, 1905.

SALMA CARUNIA CARTER

# November 23, 1964
# I Celebrate My Birthday
# End of My Teenage Years

I turned twenty years old, and many responsibilities were added as the year went on. I started working as a nurse's helper in the babies' ward. I learned to look after babies and how to feed them with bottles.

Every Saturday was the scrubbing day, and I had to scrub the ward's tables, stools, and wooden windows. Then I washed the red tile floor with disinfectant. Four intern nurses and I worked in the same department: Devashanthie, Vallarie, Haleema, and Jeyasunthari. We took a first-year nursing course, and Dayalie Sittie was our teacher. Every Friday afternoon, we attended the anatomy class that Atharavu Sittie conducted. I enjoyed these classes and almost wanted to become a nurse then, but one had to go to the government hospital to do nursing training. The other four girls that I have mentioned were ahead of me and waiting for the vacancies in government hospitals.

This training at our mission hospital was a wonderful life-learning experience. I learned what to do in an emergency and how to bind wounds. I passed the test of bandaging the different parts of the body. I also learned to take the patient's temperature and pulse, then note it on the daily charts and kept it ready for the doctor when she came on the rounds. I also learned about the various medicines used for treating different diseases. One medicine cupboard was always kept locked, and I found out later that they kept bromide in it. I had no idea what bromide was and only found out in my sixties.

Every two weeks, there was duty rotation, and we ran to see the new list hanging in the duty room. Next, I reported to the surgery theater from the babies' ward. There, my job was mainly to scrub the floor, on my hands and knees, with water and disinfectant after every surgery. After a month, I worked in the hospice center where Preena, Amy's first child, as well as Leela lived in their old age. Later on, I worked in the children's ward. There, I learned more about sick people, and I decided to become a nurse. I missed my Lola while working with others in her age group, for she left us in 1956.

One day, I saw Nura Sittie in the passage next to the ward where I was working, and I went to her and asked her if I could become a staff nurse and attend nursing training.

She told me, "No, Salma, you are born to be a teacher. We need teachers in our home school, and at the end of summer, you will come and help us in the home school."

Now I know I am leaving the hospital compound at the end of the summer. Three girls I worked with at the hospital were accepted to study in government nursing schools. They left the fellowship at the end of the summer and went to their nursing schools. The fourth girl, Vallari, was sent to work in the youth hostel in Bangalore.

The news from Nura Sittie made me happy. At last, I am going to teach at our home school, Jeevalia. Imagine this was where Vimba Sittie (Eleanor Backhouse) kicked me out in the seventh grade at fourteen years old. What a joy to go back to the same school as a teacher!

I went from the hospital compound to the school compound to start teaching in the home school. I was glad to return to my house where I grew up as a teenage girl with Shanthie Aruldasan. Here, I became an assistant to Shanthie, supervising the adolescent children's work and welfare at home. At the same time, I went to home school, started teaching different classes from grade 1 to 7, and enjoyed life as a teacher. On November 23, 1965, I turned twenty-one years old. I had grown up to be a mature young woman and was entrusted with more responsibilities. Luke 2:52 said, "Jesus kept increasing in wisdom and stature, and in favor with God and men."

At this time, I was getting to understand more spiritual things and increasing in wisdom and feeling that the grace of God was upon me. Shanthie played an important part in all this; she took me into her house when I was fourteen and helped me to grow in the Lord. My faith increased with the passing years. Her life touched me, and I felt something deep in me that I wanted to be like her. I desired to be holy and blameless before the God I worshipped, *Jesus Christ*, the Lord and my Redeemer and Savior.

In January 1966, Nesarathina Carunia, the seventh-grade teacher at the home school, fell ill and was advised to undergo surgery, so they needed someone to replace her. It was the last trimester, and these seventh-grade girls were preparing to attend eighth grade at the boarding school in June. Therefore, the fellowship had to find someone to prepare them for the next level. The council members, Nura Sittie, Shanthie Aruldasan, Christina, the principal of the home school, Vimba Sittie (Eleonor Backhouse), and Nesarathina, discussed the matter in the council meeting, where many people's names were considered. Finally, it narrowed to two, Urani and me. We both graduated from Nazareth High School two years ago. We were waiting for a vacancy in the government teachers' training school. Nesa wanted Urani to be her replacement, but Ms. Wilkinson along with Shanthie proposed bringing me back as a teacher, where I was detained from this very school in 1959 by Eleonor Backhouse. The council decided to appoint Salma after much discussion.

Joel 2:25 says, "I will restore to you the years that the locust hath eaten."

There were twenty-one students of various ages in seventh grade. It was a very humbling experience for me. Because I, who had never passed mathematics in school and barely passed it in the board examination, was now teaching math to the seventh-grade students. However, the students said they understood the math I taught and liked my method of teaching.

My students especially loved the scripture class I conducted every day for half an hour before lunch. Some who are in their sixties today still talk to me on the phone. They will speak about the verses I had underlined in their Bibles in 1966. They still use the same Bibles I underlined with red and green pencils. They say it was very helpful to them when they meditated on the various verses once they went to boarding schools and later as they advanced.

Two important verses for me are Ephesians 5:16, "Redeeming the time because the days are evil," and 1 Corinthians 15:33, "Do not be deceived: Bad company corrupts good morals." These verses were helpful to me when I went out from home to boarding school. I was able to pass them on now to this generation. I was asked to prepare them, for they were going out from the sheltered life in Dohnavur Fellowship for the first time and will see a very different world.

# CHRIST IS IN ME

Five of my students of 1966 returned in their late twenties to work in the fellowship with their credentials. I am glad to see them contributing to the community of the fifth to seventh generations with their skills and education. They are the children I helped raise and educate, as they still look up to me. My best advice to them was "Abstain from all appearance of evil" (1 Thessalonians 5:22) and "Abhor what is evil, cling to what is good."

Naraikadu (Gray Forest).
Amy Carmichael purchased a forty-acre coffee estate three thousand feet up in the Western Ghats and built three holiday houses there.

The Forest House, the first bungalow built in 1917. This was used for the men's housing for the holidays.

The Jewel House, the second bungalow built around 1919. This was used for the women's housing for the holidays. Salma enjoyed spending her summer holidays here in 1966 and 1968.

A monkey sat in the dripping rain, hey-ho, hey-ho!

Mountains dreaming in the quiet of the young moon's light.

# Naraikadu (The Gray Forest)

The school year ended in March 1966 as the summer approached. During the hot months of April and May, the fellowship arranged a vacation for the staff to go to the coolness of the nearby forest in the Western Ghats Mountains.

Amy Carmichael had purchased the land in 1917 when she was met by the owner at Mohammadeen's cave while exploring the forest. The document reveals that she paid one hundred English pounds to purchase it. She named the place in Tamil, *Naraikadu*, which means Gray Forest. Amy bought one hundred acres and built a large cottage with twelve rooms and a separate community kitchen behind it. That place allowed the fellowship's girls and women to spend their holidays in the cool mountains.

She named the house the Jewel House. A large "jewel" swimming pool was dug to hold a mountain creek's water. After some years, one could not touch the bottom of the swimming pool as it became a natural pool. For more than one hundred years, my family, Dohnavur Fellowship, has been enjoying this heritage even so today.

Amy then built a second house with another lovely swimming pool for the boys and men and a separate place for the missionaries to stay. This was located a few hundred feet below the women's cottage. There were also a few cottages built for married couples. Sirappan Annachie (Philip England) and Vibaharan Annachie (Claude Wavre), a Swiss man, both engineers, helped build the pools and small dams and the bridges around this site.

They also designed the ingenious pipe system where the mountain's cool water comes through the pipes as running tap water to the holiday houses' shower rooms and the kitchen. Amy is highly regarded in India as an early conservationist who inspired her children with the love of nature. The area where our valley lies are now considered part of the evergreen forest of South India and our range of hills, a key place for the preservation of Indian tigers.

After serving the fellowship for two years, one earns two weeks' holiday to rest in the forest. My turn to go to the forest came in the last two weeks of April 1966. I was excited about the eight-mile trek up into the mountains. The holiday season started in April and ended in June, before the monsoon—four groups of twenty-four women and six as cooks.

A total of twenty-six women would begin their vacation on the same day the previous group came down from the mountain. Twenty-four women slept in a large room, which was used as a play school for the younger children during the school season.

To go up to the foothills, we would then get up at 3:00 a.m. By 4:00 a.m., the bullock carts were lined up, and six of us packed inside a cart, sitting on the loose hay spread to cushion the bumpy ride. Then about 4:30 a.m., the carts start moving in a line up toward the mountains. As the bulls pull the carts on the unpaved country roads toward the foothills, the bells around their necks signal their presence in the dead silence of pitch-black early mornings.

At about 7:00 a.m., we arrived at the mountains' foothills and got out of the bullock carts, for they could not go any further. The ride was rough in those days, but now the staff arrives by large vans. There are lovely green pastures where the bulls can rest near the large lotus tank while waiting for the women coming down from the mountain in Naraikkadu after their two weeks' vacation.

I started the remaining three-thousand-foot climb to the house in the cool breeze of the early morning with a large bundle at my back, as some of us, especially younger ones, carried their clothing/luggage. I sang a song that I memorized at Lola's house when I was ten years old.

Make me to be thy happy mountaineer, O God,
    most High
My climbing soul would welcome the austere,
    Lord Crucify
On rock or scree, ice-cliff or field of snow,
The softness that would sink to things below.

Thou art my guide where Thy sure feet have
    trod, shall mine be set.
Thy lightest word, my law of life, O God.
Lest I forget and slip and fall, teach me to do thy will,
Thy mountaineer upon Thy Holy hill.

(Amy Carmichael)

We arrived before lunchtime and were glad to see the hot lunch ready for us by Tara Carunia (see page 37). She was in charge of the holiday cottage and responsible for its upkeep. Amy Carmichael herself started maintaining the first forest logbook. Now Tara Carunia keeps the logbooks updated and enters the things that happen every day and about the animals, birds, insects, various kinds of monkeys, and wild elephants that have been seen and heard. One day, I was sitting near the deep dark silent pool before swimming and waiting for others to come and join me. I remembered the song Amy wrote for us, her children, to sing, and I sat beside the pool and sang it.

Deena Dayalan Anantha, who was taught by assistant teacher Salma in first and second grade, standing near the logbook table at the Jewel House.

I sat by the waterfall a little while yesterday;
And I think I heard the words of its call to its
    waters far away.

For behind in the water-shed they loitered lazily;
But the waterfall it laughed as it sped on, on to
    the deep blue sea.

And it splashed on its crystal floor, and its call
    was glad and clear
"Come on, come on! It is better on before, for the
    way is wider here."

"Beckon spray!" was its quick command: I saw a
    little spray people spring,
And each one waved a little white hand I could
    see them beckoning

"Come on! It is better on before," was the Word
    perpetually;
For our river-bed widens more and more, and it
    leads to the deep blue sea

(Amy Carmichael)

## CHRIST IS IN ME

One day, the milkman, who brought milk up to the holiday cottage every morning, came and reported to Tara that a leopard suddenly jumped down from a tree on the path when he was coming up. He was so frightened that the milk canister fell from his head! We missed the milk on that day but were glad our milkman was safe. Tigers also roamed around in this area! In 1988, Naraikkadu became part of the Kalakkad Mundanthurai Tiger Reserve.

One night, I sat by the window in our house in the forest, watching the beautiful moonlight over the mountain. I remembered the songs/poems Amy wrote for her children.

### Moonlight in the Forest

Moonlight's tranquility, A shimmering ocean,
like a silver band between the misty sky
And misty land, and dreaming mountains sweep-
    ing to the sea.
The forest slowly heaves and murmurs as the low
    night-wind awakes.
The moon rides through her filmy vapors, takes
    her myriad moonbeams, strews them on the
    leaves.

### Night in the Pool

Mountains dreaming in the quiet of the young
    moon's light,
Forests, all at heart a -glimmer, and ye falls snow
    white,
And thou pool so palely gleaming like a pearl set
    in the green-wood,
Of what think ye through the silence of the night?
O ye mountains, forests, waters, have I read you
    alright?
Doth your young moon sing her story through
    the dark of the night?

> Not towards darkness are our faces, Towards the
> light creation moveth,
> Lift your heads up, Lift your hearts up to the
> Light!

I enjoyed my time up in Naraikkadu, swimming every day in the cold mountain water for most of the mornings. Then at lunchtime, some missionaries, who were also enjoying their vacation in separate cabins, came up to the Jewel House, where the girls and women were staying.

They also enjoyed swimming and joined us for the Indian lunch. Every day, something special was prepared for lunch, and I enjoyed eating and resting in the afternoons.

Then we had high tea with fresh homemade delicacies. During the second week of my stay, Vimba Sittie (Eleanor Backhouse) came up for her vacation. One day, she asked me to come and meet her in a nearby cave, so I went to see her the next morning. First, she told me she wanted to spend prayer time with me. After the prayer, she told me she was impressed with how I handled the twenty-one students in the seventh grade. Then she confessed she had misunderstood me from childhood when she sometimes punished me severely. I suppose that was the closest she would come to acknowledging that she had done me wrong.

Years later, in June 1993, I visited Dohnavur Office in London with my husband and met Vimba Sittie there. As we introduced each other, I told my husband that this lady had punished me from childhood until Margaret Wilkinson (Nura Sittie) came to my aid. Eleanor Backhouse (Vimba Sittie) did not like that and told me straight away I should not tell my husband that such things happened in Dohnavur. As I write this, I have peace in my heart and have forgiven her.

Back on the mountain, in the evening, we would go for a walk to see our garden, where many fruits were growing in abundance at that time of the year, such as guava, pineapple, and seven different kinds of plantains. They were red, green, and yellow, for they seemed to thrive in the mountain climate. I liked the green-colored plantain very much because it tasted different from the ordinary ones.

The English missionaries arranged a long trip to climb different mountains every Friday. We would leave the Jewel House at 7:00 a.m. and return by 7:00 p.m. I enjoyed the trek to a large dam in the adjacent state of Kerala and learned that we were on the other side of the mountain where the river water came through that dam. Many elephants were on that side, but we were told that everyone must stay together. The elephants may also come to bathe in the same natural pools and waterholes that we swam in at that time.

I would jump from the high rocks into the deep pools and enjoy swimming in these natural mountain pools. Someone must always be on the lookout for the elephants, for everyone knows there may be a danger if we see a lone elephant. It is natural for elephants to move as a herd. However, if one sees a lone elephant, one must take precautions, for the lone elephant could be a rogue elephant. We came back before sunset and had the hot dinner that was kept ready for us, and as we were very tired, we went to bed early.

I saw different beautiful birds and liked the whistling schoolboy's calls in the early mornings. All kinds of monkeys were swinging by their tails and replying in funny sounds as our voices echoed thru the forest. It was hard for me to say goodbye to the beautiful Naraikkadu Forest. We sang the last song together as we descended from the mountain.

The Atlas moth was found in the forest in November of 2022.

Dim green forest of a thousand secrets,
When you were planted did the angels sing?
Many things I wonder: Are they all your secrets?
Won't you ever tell me anything?
Great White waterfall, breaking through the forest,
where do you come from, where do you go?
Had you a beginning, will you go on forever?
Forever and forever will you go?
Great black glistening wall, veiled in shining glory,
Piled among the waters rock upon rock,
O to have stood and seen hands at work upon you,
Shivering you and shattering shock on shock.
Deep dark silent pool, hollowed at the fall's foot,
What do you think of all the day long?
Do you hear the thunder of tremendous waters?
Do you hear the laughter of the spray?

(Amy Carmichael)

I enjoyed the fresh, clean mountain air, and my clothes had a wonderful smell of mountain river water, which I noticed after coming down home to the plains.

# CHAPTER 13

# Bangalore, South India

In June 1966, the school term started. I was asked to move to an independent house adjacent to Shanthie's house with four other girls of my age. It was very hard for me to leave Shanthie, whom I had loved like a dear mother for the past eight years, but I was now twenty-one. I must go to make room for the other youngsters in Shanthie's house. I felt a little freer, living without the supervision of the house mother, although I had felt secure being with a house mother.

I prepared a classroom by cleaning and scrubbing the red tile floor for two new missionaries every morning. Suganthie Sittie (Margaret Holland) was a bookkeeper, and Praba Sittie (Alice Bell) was a radiographer who arrived at the Dohnavur Fellowship on October 30, 1965, from England. They were learning Tamil. Nisha Carunia, a council member, was their teacher. I decorated their study table with lovely blue morning glory flowers I picked daily from the wild. The flowers were climbing on the fence and smiling at me when I passed their classroom. It was compulsory that within two years, the missionaries learn Tamil. They had to pass an exam at the end of the second year, and only after that were they assigned jobs. Margaret worked in our main office, and Alice was sent to live in our hospital compound because she worked in the X-ray room.

In August 1966, I was sent to Bangalore to join eleven other girls. I was very disappointed not to be teaching at the school for that year. Nevertheless, one must obey the orders, or you will have no future opportunities!

This was great joy for me because I was reunited with my loving house mother, Rajamacootie Accal, who had been sent to Bangalore when I was fourteen. She was extremely happy to see me educated and grown-up. I was assigned a cooking partner and, once every two months, got the responsibility of cooking for a family of fifteen. R. Cottie Accal was in charge of the kitchen and showed me how to prepare food for the small family.

In December, another girl, Inimai Carunia, joined us. I was happy and enjoyed her company. Inimai was a sweet girl preparing to go for higher education at Women's College in Madras. I will never forget some of the songs that she taught us in Bangalore. One piece, in particular, stuck with me; it goes like this:

> Have Faith in God, commit your life to Him,
> God understands the wayward hearts of men.
> Look to the future and face it without fear…
> Have Faith in God and He will never fail.

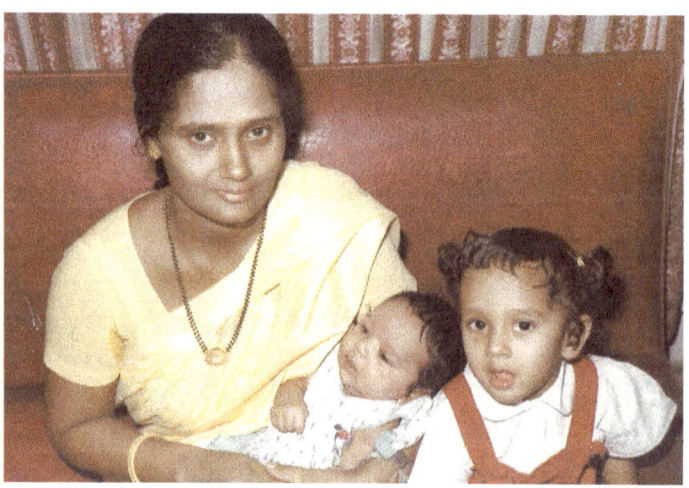

Ini, Salma's sister, with her children, Arun and Arunima

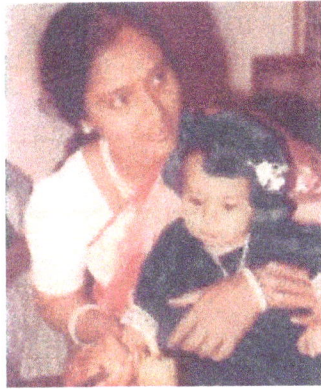 

Ini Chouguley.  Mr. Dilip Chouguley, Ini's husband.

Ini graduated from the college with a teacher's degree and, in the late 1970s, became a school principal at Dehra Doon, North India. After a few years, she married Mr. Dilip Chouguley, a lawyer in Nagpur. I consider her a sweet little sister of mine from Dohnavur.

Most of the girls, who were sent to Bangalore, ended up getting married there. However, I did not entertain such thoughts. I wanted to go for higher education and get teacher's training, for I enjoyed teaching.

The jewelry is pure gold and serves as the bank, as there are no physical banks for them to deposit their money. The sari is a rich red color. A woman of this type makes a fine bride! The ear is cut to hold the heavy jewels, which weigh so much that one wonders how the stretched lobes do not break.

For the jewels, the holes are made first and filled with cottonwood. Increasingly heavier weights are added until the lobes are long enough.

The girl is being presented for her wedding. The family jewels worn by a girl of this Vellalar class are worth thousands of rupees! These pictures are from the book, *Things as They Are* by Amy Carmichael, 1905.

Naveenaseelan with his wife, Usila Carunia, and children, John Varathan and Deepakanthie, Barnabas. The plaque on the wall reads, "Seek ye first the Kingdom of God" in Tamil. These are given to all those from Dohnavur Fellowship who marry.

John Varathan Naveenaseelan with his wife, Patmarani Carunia, and their son, Paul.

Left, in light blue shirt: Barnabas. Center, Paul and his wife, Vidhaya. Paul is holding Barnabas's son, who is his nephew. To the right, in green sari, is Barnabas's wife, Hebziba. On the far right, wearing glasses, is Usila's daughter, Deepakanthie. To her right in the blue sari is Patmarani, Paul's mother. On August 17, 2023, Paul and Vidhaya welcomed their first child, Dhayapauline into this world, who is also Usila Naveenaseelan's great-granddaughter. Sadly, on December 24, 2023, my best friend Usila passed away at age seventy-nine.

Naveenaseelan's family. Lower right: Richard and Saroruha with their granddaughter, Mercy. Upper left: their son, Selvakumar, daughter Julie and her daughter, Mercy. Julie is cooking for the family in the kitchen, as was tradition for Indian women.
In August 2022, Salma's best friend Saroruha passed away at age seventy-eight.
Below, left to right: Vasu, Selvakumar, Mike, Richard, Saroruha, Julie (Vasu's wife).

Above, left: Salma with her sister and brother-in-law, Premabanda and David.
Above, right: David and Premebanda and their sons, John and Jonathan enjoying dinner with Mike and Salma at their home in Wheaton.

Below: Salma with her beloved sister and friend, Dr. Premabanda Carunia-David.

Israel and his wife, Atharavu Carunia, with their son Zuka, in Zambia.

Salma with Zuka and Annie on their wedding day in Toronto, Canada. On the right is Atharavu, Salma's sister and Zuka's mother.

Zuka Row Irlapathy and his wife, Annie, with Auntie Salma in Houston.
Zuka graduated from Cambridge University in England with an engineering degree and now works as a general manager at Shell Oil Company in Australia.

Israel and Atharavu (Ravi) with their grandchildren, Nathan and Max.

Zuka and Annie Irlapathie.

Zuka and sons, Nathan and Max. The boys are wearing New Zealand rugby team shirts and are proud citizens of New Zealand.

## CHRIST IS IN ME

To make the Bangalore home self-supporting, we made soft toys, sold them in stores in Bangalore, and sometimes got big orders from Delhi. Each person was trained to become an expert in making one animal. I was good at making soft velvet monkeys, and it became my task to do it daily, which I enjoyed. Four of us were Lola's children: Jeevanathie, Pushpaveni, Jeyaruby, and me. We all grew up together at Lola's house, then lived under the care of R. Cottie Accal's after Lola passed away. We were again living together with our dear R. Cootie Accal for the last time and enjoyed our sisterhood, for we knew not what the future would hold for us, for some of us would marry and some would travel the world.

Left to right: Piratha, Rajamacottie (Salma's house mother), Rajamithirie, who ran the youth hostel in Bangalore.

SALMA CARUNIA CARTER

# More Disappointments

*Stand still and see the salvation of God.*

—Exodus 14:13

In May 1967, four of us were asked to come back home to Dohnavur from Bangalore. I hoped to go for teachers' training, but again, Nesarathina foiled it. She had been sent to see the school in Madras and came and told the leaders in the fellowship that the college only wanted fresh graduates from high school. I graduated from high school now three years ago, so my chance of going for the training was put on hold. That year, they sent Varisa, a fresh graduate from Trichy High School, to the vacancy. It was hard for me to swallow my tears! However, it was to be another whole year of staying at home, working hard, while waiting another year to go for the training.

I was worried about getting too old, as it seemed like all the doors were closing for me in higher education. However, I had to remind myself to learn to trust God only.

> At that time the Church bell was pealing
> God is my strong Salvation: What foe have I to fear?
> In darkness and temptation, my light, my help is near.
> Though hosts encamp around me, Firm to the fight I stand,
> What terror can confound me, With God at my right hand?
>
> (Psalm 46:1–11)

In June 1967, the school term started, and I must now wait another year before I got the teachers' training that I had anticipated since I left high school. It was my fourth year of internship in the fellowship. I was sent to the Square, the children's compound, to assist

Pangaja, for she was getting sick and had a stomach ulcer. Pangie was her pet name, and she looked after three children aged six to eight. These were Rubamalar and Ruhinie (they were sisters) and Rajavadivu. I enjoyed staying with them and nursing Pangie back to health. Every day, I mixed a special powder medicine with milk and gave her to drink every four hours per the doctor's order. Pangie had six other girls who were at boarding school, and they came home every three months for the school holidays.

In July, Nura Sittie called me and told me that the years had passed, and I needed some kind of training. Therefore, she enrolled me in the secretarial course with three other girls: Usila, Haleema, and Valarie. Meleela Sittie (Sylvia Crawley) conducted this one-year diploma course at home. She prepared us for the government exam held annually to obtain the diploma. This would be in June 1968.

We attended the class from 9:00 a.m. to noon and 2:30 to 5:00 p.m. That was in addition to my work in the children's nursery. That was not easy. It required scrubbing the floor on my knees and hands and pumping to draw water to do chores around the house and, above all, lots of plants to water in the evening after school.

I could never finish the typing speed test in the class on my typewriter. One had to press the keys hard to type. A bell rang when you reached the end of the line. Then you manually push the carriage back to starting position after typing each line, but somehow, we managed. Today, it is much easier to type on the soft-touch keyboard at the computer.

We went to Nagarcoil, a nearby town for exams, by bus and had to carry our typewriters weighing more than five kilograms (eleven pounds). There were about one hundred students in the hall, and the noise of the standard old typewriters hammering away was distracting! Regardless, one must concentrate on finishing the speed test. I was glad I finished the passage when the examiner called to stop. We waited for the result for three months, after which we had to appear for another exam, but only if we passed the typing speed test. In the meantime, I fell ill with jaundice and spent the next three months in the hospital. It gave me time to study for the exam.

In October 1968, I went to Nagarcoil for the practical exam. At this time, Dr. Nancy Robbins forbade me to carry my typewriter due to my sickness. Hence, the escort brought my typewriter to the exam hall. One question in the exam paper was "Write a letter to the prime minister of India, Mrs. Indira Gandhi; type her postal address!" I had no idea where the prime minister of India lived. A lady proctor noticed my distress, came to my desk, and asked me what the matter was. She also asked me if I was from Dohnavur Fellowship. She told me that she was Vallari's high school teacher in Ramanathapuram. I told her that I did not know Indira Gandhi's address. After five minutes, she returned to my desk and gave me a piece of paper on which she wrote the address of Indira Gandhi and told me if I was caught, not to betray her name.

Then I typed the address and finished the exam. I thanked her for the help. After many years, I had the privilege to visit the Rashtra Pati Bhavan in New Delhi, which is the residence of the president of India. Since we girls and boys were kept inside the walls of the fellowship, we did not know much of the outside world. To have known the residence of the prime minister was out of the question!

Urani and I had graduated from high school together and were still waiting to get teachers' training. But there was more disappointment for us as we did not get a seat in the training school that year. Urani was sent to help a blind student entering the Sarah Tucker teachers' training school. I remained at the fellowship. I was to do another year of internship, working in the children's nurseries and doing odd jobs such as working in the kitchen washing pots and pans, pumping gallons of water, etc. At the same time, I was also teaching at the home school.

I was very impatient to go out of the fellowship and to have a job, as my internship was getting prolonged. It was already the sixth year, yet I was supposed to find joy in it, as per the song that Amy Carmichael wrote for her children:

Hate not laborious work, Joy, joy is in it,
Do not thy duty shirk, Joy, joy is in it,
Welcome the daily round, On, and be
    faithful found,
On, and thou shalt be crowned: Joy, joy
    is in it.

I scrub my pots, I scrub my pans,
I scrub my brazes and my cans,
For work is such a jolly thing, it makes one want
    to sing

"When each duty crowds the other through the
    sultry days,
Plant a little flower of patience by our ways.
When the slothful flesh would murmur, ease
    would cast her spell,
Set our face as flint till twilight's Vesper bell.

(Amy Carmichael)

## Clay in the Potter's Hand

On June 23, 1969, I was singing the song to ease the drudgery of my work when Nura Sittie came on her bike and told me, "Salma, the results of the secretarial course have come, and you have passed."

I was very happy to get a certificate from the Government of Madras, Technical Examinations, Lower Grade. We were not allowed to do the exam for the Higher Grades. (The Lower Grade qualified you just for keyboard typing. The Higher Grade included shorthand and other secretarial skills one must know to work in a larger office, but this was not available to us.)

There was a council meeting in June 1970 where other women members discussed my future. Nesarathina, one of the council members, gave a bad report about me. She said I was not taking turns with others pushing the baby's cart in the evenings at the babies' compound. This was untrue, as I was not even working in the babies' compound but was assigned to help with three- to five-year-old children at the children's compound called the Square. I had to take them for walks every evening along with a missionary on duty from Monday to Friday. Nesa knew that any bad report about a person in the council meeting would stop that person's progress. (Margaret

Wilkinson (Nura Sittie) was like a second mother to those from the second generation through the eighth generation.)

Luckily, one day, Nura Sittie saw me pushing the wooden cart with tired, crying children from their evening walk along the public road that went past her house. So she spoke up and defended me. (Miss Wilkinson was like a Mother Superior to the fellowship.).

One day in July 1970, Shanthie told me that I needed to go and see Nura Sittie at 7:00 p.m., so I left my home at about ten minutes to 7:00. As I approached an old tamarind tree on the way to Nura Sittie's house, Nesarathina came quickly on her bicycle and stopped near me. She told me, "Salma, you should get married. Please ask Nura Sittie to give you in marriage."

I was puzzled and confused but walked on toward Nura Sittie's house, as it was 7:00 p.m.

The clock struck 7:00 p.m., and Nura Sittie (Margaret Wilkinson) beckoned me inside. I went in and sat on the floor beside her. Then she told me that a Christian man had come to ask for a bride, and she could arrange it if I wanted to get married. I immediately said to her that I had no desire to get married. At that time, I was thinking of dedicating my life to Dohnavur Fellowship and helping at the orphanage. Then Nura Sittie said there was another possibility.

"If you like, you can send an application for admission to South India Biblical Seminary at Bangarapet. If you would like to study in the Bible seminary—"

And before she could finish the sentence, I said, "Yes! I want to go to the Bible seminary!"

She told me to wait prayerfully and consider it overnight before giving a final answer in writing. Things have changed since my fifth grade teacher Navarathini's time.

I was thrilled at the thought that she had chosen me to be sent to the Bible seminary from among five hundred others. The next day, I wrote a note of acceptance in English and gave it to her. After a week, she called me to come and fill out the application form, which I did. After a short while, the seminary confirmed my admission, and I started preparing to attend the Bible seminary.

Of course, Nesarathina did not like this; she always wanted to stop me from getting higher education. She was present in the council meeting where these proposals were discussed, one about marriage and the other about studying in Bible college. That is why she stopped me near the old tamarind tree and told me to accept the marriage proposal. Hopefully, I will never hear about a chance at higher studies. Perhaps she did not realize that *God holds the key to all unknown.* Here in my life, Nura Sittie taught me a very important lesson: When taking decisions that will change the course of your life, never do it in a rush. Hear everything the other person has to say; think about it overnight before coming to any conclusion.

This decision to send me to study in a co-ed college was another path-breaking decision taken by Nura Sittie. Until then, the practice sent boys to boys' colleges, and girls to girls' colleges. They had sent two girls named Arulmani and Atharavu (Ravi) to a co-ed institution. Ravi now lives in New Zealand with her husband, and her son, Zuka, a Cambridge graduate, works as a general manager for the Shell Oil Company in Australia. Ravi and I still talk and keep in touch after all these fifty years!

All the college students got ten saris and a mattress for sleeping. Going to college was seen as a privilege and one's self-esteem increased. College education was given to only a very few among the thousands of us who graduated from high school. At that time, only two girls, Inimai Carunia and Vanasunthari Carunia, were sent to the Teachers' Training College at Madras to get a BA and BEd degree, while I was sent to the seminary.

*Bible reading is an education in itself.*

—Lord Tennyson

SALMA CARUNIA CARTER

Thousands Call For Counseling

# CHAPTER 14

# Bible Seminary

In September 1970, I went to join the South India Biblical Seminary, and Tara (Evu's friend) escorted me (Evu Accal, who bought me as a six-day-old baby to Amy). It was an overnight journey requiring a change of trains at two places to reach our destination. This will be the last time I will be escorted by someone from the fellowship, for after this, I will be allowed to travel alone.

The seminary was run by the Americans, and all the students had to buy the New American Standard Bible (Reference Edition). It was mandatory to use in the classroom. I am still using it for the past fifty-nine years. I used my Tamil Bible beside the English Bible, which helped me to understand the lessons. My favorite subjects were Old Testament, New Testament, and Theology in which I scored higher than others. The seminary had started a bachelor of theology (BTh) four-year degree course on that year. I was delighted to be the very first one from the fellowship to get a seminary degree.

The dormitory was very comfortable, and I was sleeping on a proper bed with a mattress for the first time in my life! The food was very good, and I enjoyed studying at the seminary, as good food was also provided for the soul.

My understanding of theology took me to a higher level as I learned about sanctification, one of the seven steps of salvation. I knew I was saved, redeemed, and justified by Lord Jesus Christ, who sent the Holy Spirit (Paraclete, a person called in to aid/comforter).

I joined the seminary choir and sang with them and was asked to sing high soprano with the choir director's wife, who played the piano. My voice was trained from childhood, and I was glad to be able to sing at a high pitch, thanks to Mellial Sittie who trained my voice in middle school. At this time in my life, my heart was very glad to be in the seminary.

About a month after the classes started, one day, the school principal and his wife asked me to accompany them to the railway station. We were to meet a Dohnavur Fellowship missionary couple passing by train through Bangarapet station on their way to Madras from Bangalore. The couple, Jack and Barbara Trehane, said they had a message for me from my home in Dohnavur Fellowship. The message was that I could not be enrolled for the four-year BTh degree course. This was crushing!

The principal told them that all the first-year students, whether of a two-year diploma or four-year degree courses, have a common curriculum of studies during the first year. He said that I should be allowed to continue my studies. By then, the train conductor blew the whistle, and the express train started to move and disappeared within a minute. I stood there, dumbfounded, thinking, *Why can't I take the degree course?*

I never found out for sure. I had thought that it was perhaps due to the financial constraints of the Dohnavur Fellowship. But later, I realized they had sent four girls to Madras Teachers' College for four-year degree courses. I felt so sad and rejected again. But what could I do? I had nothing of my own. I was twenty-five years old and must obey their decisions and rules, but whenever I was able to advance in education, I was stopped. I decided I would learn all I could for the time I was given. I'm glad that I am now going to learn the law of God: jurisprudence (Latin for law and knowledge) because I believe that the Bible is the ultimate guidebook for life on earth and for all eternity!

The students in the seminary came from all over India. As the State Reorganization Act of India 1956 had organized the states along linguistic lines, all spoke in their different state languages. The only common language was English, so we communicated in English, and my spoken English improved. I could speak English with the missionaries when I went home for the Christmas holidays. I returned to the seminary in January and enjoyed college life. Then, at the end of March, the seminary closed for summer vacation, and we all went home.

In July 1971, I returned to the seminary to start second year and was glad to see all my classmates. Most of them were from Kerala State, and many had the name Thomas. The tradition/church history tells us that one of Jesus's disciples, Thomas, came to India in AD 52, landed at Malabar, Kerala, and set up a church. It is known as the Mar Thoma Church or the Syrian Christian Church in Kerala. The people who live in Kerala are known as Malayalees, and their language is Malayalam.

The professors at the seminary were Americans and also Indians. Many were from Kerala. Principal Dewey taught the New Testament, and his wife taught English. Mr. Rhinehart taught theology, and I enjoyed it very much. His wife, Evelyn, taught English and was a great piano player. Mr. and Mrs. Rice taught the senior classes. Mrs. Rice also taught church history to the second year class. Our dean was Miss Pratt, who led the evening prayers.

## Sanctification

*No longer I who live, but Christ lives in me.*

—Galatians 2:20

I had been seeking to be filled with the Holy Spirit for some time and searching for it. On February 6, 1971, something happened to me, and I was deeply sad and sorrowful but did not know what it was. I cried for the whole day and finally went to see Mrs. Rice that evening and told her what was happening to me, and she prayed with me, and I felt sanctified with joy and peace. Joy is a necessary component for your spiritual well-being (Isaiah 35:10). The Holy Spirit fills you with joy! One must continually be filled with joy in the Holy Spirit (Acts 13:52). Now I have and feel the presence of the Lord God with me all the time! Every day I get up, I thank God and ask His presence to go with me today. As Moses said to God: "If thy presence go not with me, carry us not up from here" (Exodus 33:15).

> For me to live is Christ, and to die is gain. (Philippians 1:21)
>
> The fruit of the Holy Spirit is love, joy, peace, patience…self-control. (Galatians 5:22–25)

Later, on March 29, 1972, the seminary held a graduation ceremony with a special speaker from America. I was honored to be awarded the Christian Worker Certificate during this ceremony. This was at the end of my second year. Even though I could not continue for whatever reason it may be, I was glad that I had two years of college education. At the end of the graduation service, I went to the altar and dedicated my life to serving the Lord Jesus Christ. His call came to me as in 2 Timothy 4:5, "Do the work of an evangelist, Fulfill your ministry."

> Be Thou my wisdom, and Thou my true word
> I ever with Thee, and Thou with me, Lord
> Thou my great Father, and I Thy true son
> Thou in me dwelling, and I with Thee one

## Thousands Call For Counseling

Salma at South India Biblical Seminary in Bangarapet, ready to go as a missionary out into this world.

Salma with her friend, Mary.

Salma with her classmate, Sulochana.

Salma with her roommate, Sumangala.

Salma with her student friend, Tokali, from Nagaland in North India.

Salma's class.
Left to right: Mangala, Vimala, Sugirtha, Geetha, Salma, Sulochana, Jollie.

Salma with her friend, Geetha.

Seminary students in 1972. Salma is third from right in the second row.

Principal Dewey and his wife on the right side, next to Salma.

Ladies' dining room. Salma is on the left.

Evelyn Reinhardt with the other Sunday school teachers, teaching Sunday school at VBS. Salma is in the center.

South India Biblical Seminary students at Bangarapet, 1970. Salma is in the front row, second from right.

During this time at college, I saved my pocket money for the whole year and could buy a toothbrush and toothpaste for the first time. Until then, I brushed my teeth with my finger using rice-husk ash as tooth powder. I could also buy a pair of chappals because I had been walking barefoot until then. I was twenty-seven years old and had never worn shoes until that time!

At the end of March 1972, I packed all my precious and valuable class notes, files, and clothes in my steel trunk and went home to Dohnavur. I was happy with this great commission from the Lord and shared it with the leader, Nura Sittie. I also told her that I wanted to go out to work as a missionary. Even though I was trained as a secretary, I would heed the call I received at the end of my seminary studies. "Do the work of an evangelist and fulfil your ministry" (2 Timothy 4:5).

However, she told me, "Salma dear, the missionaries are not paid. You must go out and earn money and support yourself."

She also said that I could finish the bachelor of theology degree on my own when I started earning some money. It seemed like wise advice to me from her at that time. I was comforted with a verse from Isaiah 64:4, "For since the beginning of the world men have not heard, nor perceived by the ear, neither hath the eye seen, O God, beside thee, what he hath prepared for him that waiteth for Him."

The hot summer months of April and May started, and I waited to learn if I could go to Nasik in Northern India. This was where you could study and receive a certificate in child evangelism. I was very much interested in this role. I loved working with little children. Before I left the seminary, I filled out the application form to attend that child evangelism training. This application was accepted. Sadly, the fellowship sent another person: Mani Carunia, a staff worker in the children's compound. Mani had learned to speak in English while working at the American children's home in Delhi and then returned to join as a staff member at the fellowship. She was my friend and sometimes helped me with English and spelling. So at least, I was glad she got this chance to attend the training in my place.

At the end of April, Nura Sittie told me she would send me to the Vacation Bible School, VBS, at Palayamkottai for training.

The school was run by an American lady, Miss Morgan, with the help of two Indian women, Miss Leela and Miss Packiathai, whom she had trained. Four other women came to take the same training with me, and all five of us stayed in Miss Morgan's large mansion. In June 1972, I graduated and got my VBS teacher's certificate from the Church of South India, Tirunelveli Diocese. Prema, one of the girls in my class, later became a staffer there. I went to see her the last time I was in India.

Teacher's certificate awarded to Salma
from the Church of South India.

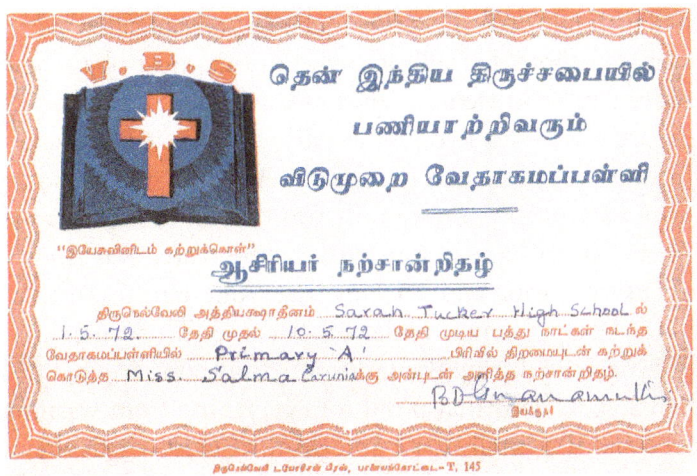

SALMA CARUNIA CARTER

# Life in the Outreach Center

In 1959, Dohnavur Fellowship set up its first outreach center to promote the gospel and help a community. This was located at Pannaivilai Village. Pramila Sittie (Olive Fuller), a Canadian missionary, was the pioneer who helped establish this center. She purchased a house and built a training center. This would then hold about ten fellowship women aged between forty and sixty. These women had little education and had never been outside the fellowship. At this center, she taught them to be self-supporting by learning to spin yarn and selling it to the weavers in about eight nearby surrounding villages.

Some also worked in the center's daycare project (*creche*). This provided childcare for the working mothers in the village when they went to work in the rice fields. They did not pay the fellowship or us for this but greatly appreciated the mission work's kindness. Every year, Pramila Sittie trained ten women to be sent to the small outposts she had established in the nearby villages and towns. There they would run the daycare projects for the children of those working women. Pramila Sittie had come to see me when I was taking VBS training in Palayamkottai. Later that year, I conducted VBS at the cathedral in Pannaivilai Village.

In July 1972, I was sent to work in the village center at Pannaivilai. It shocked me and others, for no educated person had ever been sent there. I cried for days, but one must obey the fellowship leaders, and so I went, *no questions asked*!

Before I went to live in the village, I needed to make many preparations, for the center lacked even what we considered the minimum basic facilities! Not only was there no running water, but there was also no hand pump either. The water was drawn from the well using a rope and buckets. Everyone had to go to the village pond fed by a small rivulet for bathing. This water was often muddy, especially during the monsoon and trampling by the cattle! Yes, the villagers used that pond for everything from washing their clothes to bathing their cattle and drinking, for which they would carry the water in large mud pots to use at their homes. Women needed a special dress to cover themselves when bathing in this public place. One of my friends, Tulia, made some petticoats from the torn blue saris. We would tie it under our arms to secure the petticoat when we took a dip or bath in the pool of water at the pond.

I could not take the footwear I bought proudly at the end of my Bible seminary years. No one at the village training center had shoes or chappals. I was expected to live just like the other eight sisters in our shared house. I also went back to brushing myself with burnt rice-husk ash. I had no money to buy the toothpaste. The floor of the house we lived in had to be smeared with cow-dung water every Saturday to smooth the mud and keep it in good repair. This kept the floor cool and was also believed to keep the house free of insects and germs. It took four to five hours for the water to dry, and then we spread grass mats, which served as mattresses.

I learned to spin yarn in 1959 when I had been detained from school. That experience came in handy when I joined the women at the village outreach center, as all the trainees had to learn how to spin yarn to make goods to sale. This provided income to sustain the house. Mathu Carunia and Aravinta Carunia were the fastest spinners and helped me initially. One hundred rounds of thread on the spinning wheel made one spool, and ten spools made one set, each sold for Rs. 10.

In the training center, we led a very simple life, just like the poor villagers living without luxury. Once a month, Pramila Sittie would take three of us to buy provisions from the nearest small town. On our way back, we walked six to eight miles, carrying the heavy grocery basket on our heads. It is much easier to carry the load on our heads than to carry it any other way. This is especially necessary on the narrow tracks between villages and through the jungles.

I enjoyed staying there with all the different and older Carunias (sisters) with whom I had never shared the same house at the fellowship. All of them became my friends during this time. The training ended at the end of September. After a stay of only three months, I returned with all the other trainees who had completed their year-long training. And my heart was singing:

> God is still on the throne. He never forsakes His own, though trials may press us and Burdens distress us, He never will leave us alone, His promise is true, He will not forget you.

(Scripture Union, London)

Pramila Sittie (her Tamil name) came to the bus stand to see us off. There, she handed the bus-fare money to Neelananthinie Carunia and told her to buy tickets to Dohnavur for the nine of us. Yet Neelananthinie was afraid and told me she did not know how to calculate the fare or get the change, as she had never seen so much money and asked me to help her. I agreed, bought tickets for everyone, and gave her the difference once we sat inside. She provided an account that I helped her to the fellowship office after we reached home.

Let me tell you more about how Pramila Sittie tried to educate these women—individuals who had never gone to school outside of fellowship or interacted with people from outside. She conducted classes every evening for the whole year and taught them different subjects. She also held an examination at the end of the year. Pramila Sittie purposely gave Neelananthinie the responsibility of handling the money and being the group leader as part of the practical training, as she was the oldest. However, Neela was afraid to talk to the bus conductor, for these were single women who had lived in a sheltered place all their lives and had no contact with men.

They were now well over fifty but did not know how to do the sums. But that did not mean that they didn't have any talents. Neela worked at the fellowship hospital laundry for the past thirty-four years and was very good at that job. She woke up early to fill three large cement tanks with boiling water before 7:00 a.m. Afterward, she washed the clothes and piled them up neatly folded outside of the laundry for the nurses to collect by the evening. So here we see Neela had a different talent than me, and I respect her for that.

# CHRIST IS IN ME

At the bus stand, we met the next set of trainees going to the village center. To my surprise, one of them was Nesarathina Carunia! Her face was very red from crying, as she didn't want to go, but one must obey the fellowship rules. She asked me about life in the village, and I told her it was a very simple life I enjoyed. If she gets used to it, she will be okay. It later transpired that the time was coming for Pramila Sittie to retire and return to Canada in a few years. The fellowship council decided that Nesarathina would be the one who would take over the job from Pramila Sittie at the training center. So they sent Nesarathina to learn how to do the job from Pramila Sittie.

It was not only about the retirement of Pramila Sittie but the time when the government of India asked all missionaries to return to their own countries. The fellowship had to prepare the Indian leaders to take up all the leadership positions. Things were changing at the fellowship in other ways too. Now boys were no longer being adopted by the fellowship.

Amy Carmichael seems to have written this poem, for her children, just for such an occasion:

New-born, the world swings forth at Thy command,
The falling dewdrop falls into thy hand,
God of the firmament's mysterious power,
I see Thee thread the minutes of my hours.

I see Thee guide the frail, the fading moon,
that walks alone, through empty skies at noon,
Was ever way-worn lonely traveler,
But had Thee by him, blessed Comforter?

Out of my vision swims the untracked star,
Thy counsels, too, are high and very far.
Only I know, God of the nebulae,
It is enough to hold me fast by Thee.
(Amy Carmichael)

Lamentations 3:26 says, "It is good that a man should both hope and quietly wait for the salvation of the Lord." Amen!

The Dohnavur Wheel.
This explains the work performed around the Dohnavur Fellowship.

*May the mind of Christ my Savior live in me from day to day,*
*By His love and power controlling all I do and say.*

—Kate B. Wilkinson

# CHAPTER 15

# Institution Life: Every Day New Experiences

All nine Carunias reached Dohnavur and waited for new instructions. The next day. only Neelananthini returned to her old place of work in the hospital. The rest were given a change from their previous work stations. All were in good spirits, for it is considered that one is serving the Lord by participating in the work in the fellowship around the compounds. Aravinda was assigned to work in the kitchen of what had been, till then, the small boys' compound called Vistara, where now I was given a house to stay with eight others. My former homes were now being filled with younger ladies.

All my life, I have stayed in the school compound called Round or Square, which are children's compounds for girls. This was a different experience staying at the new compound, but my best friend, Karunaileela Carunia, was already there to welcome me. So we renewed our old school friendship and were happy to stay together in the same house. Nisha Carunia was the head of the compound. About fifteen little boys aged four to six still lived in Vistara under Packiavathie Carunia's care, and Vanessa was her helper. Later, all the boys went to live in Vanacharbu, and the houses in the Vistara, which used to be the small boys' compound, were filled with retired women.

The next day, I met Nura Sittie about my next assignment. First, she told me that Pramila Sittie had sent a good report about me, then she said that she had *decided to upgrade the school and make* the Jeevalia school now teach up to eighth grade. This would be for the few girls who, for different reasons, could not go to a boarding school each year. She wanted me to be their teacher! Seven were twelve- to fourteen-year-old girls: Ponmalar, Rathnakumari, Jothibai, Jeyarani, Rajaseelie, Balamathy, and Inbarani. I knew these girls well as I had worked in their nurseries, helping their house mothers, and seen them grow up.

I remembered that day in June 1959 when Nura Sittie told me I had been expelled from the Jeevalia home school and was sent to hard labor for a year! Today, in October 1972, I stood on the same spot on the red tile floor, and Nura Sittie was telling me that I was to be a teacher in the same school from where I was expelled in 1959.

I was amazed at how things had changed from my time! Now, they did not expel them from school but kept these girls (known as the odd girls) with those too young to go to boarding schools. Thus, I, Salma, became their teacher! It was unbelievable, yet I knew I was cut out for the job. It was God's plan, and I stepped into it with great confidence as He had equipped me. Joel 2:25 says, "I will restore to you the years that the locust hath eaten."

I enjoyed teaching the eighth graders as I loved them as my own, and they are still in touch with me and remember those days of scripture classes that I taught. I had underlined certain verses in their Bibles, such as Ephesians 5:16, "Redeeming the time because the days are evil." Five of them are married and have their own families. Balamathi lived in Dubai with her husband, who has his own business. Her two children work in India: the elder daughter is a medical doctor, and the younger is a chartered accountant. Inbarani lives in Madras with her family, and I enjoyed visiting her a few years ago. She works as a nurse in a hospital, and her younger daughter is trying to become a pilot. Her eldest daughter has gone to New Zealand and works as a nurse there.

Jeyarani is married and settled in North India. R. Kumari is married and lives in Madras with her family. She works in the school for the hearing impaired. She lost her husband in 2022. Ponmalar is working in a very responsible position with a mission up in North India. She is the secretary of a charitable trust that runs a small village school with about seven hundred students. Rajaseelie offered her service in the fellowship and worked as a head cook. These are my beloved children in whose life I played a part in 1972–73. Seeing my kids doing well in their lives brings me much joy! Please see that poor orphans can be so successful and bring much joy. God be praised!

As I wrote this, I got the sad news that Balamathy, whom I taught in the eighth grade, died on September 26, 2020, of SARS novel coronavirus-2 (COVID-19). This global pandemic was first detected in Wuhan, China, in November 2019 and soon spread across the globe, with more than 35 million infected and more than a million deaths. Also, more than 300,000 infections and 7,500 deaths were reported daily.

Every morning, the school started at 8:00 a.m., and the staff assembled in the staff room at 7:45, got down on their knees, and said the *Prayer of St. Francis of Assisi* together:

> Lord, make me an instrument of your peace; where there is hatred, let me sow love; where there is injury, pardon; where there is discord, union; where there is doubt, faith; where there is despair, hope; where there is darkness, light; and where there is sadness, joy.
>
> O Divine Master, grant that I may not so much seek to be consoled, as to console; to be understood, as to understand; to be loved, as to love; for it is in giving that we receive, it is in pardoning that we are pardoned, and it is in dying that we are born to eternal life. Amen.

I started my class with an English song, as they all stood up (in India, students stand when the teacher enters the classroom), and together, we sang:

> Father, we thank thee for the night and the pleasant morning light,
> For rest, food, loving care, and all that makes a happy day.
> Help us to do the things we should, to be to others kind and good,
> All we do in work or play is to grow better in every way.

I was teaching all the subjects. We did a project in geography class to help the students learn better. We brought mud and bricks into our classroom and made a map of India on the floor. We marked each state with different colored sawdust. This way, they could learn the names of all the states, their capitals, and the languages spoken in each of them. Then we made the national flag to mark the capitol of India, New Delhi. As I write, there are 28 states in India, with 22 official languages, but 121 total spoken languages, coming from 270 mother tongues!

Then I introduced show-and-tell to the class, which they had never heard of before. They had real fun in that class and enjoyed it. In math class, I brought some real money (a little bit I had) with one or two rupees and pennies. This way, they could see the Indian currency notes and coins. In Dohnavur, we grew up not handling any money. We no longer had to learn about English money: pounds, shillings, and pence. Also, on April 1, 1957, India adopted the centigrade gram second (CGS) instead of the foot pound second (FPS) system (Fahrenheit). I would explain the common denominator and how to do the sums of banking with lending, borrowing, interest, and so forth. I was good with the tables and geometry and could teach confidently. I was pleased that all the students understood everything I taught in math class, as well as in all other subjects.

# CHRIST IS IN ME

The last period before lunch was the scripture class, and I took them outside the classroom to a quiet place near the garden. We all sat in an empty sandpit under the margosa trees, where it was cooler. We enjoyed seeing different birds resting in the shade of the trees and studying the scripture lessons together. Then we prayed together when we heard the school bell to end the class at noon for the lunch break.

The days passed quickly, and soon we were in the third quarter of the last trimester. I was busy preparing the eighth grade for their final exam, which they would take in the last week of March.

Nura Sittie called me at the end of February 1973. She asked me to sit on a chair close to her. I wondered what was happening because we always sat on the floor. She told me that the fellowship had received an application form for the post of assistant dean, Ralston Manor Hostel, in Wynberg-Allen School, Mussoorie, North India. It appears that someone in the school had read one of Amy Carmichael's books and wanted the fellowship to send a woman from the fellowship to work in their school. She also told me that all three council members: Shanthie Aruldasan, J. Christina, and Nisha Carunia, had agreed on my name for that job! Nesarathina was sent to the village center, so she was not there to ruin my chances of getting a job and advancing myself!

Then Nura Sittie asked me if I would like to go and take that job, and I immediately said yes! So she put the application form in front of me and helped me to fill it out. I was glad my long wait to hold a job outside the fellowship had finally come to an end. I was reminded of the song that Amy wrote for us, her children:

Psalms 31:15 says, "My times are in thy hand."
I am the God of the stars: They do not lose their way,
Not one do I mislay;
Their times are in My hand, they move at My command.

I am the God of the stars, Today as yesterday;
The God of thee and thine Less thine
  they are than mine
and shall mine go astray?
I am the God of the stars: lift up thine
  eyes and see
As far as mortal may
Into Eternity; and stay thy heart on Me.

## Corrie ten Boom

In the meantime, as usual, I continued to teach, waiting patiently for the good news. In the scripture class, I told my students about *the great missionary* Corrie ten Boom, whom I met when I was ten years old, studying in fifth grade.

One day in 1955, at 9:00 a.m. school prayers time, the church bell rang, and we all assembled inside the church and sat line by line. There was a long table in front of us with some objects, and next to it, there stood a white woman.

She told us that her name was Corrie ten Boom. She was born in Amsterdam, Netherlands, on April 15, 1892. She was the youngest of four children. Her father, Casper ten Boom, was a watchmaker. When Corrie was still a baby, the family moved to Haarlem, where he inherited the family watch shop. The ten Boom family were devoted Christians who dedicated their lives in service to God and their fellow men. During the Second World War, the ten Boom home became a refuge, a hiding place for those hunted by the Nazis. Sadly, they were betrayed and arrested. After ten days of imprisonment, Corrie's eighty-four-year-old father died. Corrie and her sister Betsie were transported to Ravensbruck concentration camp. Betsie died in December 1944, but Corrie was released due to a clerical error. During the next thirty-three years, Corrie traveled to sixty-four countries preaching Christ's message of forgiveness and love. I saw her when she visited my home Dohnavur Fellowship in South India. Her message was simple: "There is no pit so deep that God's love is not deeper still" and "God will give us the love to be able to forgive our enemies."

Corrie ten Boom told us students from third to seventh grade that Jesus is the light of this world, and we children must shine as a lamp for Him. As we children fixed our eyes on her and listened with rapt attention, she held a demonstration with the objects that were on the table: a flashlight, some rags, and some batteries. She put two flashlight batteries inside the empty torch, flipped the switch, and the light came on. Then she shone it at us, and we children were amazed by the flashlight's light!

We had never seen anything like this before! We only knew of the hurricane lamp we used every day after sunset. Then she opened the flashlight, took the batteries out, and replaced them with rags, then she switched it on again and turned it toward us, but there was no light this time. And thus, she demonstrated that the flashlight needs powerful batteries. Similarly, we all need God's power that forgives and cleanses us from sin. His power makes us strong in our faith in Him, and we can be a light shining for Jesus Christ, our Redeemer. At the end, we all sang, "This little light of mine, I am going let it shine. Let it shine! *Let it shine!*" Later in my life, I read her book, *The Hiding Place*.

As I think about my life in Dohnavur, I realize we were blessed in extraordinary ways. Outwardly, we were living a very simple life, but spiritually, we were richly blessed. The small village of Dohnavur is twenty-seven miles from the nearest railway station. It was 410 miles from the nearest airport. Yet we had the most distinguished people visiting to see the spectacular work done by Amy Carmichael. I remember another great man who visited Dohnavur Fellowship.

One day, when I was nine years old, at about 5:00 p.m., I was watering the blue plumbago flower garden. Suddenly, a motorcade passed down through the public road in front of our House of Prayer. Everyone started shouting that Billy Graham was passing the school compound, so we ran and waved to him. In 1953, Billy Graham came to India. He had heard of Amy Carmichael's amazing work in India. So when he had a crusade in the big city of Palayamkottai near us, he came to see the famous children's home of Dohnavur

Fellowship, established by the greatest missionary of the twentieth century, Amy Carmichael.

On that Sunday, we had a big praise meeting as we thanked the Lord for his big gift to the fellowship. It was the offering from the South India Crusade. In those days, I never dreamed that one day. I would be in America and work in one of his crusades! This occurred in 1983 at a crusade in Tallahassee, Florida. At that time, my husband was studying at the Billy Graham Center at Wheaton College. The crusade was broadcast from Florida, but I worked for the crusade by phone at Wheaton College. I was a telephone counselor and prayed with many people.

I feel sad that I did not make any effort to go and see Mr. Graham when I came to America; it is too late now since he passed away on February 21, 2018.

I now plan to visit the Billy Graham Library and want to donate my husband's PhD thesis about "How Christianity Spread in the Non-Western World." There it will be useful to people who come to read about spreading the gospel.

Salma visiting her eighth-grade students (class of 1972). In the slate gray dress is Balamathy, whose house they are in. She passed away from COVID-19 a few years ago. She left behind two children, one of whom is now a doctor, and the other a chartered accountant. Balamathy's husband, a businessman in Saudi Arabia, often tries to donate money to Dohnavur Fellowship. He also helps others who have no place to go.

Salma with Balam's church congregation in Madras.

Srinivasan, Balamathy Carunia's widower. For the past two years, he was sending a large amount of money to Dohnavur Hospital to be used for purchasing medicine. After his wife's death in 2020, he created the Balam Foundation in her name to aid Dohnavur girls in advancing their careers. God can use anyone to fulfill His purpose on this earth (like Cyrus, the king of Persia), but Srinivasan's kind offers to help the fellowship have been rejected several times, due to his different beliefs, even though his wife, Balam, stood firm as a Christian until the end, as he didn't interfere.

Difficulties afford a platform upon which God can show Himself. Without them we could never know how tender, faithful the almighty God is. How much we may and ought to trust Him.

(Hudson Taylor)

Salma counseling by phone for the Billy Graham crusade while working at Wheaton College in Illinois, USA.

## My Precious Notes Destroyed

When I returned from the Bible seminary, I was disappointed that I could not complete the four-year degree course. Remember, I told you how Nura Sittie consoled me by saying that when I got a job, I could save my earnings and return to the seminary to finish the course. This seemed to be good advice, so I took all of my notes I had spent hours and hours on researching, my valuable treasure, and bound them together. I then asked Shanthie, who worked in the school office, to keep them in a safe place. She gave me an empty shelf inside a wooden locker in the school office. I stacked all my college files there, hoping to take them with me one day when I went outside to earn money and stand on my own feet.

In March 1973, the acceptance letter for the teaching job I had applied for came, and Nura Sittie called me to her office. She told me that I had to report for duty at Wynberg-Allen School immediately, as the school had already started its first semester. I was so happy!

I started to pack my things and went to the school office to take my precious notes and found that they were not in the locker where I had placed them! I was beside myself and started to inquire from those working at the school office; they all denied seeing them. I went up and down the school compound, searching everywhere, even in the large bin where we threw our wastepapers, but I could not find my Bible seminary notes. The fear of losing my valuable notes started to creep up on me, and I was shaking but still willing to say like Job 13:15, "Though He slay me, yet will I trust Him."

Then I saw three large sacks of wastepapers ready to go and be sold to the wastepaper collectors as the school year ended. Evunithie Carunia was overseeing it, and she had filled the sacks. As we were teachers together in the home school, I knew her very well. She was kind and talented in music, and I liked her. She agreed to help me find my college files, so we went and searched everywhere; she emptied all the sacks for me and searched for my notes, but we could not find them in those sacks.

This area around the school office was not a strange place to me. For years, I had watered the lovely orange flowers that bloomed on its trellis at the west side of the office. And I have swept around the office every Saturday year after year, as I lived next to the office. Not finding my papers in the office, I went to check if someone had thrown them outside, on the premises, and there I saw a burned spot on the ground in the backyard.

I called Evunithie, showed her the black spot on the earth, and asked her why it was charred, for it seemed someone had burned something in that very spot.

No fire or burning was allowed anywhere in the fellowship premises except in the kitchens where the food is cooked. I knew something strange had happened in the backyard of the office. I was hurt and saddened because I suspected someone had burned my files in that place. I started to cry and felt helpless. Then I thought of attending the fellowship leader, Nura Sittie (Margaret Wilkinson). So I spoke to her and Shanthie, her assistant leader. I told them something had happened to my precious college files kept in the school office.

Shanthie quickly went and inquired the office staff about my files. She was told by Pingla Carunia, who assisted Nesarathina in the office, that *Nesarathina had ordered her to destroy Salma's college notes!* Pingala had burnt them all in the backyard of the school office instead of putting them into the wastepaper bin. This all happened just a day before Nesarathina left the fellowship for a year to work at the village outreach center.

I could not believe what happened every time I got a chance to go forward or advance in my life. Who can I go to and cry for such cruelties? Nura Sittie and Shanthie saw the wicked deed but were helpless. In my distress, I started to sing Psalm 91, "He who dwells in the shelter of the Most High will abide in the shadow of the Almighty. My refuge and my fortress…A thousand shall fall at thy side and ten thousand at thy right hand: but it shall not come nigh thee." I took comfort in these words from the Bible, for I always know where to run when I am in trouble. "We are afflicted in every way but not crushed, Perplexed, but not despairing Persecuted, but not forsaken, struck down, but not destroyed" (2 Corinthians 4:7–8).

*May the Word of God dwell richly in my heart from hour to hour,*
*So that all may see I triumph only through His power.*

—Kate B. Wilkinson

Sunithie, Sashi, Sarovinda Carunia, Salma's seventh grade (1966) and eighth grade students (1972).

Rathnakumari Carunia.  Ponmalar and Salma.

Lalithabai Chelladurai.  Lalithabai's son, Duke, with Mehala Carunia.

Ruhini Carunia-Emanuel, who Salma took care of in 1969. She still calls Salma to thank her for her loving care. See page 303.

Rajaseelie Carunia, one of Salma's eighth grade students, playing keyboard with contributions from Salma's book club in Texas.

Ruhini's son, Johnny, who works as an engineer in Holland, with his wife, Rita, and their daughter, Emilia.

## SALMA CARUNIA CARTER

Time for me to leave behind my blue Dohnavur uniform!

*May I run the race before me strong and brave to face the foe,
Looking only unto Jesus as I onward go.*

—Kate B. Wilkinson

Goodly my heritage, fair is my lot.

Amy Carmichael's birthday feast, December 16.

Dohnavur Fellowship House of Prayer (church building).

May the mind of Christ my Savior live in me from day to day,
By His love and pow'r controlling all I do and say.

May the Word of God dwell richly in my heart from hour to hour,
So that all may see I triumph only thro' His pow'r.

May the peace of God, my Father, rule my life in everything,
That I may be calm to comfort sick and sorrowing.

May the love of Jesus fill me as the waters fill the sea;
Him exalting, self abasing ~ this is victory.

May I run the race before me strong and brave to face the foe,
Looking only unto Jesus as I onward go.

May His beauty rest upon me as I seek the lost to win,
And may they forget the channel, seeing only Him.

~Kate B. Wilkinson

## CHRIST IS IN ME

Goodly my heritage, fair is my lot,
Wonderful Master, art Thou,
I, who am least of the things that are not,
Sing with the bird on his bough;
Sing of the love that unfathomed, untracked
Led me, will lead, evermore.
True is Thy word; not a good have I lacked,
Lord, I adore, I adore.

Oh, make my fallow-land soft with Thy showers,
Sunburnt and hard though it be,
Grant it a springing of corn and of flowers,
So let it blossom to Thee;
So let it blossom that Thou shalt forget,
Jesus, my Lord, crucified
Thorn that once wounded Thee, pain that beset,
Travail of love satisfied.

(Amy Carmichael)

Be Thou my vision, O Lord of my heart
Naught be all else to me, save that Thou art
Thou my best thought, by day or by night
Waking or sleeping, Thy presence my light

Saying goodbye to my Dohnavur family to go abroad to study.

Dr. Ponnalari Carunia seeing an outpatient in her office.

Usila (in white and red sari), Salma's good friend who passed away in December 24, 2023.

Sellarani, one of Salma's seventh grade students, who later became a member of the staff at Dohnavur Fellowship.

Nanthamani Accal, whom Salma helped at the little boys' compound. Among the boys were Kumar, Chandran, and Prathaban, whom Salma assisted with during one summer holiday.

Salma with her beloved Pakiavanie, who passed away on September 5, 2024 at age 68.

Sarovintha (left), one of Salma's seventh grade students, who is now the vice president of the Dohnavur Fellowship. To her right is the housemother Tulia, and behind them is Balarani, one of Salma's fifth grade students.

Saroruha Manjirie with her grandson.

Ubahariecottie, Salma, and Valerie.

Salma leaving by train. Farewell, Dohnavur!

## CHAPTER 16

# A Job at Last! In the Himalayas

On Saturday, the news of Salma going to work at Wynberg-Allen School, way up in the Himalayas, came out in the weekly newsletter. Now the fellowship family and everyone came to know that I would be leaving home by the end of March. My eighth-grade students were very much disturbed as I would leave them just before their annual exam. They all came to the class crying on Monday, but I encouraged them by saying that life goes on, and we all need to progress and go forward in our lives, and they, too, will soon forget me as they move in their own lives. I told them to concentrate and prepare well for the final examination. My heart ached to leave them then, but I also believed God was directing my path and my future!

These students never forgot me. For example, as I am writing this story today, April 2020, I received an email from one of the girls, Ponmalar Karuniya. And she wrote:

> My dear Sammakka, how are you? By the grace of God u r safe. I am thinking of you every day. God is with you. He will never leave u. & not forsaken u. I never forget ur love & concern. Really u lead us very kind. God will give a reward. Take care of yourself. Eat well. Love & 😋 kisses.

> Send some gifts to me. U r my best gift. That's enough for me.

12/25/2023
ponmalarkaruniya@xxxxxxx.com

I ran to Kirubai's house to tell her I finally got a job outside the fellowship. However, she had already seen it in the Saturday newsletter. *I hugged her tight, not knowing when I would see her again.* She was now sixty-five years old and frail. Rajarathinie, who also had loved me dearly, had already passed away. I saw Kirubai for the last time when I came home for the Christmas holidays in December 1973.

I went to the school office as they were packing my steel trunk. I was given five new colored saris and a matching blouse from our sewing room. Then I put in all the rest I had, which was not much. However, I had to return all my blue saris to the sewing room. These dear blue uniforms have been with me since I was two, and now the time has come to leave them behind. I now can wear color saris, not the fellowship's blue uniform. *My life was changing from living the sheltered life of Dohnavur.* Now I can earn some money for the first time in my life, which sets me free from depending on the fellowship. I am twenty-eight years old and want to be free to think and make decisions for myself!

There was lots of space inside my new trunk, and I missed packing all my seminary notes. But at that time, I came across this verse in 2 Corinthians 3:6, "You are a letter of Christ, written not by ink, but with the Spirit of the living God, not on the tablets…but of human hearts." This message brought great peace and joy to my heart. Finally, I was able to let go of my treasured seminary notes and files because the words were already written in my heart and mind by the Holy Spirit. What a great revelation, as God's Word is written on the tablet of my heart, and no one can ever destroy it!

Nura Sittie found a travel companion for me, Miruthu Carunia, another Dohnavur girl who had come home on vacation and would return to her job in New Delhi at the end of March. She said having a travel companion who knows the way to Delhi would be good, as I have never traveled to North India. Miru worked at Signal Home in Delhi, run by two American ladies, Jean and Jacky. After reaching Delhi, Jean agreed to take me to the railway station to put me on the next train that leaves New Delhi and goes to Dehradun, located in the foothills of the Himalayas. At that point, I will be met by another Dohnavur girl, Pushpa Carunia, working at the Woodstock School above the Wynberg-Allen School. She will take me to Mussoorie, my final destination, by bus.

The days passed, and the big day of my freedom, leaving home to hold a job, finally arrived. My friend Karunaileela opened the large green gate separating the compound we lived in from the outside world! We could see everything happening on the outside near our workshops. Under the big tamarind tree stood a hand-pulled cart with my new steel trunk, containing all that I possessed, my colored clothes and things from the fellowship, ready to go to the bus stand. All my friends and loved ones came to say goodbye. They all kissed me, wished me well, and prayed for travel mercies, for I am going to the other end of India, a journey that will take four long days and nights by express trains. Even though I had been waiting for this day all my life, I now felt very sad to leave my dearest mother, Grace/Kirubai.

As I waited at the green gate, suddenly, Meleela Sittie came on her tricycle. She asked why the forbidden green gate was opened wide. My friend Karu told her it was to allow Salma to go to the bus station as she now has a job outside the fellowship. Meanwhile, my travel companion, Miru, arrived with her luggage and a real leather suitcase! I dreamed of buying such a wonderful thing with my own money one day.

Finally, after *waiting eight years*, my long-awaited day to leave the fellowship had arrived. I said goodbye to my large family of nine hundred and started walking to the bus stand, empty-handed and with not even a paisa (penny) in my pocket but with a song on my lips:

Because He lives, I can face tomorrow,
Because He lives, all fear is gone,
Because I know He holds the future,
And life is worth living just because He lives.

(Bill Gaither)

Meleela Sittie came to the bus stand to see me off. My travel companion, Miru, purchased my ticket with the money the fellowship entrusted with her. One of our workers hauled my steel trunk up to the rack on top of the bus. I sat inside the bus thinking about the future. As the bus started to move, I saw Meleela Sittie waving goodbye to me.

After two hours, we reached Tirunelveli. Miru bought two tickets for the overnight journey to Madras by train. The next morning, we arrived at Egmore railway station. We went to the Madras Central Station to catch the train to New Delhi. Miru again bought two tickets, and we settled on the wooden bench meant to seat three passengers but soon had eight! Some passengers were even sitting on the floor of the compartment. The train was overcrowded. Miru said, "Welcome to the real India you will see and experience from now on."

As the train began to move, I looked out the window and saw a vast empty plateau on both sides, red dust for miles and miles, and some sand dunes. Then, to my surprise, I saw a bunch of peacocks dancing on the rocks!

I had no idea it took so long for the train to reach New Delhi. I spent hours sitting and trying to sleep upright on the hard bench. It took more than forty hours, and I finally arrived in New Delhi late in the afternoon, after a journey of two nights and one whole day!

Miru helped me to get our luggage down, and Mama Jean met us. She drove us to her children's home, Signal Home, where Miru had been helping her. After dinner, Jean took me back to the train station. While on our way, I noticed she stopped the car when the traffic lights changed to red, then drove on when it turned green. I was very surprised to see the traffic lights for the first time in my life, and I wondered who was turning the lights on and off. I couldn't see anyone switching the lights from green to amber to red! Jean hired a porter at the Delhi railway station to carry my steel trunk, then she bought the ticket and settled me on my seat.

I was very tired after traveling for those nights without much sleep, as no reserved sleeper berth was booked for my travel. At 11:00 p.m., the Dehradun express train started to leave the junction. It was so dark outside that I could not see anything. Soon, I felt that the train was steadily climbing up and blowing the whistle often. It was also becoming very cold. Then at dawn, I saw the high mountains as the sunlight danced between the boulders, and a splash of greenery appeared with very tall trees among the large rocks. Early in the morning, I reached Dehradun, the foothills of the mighty Himalayas!

The scenery was breathtaking and very beautiful, with the colors pink, red, yellow, and white rhododendrons waving in the cool mountain breeze, *welcoming me to my new world.* They were blooming all over the forest as they could be spotted atop the trees. I had never seen such rhododendron trees before in my life. Oh, it was a beautiful scene I enjoyed before the train reached the Dehradun station. When I arrived, I saw Pushpa waiting to receive me. Finally, at the foothills of the Himalayas, going higher in the mountains required a bus trip, for the train went no further.

Pushpa Carunia was an older Dohnavur Fellowship sister. I knew she was working at Woodstock School in Mussoorie on the same mountain while I would be at Wynberg-Allen School. After breakfast and coffee, we started the twenty-one-mile bus journey from Dehradun (elevation 2,140 feet) to Mussoorie (height 6,520 feet), a climb of 4,400 feet. This was the first time I had gone up a mountain, and the bus was moving slowly on a narrow winding road with several hairpin bends. The road was paved but still rough. The view from the top was breathtaking, but looking down from the window was terrifying, as the bus seemed to be traveling on the edge of a chasm! Whenever I saw another bus coming from the opposite side, my heart missed a beat. It seemed to be trying to pass by the edge where it hardly had any space to pass.

When the bus reached the stop nearest to the school, Pushpa called for the bus to stop as we had to get down and walk the rest of the way to our destination. A porter was standing to help with the luggage, and Pushpa engaged him to carry my trunk. It was fascinating to see the way he held the baggage. It was on his back, suspended by a strap wrapped around the chest and then up over his forehead. This way, he could balance climbing up and down the mountain and take the shorter but steeper hilly track rather than the long winding road. In the plains, I had seen the coolies/porters carry the luggage balanced on their heads.

It took two hours for us to walk to the Wynberg-Allen School. I was taken to a hostel called *Ralston Manor*. Susan D'eath, from England, was the dean, and I was to join her as an assistant dean. At last, I arrived at my destination after traveling for four days with little sleep and felt exhausted.

The school principal came to the hostel to welcome me. However, I felt dizzy due to the pressure change in the high mountain. I asked him if I could sit on the chair, for I was taught to stand up in the presence of the leaders, principals, and all who had authority over me. Mr. McMillan, the Australian principal, understood and allowed me to sit and then gave me a big welcome to work at their school

After a little rest, Susan Preston took me around the hostel. The British originally built it for their soldiers and now used to accommodate the Tibetan sponsored students, about fifty boys and girls (the children of Tibetans living in India after China invaded Tibet) studying at the Wynberg-Allen School.

Tall fir trees and mountains and valleys surrounded the beautiful stone building. One could see Buddhist monasteries in the distance. I often saw the monks passing through the road near our hostel, wearing their maroon-and-orange monk's uniform. I had landed at one of the most beautiful valleys in the Himalayas, as Mussoorie is also called the queen of hill stations. Susan showed me my room, which was prepared for me. Pushpa had placed a thick quilt on my bed. This warmed me up, and I rested for the remainder of the day.

Pushpa had made my bed with a lovely quilt and bedspread, as she knew I had no money to buy any bedding. It was still very cold, even though it was spring and the snow was melting on the higher peaks of the Himalayas. My immediate concern was that I had no clothes besides the seven cotton saris packed in my trunk. I needed to get some winter clothes and socks and shoes urgently.

When I opened my trunk, which the fellowship had packed, I was surprised to find my English Bible, which I had got at the Bible seminary and all the documents that I had to submit to my employer, including my high school certificates and some letters of reference. This was the first time I saw my Secondary School Leaving Certificate examination mark sheet, as all these documents were kept in the school office at the fellowship. So now, I looked at my scores and was amazed to see a higher score in math, which I never got throughout my high school exams!

Almost eight years have passed since I took my high school exam, and only now do I know how many marks I scored in each subject. Another thing that I never saw till then was the letter of appointment from Wynberg-Allen School. The fellowship, which is my home, the parent of us orphans, was the only one that can correspond with the school. The letter contained my job description and also details of my salary. I was to care for about fifty boys and girls aged five to twelve, and my job also required night duty when the occasion arose. This letter of acceptance by the school was never shown to me.

I was surprised that the fellowship told the school how much they should pay me! I was to be paid only 200 rupees per month (US $25 at that time) even though the school had offered to pay a much higher salary! The school fixed my salary at 200 rupees at the fellowship's request, out of which the school deducted Rs. 75 toward the food charges. Then, I got 125 rupees every month in my hand. I had never seen so much money and was *very happy* and thanked God for everything.

The children and I got acquainted quickly, and they all became like my own. The children in the school called me Auntie Salma. I did some child evangelism among them, for I was trained to be a child evangelist. Susan asked me to take prayer for the children in the evenings, where I taught them about fifty children's songs with lots of actions. The children enjoyed singing songs with activities along with me. Every day, I told them a Bible story, prayed with them, and tucked the little ones into their beds for the night. In the morning, K to sixth-grade students climbed the mountain to Wynberg School, and the seventh grade went to Allen school, which is on the other hill. After breakfast, they leave the hostel at 7:30 a.m. and return by 4:30 p.m. after having their afternoon tea in the school dining room.

That is where they also get their lunch (rice and curry) at noon. By then, the hostel cook has prepared their evening dinner, which they eat at 6:00 p.m. I taught them some thanksgiving songs, which they sang before their meals.

While they were away at school, I would make beds, tidy up their dorms, iron and fold the boys' uniforms, and have a few minutes to read and study.

## Incident at the Swimming Pool

During summer, Susan asked me to take all fifty boys and girls to the swimming pool at Allen school. I took them up the hill, and when we arrived at the swimming pool, I told everyone to stay in the shallow part of the pool. The other end of the pool was twelve feet deep. I did not want anyone to go into the deep end whether they could swim or not. I knew children's instincts and that young boys, in particular, are often intent on trying something adventurous.

Three older boys, Owen Carla, Sonam, and Ronald Grandy, came to me and asked whether they could dive into the deep end. I asked them whether they knew how to swim, and they said yes. I did not know them very well, for Susan looked after the boys, and I looked after the girls at the hostel. I cared for the twelve-year-old boys only once a week on Susan's day off when I managed the whole crowd.

Ronald saw how Sonam was jumping into the deep and enjoyed swimming in the deep water and came to me and asked whether he could jump. I again asked him whether he could swim, and he said, "Yes, Auntie," so I let him go. I was standing between the shallow and deep parts of the pool. Suddenly, I heard the high school boys standing at the top of the pool balcony, yelling and screaming, calling, "Auntie! Auntie!" One of them was Ronald's elder brother. I looked up, and they all pointed at a boy drowning at the deep end.

I rushed, dove deep, swam toward the boy, and tried to lift and pull him out. But he weighed a little more than me. I struggled to pull him up, then got hold of him tight and somehow tried to swim underwater toward the shallow end while the drowning boy tried to pull me down with him! I was saying my last prayer as I thought this was my last day on earth! Suddenly, I saw the boys on the balcony clapping their hands. Then I thought I might have reached the shallow part of the pool, so I tried to stand on my feet, and sure enough, I stood up with the boy.

He was frightened but glad that he was safe. What an adventure! It reminded me of when I was in the fifth grade. I had saved my classmate Jeyavallie who was drowning in the irrigation well where we learned swimming at home in Dohnavur Fellowship. I was so glad I was still alive that I hummed a song I learned from my children at Wynberg School.

> Each day I'll do a golden deed,
> By helping those who are in need;
> My life on Earth is but a span,
> And so, I'll do the best I can.
>
> Life's evening sun is sinking low,
> A few more days and I must go,
> To meet the deeds that I have done
> Where there will be no setting sun.
>
> To be a child of God each day,
> My light must shine along the way;
> I'll sing His praise while ages roll
> And strive to help some troubled soul,
>
> The only life that will endure,
> is one that's kind and good and pure,
> And so, for God I'll take my stand:
> Each day I'll lend a helping hand.
>
> (William Matthew Golding)

# CHAPTER 17

# Tibetan Children
## Linda Kalsang

I still remember some Tibetan girls' names, even after more than forty-five years, Linda Kalsang, Lindsay, Yongsoom, Yunchen, Rinsen, Nutroup, Kusang. The first three were in kindergarten, and the others in first to third grade, then fourth to fifth grades. I developed a special liking for Linda Kalsang. She had lost her father when fleeing to India from Tibet.

Her mother is a Christian who was working at the Moravian Institute somewhere on the other side of the mountains. Linda was always interested in the Bible stories and the songs I taught. She was a poor but happy child with great humility and respect for others. I never saw her fight with other children, as it sometimes occurs in a children's home or boarding school. She had only one good frock beside the school uniform, which was a gray tunic/skirt with a white blouse and a green tie with gold stripes. This is how I would dress her on special days.

Today, I wish I had the money in those days to buy her another little dress. But I was also poor and did not have much money. Hundreds of Tibetan students attended the Wynberg-Allen School, but as far as I know, only one, my dear little Linda, responded to Christianity and grew up as a Christian. Still, there could have been other Christians that I didn't know of at that time. There was a boy named Yacob Tshering in the same hostel where Susan looked after them when I was looking after the girls.

In 1993, one cold November afternoon, while I was climbing the stairs at the Library of Edinburgh University in Scotland, UK, where my husband was doing his PhD, I saw a sign that said Retired Missionaries and noticed an old lady sitting and reading in that small room, so I went inside and introduced myself to her. She said her name was Betty, and she was a retired missionary who had worked with Tibetans in Nepal!

I jumped at the chance to talk about the Tibetans. I told her that I knew a Tibetan girl, Linda Kalsang, who was in the boarding school at the Wynberg-Allen School, and that I took care of her from K to sixth grade. I also told her that Linda was the only Tibetan Christian that I knew in my time at the school. Then to my surprise, Betty showed me a wedding picture of a girl, and I asked, "Is this my little Linda Kalsang?"

I thought I recognized her right away.

The lady said, "Yes this is Linda Kalsang, now married to Jacob. Both are working as missionaries in Nepal."

Oh, how my heart jumped with *great joy* for the little girl whom I knew when I worked in the school from March 1972 to October 1978. Betty gave me her address.

I wrote a letter to update Linda since I left the school to go and study in America in October 1978. Linda wrote back to me on February 4, 1994, saying, "Dear Aunty Salma," and she gave me all the news about her family. Linda said she is working at an orphanage in Nepal along with her husband, Yacob Tshering, as a missionary, caring for twenty-six children. She was also teaching in the school as she completed her BA degree and ended the letter praising God for joining them in marriage and for their work among the Tibetans. I treasured that precious letter from my little Tibetan girl *Linda Kalsang* whom I left behind in India forty-two years ago. This is a proof that Christ's kingdom joins all of us from the four corners of this world! Amen.

I quickly settled into my new job and found joy in the ever-changing mountain climate. In summer, we enjoyed the flowers of the woodlands and the mountains. During autumn, we went down the road trampling the colorful red and yellow leaves. The autumn in the Himalayas was very bright, and the colors of the trees of the mountains were breathtaking. Hearing the children from different countries speaking several languages mingled with the cool air was joyous. Everything refreshed one's body, soul, and mind.

The monsoon rain started in September, and the great River Ganges flowed from the high mountains. November approached with its cold wind, and the time had now come for us to pack our trunks and leave the mountain before the harsh winter set in. Susan and I checked all our children's trunks as we brought them down from the loft. Every chest had a list of things checked and marked when they arrived at the school in March. Now it was our responsibility to see all of their clothes and things were packed safely back as the staff checked item by item to send them back home. Any missing items on the list had to be reported to the parents. In mid-November, the school was closed for the long winter vacation.

## Children's Parents

China annexed Tibet in 1951. There followed a large-scale suppression of the political and religious rights of the Tibetan people. The fourteenth Dalai Lama, the spiritual and temporal head of the Tibetans, escaped to India in 1959 after a failed Tibetan uprising. There were thirty-nine settlements or camps for Tibetans in India, where they were provided free education. However, most Tibetans lived in McLeod Ganj, near Dharmashala, in the Himalayas. It is also the seat of the Central Tibetan Administration or the Tibetan government in exile. In 1989, the Dalai Lama received the Nobel Peace Prize.

When the parents of the Tibetan kids came to visit or pick up their children, I would meet them. The parents were always polite and bowed with their hands in praying positions to greet me. They also do this when they say goodbye and leave their children with us.

Some wore the lama dress of a monk, which is orange or maroon. The color signified their religious positions.

The Indian children travel by school van. It takes them to the big bend in the mountain, where they get the bus to Dehradun at the foot of the mountains. Two of the school staff will escort them to New Delhi and put them on the trains to their destinations wherever they have to go home for the winter, where their parents will meet them and take them home on the other end.

The mother of my darling child, Linda, came to pick her up. It was always pleasant to meet her dear mother, who wished for a better life for Linda as she needed an education for the future and hoped she could attend high school.

My appointment to this school was due to the resignation of a British nurse, Beryl Norman. She had worked as the dean of the hostel for many years and resigned in 1972 to work at Manali hospital. Later, she adopted some Tibetan children, including Rinsen and her brother. Every year, she drove a jeep from Manali hospital to Wynberg-Allen School, a distance of more than three hundred miles, to come and pick up about eight of the Tibetan children who lived with her. Driving to the school took about three days to pick up the children.

Auntie Norman was a hardworking missionary who supported these orphan boys and girls and taught them many things as they grew up under her care. In 1994, I heard that my little girl Rinsen became a medical doctor. She started working at the same hospital in Manali, where her adoptive mother, Beryl Norman, was a nurse. Auntie Norman passed away in 1995, surrounded by many of her Tibetan children, as she was a great missionary to them.

In mid-November, the school closes for the long winter vacation and reopens at the beginning of March. It is time for me to leave the mountains and return to the fellowship located in the plains of South India. The dean, Susan, was returning to England to get married, and we both said goodbye.

Susan and Roger Preston's wedding day, 1973.

The Prestons' three children.

Today in June 2020, as I was sorting out the things that I brought with me from India on October 29, 1978, to my surprise, I found a Wynberg-Allen School voucher: Paid to Miss. Salma Carunia. Payment on a/c (air conditioning) first-class fare (train) from Tirunelveli Junction to Dehradun. Amount: 264 rupees. However, I was not sent on the air conditioned car that the school paid for. The school had booked my ticket from Dehradun to Tirunelveli and given me an advance fare for the return journey. The school policy was to pay return travel expenses for their employees, which was another blessing at that time. This was the first time in my life that I had a reserved sleeping berth on the train and could sleep on the three-day journey.

I felt so happy to come home for the first time from my job and arrived with many gifts. I had saved some of my monthly salaries to take something for my friends and the eighth-grade students, whom I left behind before their annual examination. They also came home for their Christmas vacation, and I was glad to see them now as they had become boarding school students. But mostly, I wanted to see my ailing beloved mother, Kirubai, who had looked after me since I was a baby. She loved me so dearly by showing a birth mother's love to me all those twenty-eight years.

I arrived home in the afternoon by bus, ate, and rested. I could not run to see my dear Kirubai as usual. She was no longer at her home but had been admitted to our hospital. I had to wait till the visiting hours to go to the hospital to see her. At 4:30 p.m., I went to the hospital and was shown her ward. And I went inside and hugged her and was pleased to see her again. I brought some fruits, especially apples, which were impossible to get deep down in South India. A nurse told me that Kirubai was very excited at the news of me coming home, as Kirubai's pulse rate went up. I am glad she got to see me growing up and finally to know that I got to settle down with a very good and responsible job that I enjoy, even though it took me far away from home. Every evening, I went to the hospital to spend time with her.

During my vacation time, the school sent my salary by money order to my home, and I have one receipt of a money order that they sent which I have kept till today. It is dated February 7, 1977. The amount was 332 rupees after five annual increments. Oh! What a simple and humble life I lived with little money. I used the money to buy things for my many orphan sisters and friends in the fellowship at my home.

When my vacation was over and the time came for me to return to my job at the end of February 1973, I said a final goodbye to Kirubai. We hugged each other, for I knew that I might not be able to see her again on this earth, for she had become very weak. On September 6, 1973, my beloved mother, Kirubai, passed away. I thank God for keeping her alive to see me as I settled down with a very good job and am living a life of witnessing for God.

On February 25, 1974, I took the Madras express train from Tirunelveli to Madras after saying goodbye to my Dohnavur Fellowship family. It was hard to say goodbye to my friends, for I knew I would not come home till the end of November.

A vanload of them came to the Tirunelveli Junction with my beloved sister, Dr. Ponnalari. She was now working as a medical doctor in our own fellowship hospital, seeing hundreds of patients on outpatient days except on Sundays. She did this work without any payment from the fellowship, which had paid for her education. She told me she happily serves the Lord in this fellowship mission hospital. Once all of the missionaries from England, who worked in this hospital, retired and left for their own country, Dr. Ponnalari took full responsibility for the hospital, doing surgery twice a week and whenever it was necessary. Once, my husband and I witnessed her deliver twins by cesarean section. Dr. Ponnalari was a very skillful surgeon.

I settled into my sleeper berth. At 5:00 p.m., the train started to move slowly—blowing its whistle constantly. Everyone, including Dr. Ponnalari, was waving goodbye from the platform. Slowly, they disappeared from my view, lost amid the heavy smoke in the hot Indian air.

I arrived in Madras the next morning, where my childhood friend Saroruha, who lived there with her family, met me and took me to her home. I enjoyed the good Indian food that she cooked. I rested and returned to the Madras Central Station at 6:00 p.m. to catch the express train to Delhi at 8:00 p.m. I got into my berth, for I would be on this train for two nights and a day. Saro and her family waved goodbye when the train blew its whistle, and the conductor slowly waved a green light as the train left the station.

The train was jam-packed with people. I was glad that this time, I could book a sleeping berth where I could stretch out and sleep. The school paid my travel fare. Jeevanathi met me in Delhi and took me to her home, where I enjoyed another good meal of chicken curry and rice. Jeeva, Dr. Ponnalari, and I grew up together under Lola's care as children. Jeeva lives with her family in Delhi as her husband was an Indian Army Armored Corps Officer. After some rest, they took me to the Delhi railway station to catch the Dehra Dun Express, which left at 9:00 p.m. I settled down on my berth for one more night's journey.

Jeevanathie Carunia-Alexander in 1975 with her children, Mercy (who graduated from Oxford and taught biology at Cambridge before returning to India) and David (who became a fighter pilot in the Indian army and is now retired).

Atharavu Carunia with her friend Salma in Texas, 2010.

Salma's sisters, Dr. Ponnalari and Chinnamal Carunia.

Left: Karunaileela Carunia and Salma. Salma was celebrating her last Coming Day at home, age thirty-three.
Right: Mani Carunia and Salma. These dear friends gave moral support to Salma before her voyage to America.

Pushpamanjiri and Silas's Wedding
Most of the Dohnavur girls came for the wedding.

Front row: Rachel, Nancy, daughters of Enoch;
Mercy and David Alexander.
Middle row, starting with second: Karuniapu Enoch, Muthani Carunia,
Santhaevu Carunia, Pushpa and Silas. Memani, Urani Carunia.
Back row, starting with third: Salma, Chinnamal,
Jeyabala, Punitha, Vallari Carunia, Jeevananthie.

Salma with her friend and sister, Vallari Carunia.

# CHAPTER 18

## A Very Big Responsibility

Upon my arrival at the school, I went to see the supervisor, Irene Rudling, who was in charge of all the hostels. She assigned me to a large dorm with about seventy children from K to sixth grade! The dorm had bunk beds arranged in rows from one end to the other, with some gaps in the middle for me to walk up and down to keep an eye on the children on both sides. I was overwhelmed by the big responsibility. Yet I thought, I am now twenty-nine years old and have great self-confidence. I can do this job, even though it appears to be very demanding.

All the staff reported for work a day before the school reopened, and a staff banquet was held at Allen school in the evening. I went with my supervisor Irene and the middle school principal Denise Earthy as all three of us lived on the second floor of the same building as the children's dorm. We climbed over the mountain to reach Allen High School. The school office and the principal's residence are also on that mountain. The butlers served us a delicious three-course meal which everyone, including me, enjoyed very much as one does not get that kind of rich food every day.

The next morning, the children arrived at the school with their parents. I welcomed them to my dormitory and told them to choose where they wanted to sleep on the bunk beds. I put all the K to second-grade kids in the lower bunks where they were safe from falling.

Children brought their own pillows and quilts. I made it a point to learn every child's name. I ensured that they all had six gray cotton tunics and two worsted tunics or skirts, six white long-sleeved blouses, a green with gold stripes school tie, and a dark green blazer for the winter season. This was the Wynberg-Allen School uniform for the students. The school billed those who did not bring uniforms with them. Mr. Thomas was in charge of the tailors who made their school uniforms.

I was responsible for maintaining discipline in the dormitory. The children got used to me quickly as I now actively show love and tender care in their parents' place and will take care of them throughout the school year.

The children in my dormitory were a mixed lot, mostly Indians. However, they did not all speak English as they came from different countries like England, Thailand, and Saudi Arabia and spoke in their national languages. Some were from other regions of India and spoke in their regional tongues. Also, there were a lot of Tibetan children. The first few weeks after the children arrived were hectic. Besides the day duty, I had to sit with them throughout the night to comfort many kids who had come to school for the first time and cried as they missed their parents and their homes.

One Tibetan girl, Somo, admitted to kindergarten class, wailed loudly every night. Since I could not understand the Tibetan language, I got one older Tibetan girl to help me comfort her. Somo arrived with nothing except a small bundle which she kept under her pillow. I provided Somo with old uniforms that fitted her and ensured she had adequate supplies of socks, shoes, etc. I found some steel trunks in the loft and gave one to Somo to keep her uniforms and other items she now possessed, and her smile was encouraging. Somo started communicating with me and others within a month and settled down happily. Ultimately, she became a very good student and graduated from high school.

Two girls, Arvind and Kitty, came from Hounslow, England. Kitty was five years old and always got ready early in the morning, wearing her school uniform and black shoes. These were polished by the two workers, Rose and Ganga, who came to work at 6:30. They assisted the children in getting ready for school.

I reported for work at 7:00 a.m. As soon as I opened the door, Kitty came running, took me by my left hand, and did not let it go. So I used my right hand to comb the hair of some of the girls! I understood that the child was trying to find security in the new environment. Kitty was a very sweet little child. At the end of the school year, they returned to England, leaving all their uniforms and clothes behind, with me, saying they did not need them anymore. They did not come back the next year. I knew Somo was outgrowing the tunics she had. Another Tibetan girl, Youngchen, who came to me the next year, could also use them. I always tried to ensure the poor ones had adequate supplies to start school. The supervisor also helped me with providing necessary things for them.

One more girl was added to my dorm a week after school started. Her name was Meenakshi. I gave her a place to sleep as she arrived after sunset. The next morning, I learned that she was the daughter of the king and queen of Alwar, Rajasthan. She was Princess Meenakshi. Meenakshi was very humble and never showed that she was a princess. She mingled freely with the other kids and lived the same simple dorm life as others. This was her first time away from home.

Once a week, her chaperone came to pick her up as she went home to the summer palace on weekends. It was located right below our mountain. Once, she invited me to visit her palace. So one weekend, I went with her in her car. There I saw two lions inside a fenced area! There were three huge dogs, and one came bounding toward us, and I was much afraid, but Meenakshi called "Shefan," and it calmly went to her. I was thankful!

Princess Meenakshi, from Alwar, Rajastan, at her summer palace with Auntie Salma in Mussoorie, UP, North India. She was studying at Wynberg School, where Salma was a dean.

During summer, the children have a two-week break from school. One day, during this break, Meenakshi told me she wanted the whole dormitory to come and have fun at her summer palace. So I arranged it, and off we went. We climbed up and down the mountains and finally arrived at her summer palace by following a wide winding road. The kids were served snacks and drinks by her large entourage of staff. All the children enjoyed playing around. Princess Meenakshi was under my care for the next two years as she continued fourth and fifth grades at the Wynberg-Allen School. In September 1978, she lost her father, likely due to politics. That October, I resigned from school and went to America to study. Later, I heard that she also did not continue in Wynberg-Allen School.

These are the precious children who had been trusted to my care. I was to give security while they were away from their parents for nine months. Some found the discipline and the school rules and regulations hard to obey. They all came from different backgrounds, but it was my duty to oversee the well-being and harmony of the children. One needed the wisdom to deal with those who found difficulty adjusting to the environment of boarding school. This was a different kind of boarding school from the one I attended and received my education from in South India. This school had children whose parents were wealthy and came from a high and privileged society. Some were used to more attention and getting their own way with things. I had to discipline a few of them but in a very tactful manner.

This year, I had about fifty children from third to sixth grade in my dormitory, and I spent time with them every evening. After dinner, the children climbed on their bunk beds. I taught them some songs with action, and sometimes, they even jumped from their beds, singing to their heart's content. It was a very pretty scene, and I was happy to see each child going to bed with a happy heart. I also had some story times with them where I told them stories from the Bible, which they listened to with lots of enthusiasm.

Most of the time, children from K to second grade also came to my dorm to enjoy the bedtime Bible stories and singing choruses with actions that I taught. Saturday evening was playtime, and we went around the school playing hide-and-seek. Children loved it. On Sunday evenings, they entertained me with skits based on the Bible stories which I had told them during the week, and they used their imagination. They used their counterpanes (a green bedspread, the school uniform's color) for the backdrop to make it look like a real stage.

I enjoyed spending time with my girls in the dormitory, along with taking care of them. I enjoyed looking after them and caring for their well-being. I might have shaped the lives of some children who said they wanted to be like Daniel, bravely standing among the lions in the den, protected by his God, or be like David, who killed the giant with a sling and one stone. Some children are still writing to me as they said they found me (Auntie Salma) through social media after fifty-one years!

They still remember the Christmastime they enjoyed at the dorm, singing carols and the evenings that I spent with them telling the Bible stories before they went to bed. I stayed true to my calling as a child evangelist. I was able to minister to hundreds of children in the way St. Paul says, "In season and out of season, get the gospel out and spread into the world."

Yawlark and Rhomphon were identical twins from Thailand who joined the school in third grade. I could never tell them apart and always mistook one for the other. Finally, I figured them out, for Yawlark was the one who never got into trouble! Both were very sweet kids wearing identical dresses, which made it harder for me to tell them apart. When they returned to school for fourth grade, they came to me privately and asked me for a Bible, for they wanted to read the stories that I told them in the evenings at bedtime. I told the supervisor, and she got me two Bibles, and I gave it to them. When the twins returned to school from their winter vacation, they ran to me and asked me for another Bible. They told me that they had taken it home and used to read it every night, but one day, the family removed it from under their pillows, so they do not have it anymore. The following year, I told them to leave the Bible with me when they went home so I could keep it for them.

In February 1992, I met the twins and other Thai girls, who were Harmeet, Mohinder, Varinder Kumar. They all were in my dorm at school. We stayed at my darling Harpawan Kukreja's house for three days when I stopped in Thailand with my husband on my way to China, where we worked as English teachers. I could not see Kiranjeet, but she called me and spoke to me on the phone just before I left Thailand, saying she had given birth to her first son a week before. As per the custom of the Sikh religion, she has to stay home for forty days and cannot come out. I wished her well with a lot of love.

I hope that I can go and see them again, maybe after I get to publish my story. Today in June 2020, I talked to Pawan, and she told me that everyone is going to Kiranjeet's house the next day for the dedication of her new house. I told her to please give them all my love and my new email address. The twins have now grown up and have children and grandchildren. They are still corresponding with me from Thailand. *Oh, how time flies!*

In my third year, Diane Bailey, who came from Australia, was appointed to look after the younger children, and as she worked with me, we became good friends. I still remember our days playing Scrabble in my room after we put the kids to bed. In the morning, she made poached eggs for me to go with my breakfast, which I liked.

Left and upper right: Salma exploring the Himalayas.
Lower right: Salma with Diane Bailey.

Wynberg-Allen children from all around Europe and Asia, who were under the care of Auntie Salma Carunia.

Kitty, Kajil, Yanchen, Anjilie, and Arvind, with Salma.

Harpawan Narang, Reena, Swarnalie. Kiranjit, Beena, Yshi, Prathima with Auntie Salma.

Tshering, Tarvinder, Kulvinder, Nutrup, Rinsen. Anne, Sunitha, Yangzoom, Princess Meenakshi.

Tanyavarya, Abba, Anna, Kamalajit, Zeena, Rinsen, Suchdev. Katarie, Kiran, Mohinder, Eunice, Mandeep, Harmeet. Sharon, Linda Kalsang, Reena, Amithindar.

Mandeep, Rinsen, Nutrup, Eunice.

Wynberg staff. Lower row, center: Irene Rudling, supervisor of the four hostels, and Denise Earthy, principal. Back row, wearing glasses: Ms. Thomas. Salma is in the middle of the back row.

Irene Rudling with her hockey team: Tarvinder, Pinki, Grace Thomas, Anitha, Renu Vig.

Harpawan Narang and family with Auntie Salma in Thailand

Harpawan and Harmeet with
Auntie Salma, 1991.

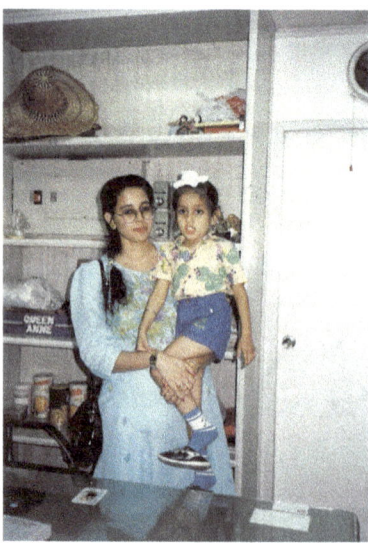

Yawlark and her husband and family in Thailand, 2016.

Rhomphon in Thailand, 2016.

Twins Yawlark and Rhomphon in Thailand, 2016.

# CHAPTER 19

# A Great Prophecy Comes through Mr. Thomas

One day in June 1975, I went inside my room after I got the children ready for school and sent them downstairs for breakfast. I spent some time reading my Bible and books for meditation, such as *Streams in the Desert* by Lettie Cowman, *Edges of His Ways* by Amy Carmichael, and so forth. Everything I read on that day pointed toward *God's sovereignty*. Psalm 93 and Hebrews 10:23 says, "Let us draw near with a sincere heart in full assurance of faith." Romans 11:29 says, "For the gifts and the calling of God are irrevocable."

God's call and choice for my life were very clear to me. Second Peter 1:10 says, "Brethren, be all the more diligent in making certain about *His calling and choosing you.*" I got down on my knees and started to pray. Then I got a clear message. God has a different plan for my life in the future, which had not yet been revealed to me!

All I knew in my heart was that I would leave this place. It will cost my job and the secure location that I now have. I loved my job, looking after these dear little children and being a child evangelist. I prayed, "Lord! Please do not take me away from here." I still struggled on my knees and finally threw up my arms and said, "Lord! Thy will be done!" And there came a great peace in my heart. I had experienced hearing God's voice before as He directly spoke to me. To hear God's voice, one must walk closely with Him. Isaiah 35:8 says, "The highway of holiness."

By now, Diane, who made my breakfast, was waiting at my door, knocking, wondering why it took me so long to come for breakfast. I told her that in my devotion, God has spoken through His words to me. He has a new plan for my life. Then, I told her maybe I will know what this new plan is when our mail comes at 2:00 p.m. Diane said, "Let us wait and see."

At 2:00 p.m., mail was delivered to my door, and I quickly opened and read them all, especially the ones that came from my home, but no revelation arrived. However, I cannot ignore that God did talk to me that very morning.

The children returned from school to change into their play clothes to go down to play in the playground until the dinner bell rang. After all of them had gone to play, Diane came and asked me to go to the town to get some vegetables, bread, and other groceries. When we left for shopping at about 5:30 p.m., she inquired if there was anything in my letters about my future. I said no. But I knew that God did speak to me in the morning! We climbed up and down the mountains to reach the town and bought groceries.

We returned to school before it got dark, for we both had to be on duty in our dorms before the children returned from dinner. We entered the playground through the school gate and saw the children playing. It was almost 6:30 p.m. Two staff members were sitting on the bench supervising the playground activity. One of them was Mr. Thomas, the school clothing manager and the storekeeper. He also ran the tuck (sweet) shop. His wife, Ammani Thomas, was in charge of the School kitchen and children's dining room. They had a daughter, Sharon, who sometimes came to my dorm to play with her classmates. Their son Steven was in Allen High School.

When Mr. Thomas saw us passing through the playground, he called out loudly to me and said, "Salma, I have to tell you a very important thing." So we walked toward the bench where he was seated. Mr. Thomas said, "Salma, last night, God told me to tell you that you must go to the Bible college/seminary."

I was dumbfounded. *Oh, mercy! Can this be?* I thought. Finally, I looked at Diane, who seemed equally surprised.

I gathered my thoughts and told Mr. Thomas that I had already attended the Bible college that his wife had participated in many years before in South India. Then Mr. Thomas said, "You must go abroad this time."

I said, "Oh, dear Mr. Thomas, I am an orphan from an orphanage without money apart from the very little I am earning now, for which I am grateful. I will not even be able to obtain a passport." Then Mr. Thomas told me he could not go to sleep last night after receiving this message from the Lord and was looking for me for the whole day to deliver *this very message*. Now that he has delivered God's message to me, he can sleep well tonight.

Then Diane and I went upstairs to discuss how God has prepared me this morning for this message about the big change that may come upon my life. Diane, from Australia, immediately suggested WEC Wycliffe Bible College in Australia. I could not fathom how I would surmount so many difficulties. But then I recalled the song I was singing in the fellowship's God's Garden in 1959 when I was detained from the home school:

> God holds the key to all unknown, and I am glad,
> If other hands should hold the key, or if He
>     trusted it to me,
> I might be sad.
> Enough this covers all my wants, and so I rest!
> For what I cannot He can see, and in His care, I
>     saved shall be,
> Forever blest.

(Joseph Parker)

That evening, Diane and I played Scrabble as usual. I wondered how this mystery would work, but I was sure only God could make it possible. Also, I know that no one else could do it for me from a human point of view!

My room was between two dormitories where about one hundred children were fast asleep. They were secure in knowing that if any of them needed help or was sick, Diane and I could immediately attend to them. Even though the path down the mountain to the school hospital was dimly lit and had other lurking dangers (bears and the Himalayan leopard can cross this path), we would take the child to the sick room, where a nurse stayed for twenty-four hours. I also went to bed with the same confidence, trusting God to care for all my problems.

The next morning after I had done all of my work at the dorm, at about 11:00 a.m., I went to the staff quarters to meet my friend Ruth Bradby, an American from Minneapolis, Minnesota, USA. She was married to a British man named Hugh Bradby. They had a son named Mark, and sometimes, Ruth asked me to babysit him when she went to the town to get things. I knocked at the door, and Ruth answered, so I went inside. When I entered her flat, I saw two magazines on the floor and picked them up. They were Time magazine and Christianity Today, from America.

*May the love of Jesus fill me as the waters fill the sea;*
*Him exalting, self-abasing—this is Victory.*

—Kate B. Wilkinson

Hugh and Ruth Bradby with their children, Mark and Kirsten.

After telling her all about Mr. Thomas's prophecy that I should go to a Bible college overseas, I told Ruth that Diane, my friend who works with me in the children's dorm, wants me to go to WEC Bible College in Australia and plans to help me financially. Then Ruth said to me, "Salma, you must try to go to Bethany Theology and Mission College in Minneapolis, Minnesota." As I was talking to her, I flipped open the first page of Christianity Today I had picked up when I entered her house. It had Bethany College's address on the first page!

*What a coincidence!* My worries about how I could ever realize such a dream crowded my mind. But suddenly, I recalled Romans 11:29, "The gifts and calling of God are irrevocable." Why is it so hard to believe? Where is the strong faith I had from my childhood? Isn't *faith* the substance of things hoped for, the evidence of things not seen? (Hebrews 11:1). I then poured out my fears to Ruth.

The Bradby family.

The Bradbys: Kirsten, Robin, Ruth, Hugh, and Mark.

"This idea of going abroad is *too much for me* to comprehend, *to America!* My English is not good enough to study in America."

I begged her to forget the idea of me going abroad. I also told her I might survive in England or Australia because the missionaries who helped raise me at the Dohnavur Fellowship have returned to their own countries. I said, "They might help me, but the idea of a girl making decisions about her future is unheard of in Dohnavur Fellowship." When I had finished, Ruth calmly looked at me and told me to think about the miracles that can happen if God wills it. She then went shopping as I remained and played with her son Mark for an hour or two.

A month later, I received an application form from WEC Bible College. I filled out the simple application form and sent it along with some letters of reference from people who could vouch for me. I got one from the pastor of the church and two from my colleagues, Diane and the headmaster of Allen High School, who were both from Australia. One of the references had to be sent from home, Dohnavur Fellowship, so I sent one reference requirement paper to my home at the fellowship.

Later, when I was home for the winter vacation, Margaret Wilkinson told me that she had sent a good report about me to the WEC. She also told me that a Dohnavur missionary Arul Sittie (Kathleen Grant), who knew me from my childhood, when I studied in kindergarten at Jeevanantha home school, had retired and settled in Australia. She was glad to hear the good news that I had applied for admission to WEC Bible College.

In the meantime, the end of the school year was approaching fast, and I was busy preparing my students for the winter vacation. At this point, I took the time and apply for a passport. There were many questions that I had to answer, and I finally filled out the eight-page application form and sent it to the passport office in New Delhi. During this time, all the children's trunks had to be brought out of the box room for a final check of the clothes and goods they had brought from home. The checklist must be completed and missing items noted, while all else is placed inside the box for their parents to see.

*May the peace of God, my Father, rule my life in everything,*
*That I may be calm to comfort sick and sorrowing.*

—Kate B. Wilkinson

It was now November 1975, and it started to get very cold. There is no heat in the dorm or classrooms, so everyone wears heavy coats. All the kids wear warm clothes, and I ensure they are cozy and covered with warm quilts in their beds at night. I received a letter from WEC Bible College in Australia in the first week of November, expecting good news. I opened it. It read that they *did not accept* me to study at their college. I was crushed and showed the letter to Diane. This was a great disappointment, but I must trust God alone, for His ways are not mine. I remembered the song based on Psalm 18:30–32:

> As for God, his way is perfect.
> It is God that girdeth me with strength and maketh my way perfect.
> As for God, His way is perfect: This is my song.
> When I called on Him, He heard me, For the battle did He gird me,
> In my weakness made me strong; This is my joyful song.
> And my way He maketh perfect: This is my song.
> Uphill, downhill, though it windeth, Often through the mist that blindeth,
> All day long and all night long; This is my joyful song.
> Perfect Leader of thy people, Thou art our Song.
> Thine the love that never faileth, Thine the power that all prevaileth;
> Lord, in Thee our hearts are strong; Thou art our joyful Song.
>
> (Amy Carmichael)

The next day, I told my friend Ruth Bradby about the disappointing news I received from WEC Bible College. Ruth again encouraged me to write to Bethany Missionary College in Minneapolis,

Minnesota, America. I thought and prayed about it and finally got the courage to write to Bethany Missionary College, asking Ruth to correct my English. She agreed, and I wrote a letter to Bethany College about my desire to enroll and study in the missionary training course. Then I took the note to her, and she typed it on the form, and we mailed it. (I still have a copy of the letter I wrote in 1975 in my files.) Then, it was time to go home for the winter holiday, and I took the long train journey back home to the Dohnavur Fellowship. I arrived in three days.

While home, during winter vacation, I went to see the leader of the fellowship about the matter of the application for my passport. I had filled out all the columns except the place (the box) for the father/guardian's signature, which was blank. Since Dohnavur Fellowship was my home and I was an orphan, I needed the signature of the guardian, which, in my case, was the Dohnavur Fellowship.

Our leadership head, Nura Sittie (Margaret Wilkinson), and the council refused to sign it. I was told they do not encourage their children to go abroad.

I thought, *If God can talk to Amy Carmichael and all the missionaries who came to serve God in Dohnavur Fellowship, then why can't I, who heard the same missionary call from the same Lord, go overseas to study to become a missionary or wherever God leads me?* Therefore, I thought their unwillingness to sign my passport papers was unfair, but I dared not ask them why, for no questions were allowed to be asked. I was helpless and had to send my application papers without their signature.

Salma with Denise Earthy, Wynberg school principal, in England.

Salma's friend and sixth grade teacher, Shanthie Gnanaolivu, standing on the terrace, against the Himalayas at Wynberg-Allen School.

Om Prakash Verma, his wife Kamal, their children, Vinod, Jyotsna, Hithender, with their wives and children.

# CHAPTER 20

# The Trials and Miracles in Making My Passport

On November 23, 1975, I turned thirty-one years old. The months passed, the winter holidays ended, and I returned to my work at school. I struggled to find anyone willing to sign my papers. But I knew that only *one* person could do it, the only one I could trust. That will be my Lord and Savior, Jesus Christ. In the fellowship orphanage, where I grew up, they taught us that God is our Father. Since I was a child, I knew there was an unseen Father we could cry to for help. Psalm 10:14 says, "Thou art the helper of the fatherless."

The year 1976 was passing quickly, but I still kept my hope in the Lord, waiting for Him to work it out. In the meantime, I received a very long application form from Bethany College America in spring. There were one hundred questions to answer, and I took it to Ruth, whose idea was to apply there in the first place. I had never seen such a long application form for anything in India! I was really intimidated by it. However, Ruth encouraged me to fill it out. But I needed to ask her about the meaning of some of the words I could not understand.

For example, there were questions concerning alcohol and drugs. I told Ruth I did not know these things. Then I asked her the meaning of alcohol and what marijuana is. She said, "Salma! If you do not know what they are, answer the question *no*, for it doesn't concern you as a person." Then I wondered why she would not tell me what they were. Later, I learned about these evils from watching TV in America. Even my American husband never explained such things, for he said, "Salma, you are clean and pure in your heart and mind, and I do not want you to know of these things which can corrupt you!" I am glad I never touched them!

At the end of the summer of 1976, I sent my application to Bethany College, Minneapolis, Minnesota, USA. Time passed, autumn gave way to winter, and it was time for the school to close for the winter vacations. I packed my things and went directly home. The girls of the Dohnavur Fellowship were not allowed to go anywhere or to visit anyone on the way back from their workplace. I had asked permission to visit South India Biblical Seminary, where I had studied. However, I received a telegram from the fellowship saying, "Come home straight away."

I hoped my acceptance letter from Bethany College would have come by now. Indeed, it had. Bethany College wanted me to join in September 1977 and sent the letter to my home address. But the fellowship sent it back to Bethany instead of redirecting it to me at Wynberg school where I was working or keeping it with them until I came home for winter vacation.

My birthday came on November 23, 1976. I turned thirty-two years old. I was at home for Christmas and standing at the portal of the New Year 1977 and trusting God. The sky rolled back its winter blanket. The spring arrived with green-colored leaves announcing new life and putting forth colorful flowers. It was also time for me to go back to my job. I left home in March but still had found no one to sign my passport application as my guardian/guarantor.

The first night of the staff's arrival was the staff banquet as the school welcomed us back. Most of the team knew about the prospect of my going to study abroad, but I had no news to give them, for everything seemed to be standing still for the past two years. Two days after that, the students arrived with their parents. I had fifty boarders in my dorm from grades 3 to 6. Most of my children knew me well. This was my fifth year, and most of my girls have been with me since they came as second graders. And as the years went by, I got to know them well and loved them as my own, for they were with me for a whole nine months each year. I was good with that age group of children, even though some did find the school discipline hard.

## Mr. Verma Offers to Help

A little girl named Jyotsna was from New Delhi and came from a well-to-do family. She joined the school in the third grade and was now in the fifth grade, so I had her in my dorm. She found the school rules and regulations hard to obey. However, my job was to maintain discipline and treat everyone the same. I tried to keep every child happy in my dorm and looked after their welfare without discriminating between the rich and the poor.

In June, the students got a two-week summer vacation. As the plains in India were extremely hot during the summer months, the parents of the Indian students usually come to the hills and take their children out for a holiday in the mountains.

Many children, particularly those from Thailand, stayed at the dormitories, so I tried to occupy them with various activities. I took them for picnics, where they took a sack lunch, and we trekked together. Sometimes, we went to the Wynberg stream to swim. Once, I took them to Skinner's farm, where the school got milk from. We also went to St. George's swimming pool, and the kids enjoyed swimming and the outdoor activities. In the evenings, I organized activities in the dormitory to ensure they enjoyed their vacation time with me at school.

*May the Word of God dwell richly in my heart from hour to hour,*
*So that all may see I triumph only through His power.*

—Kate B. Wilkinson

After the summer vacation, parents drop their children in the hostel. The next morning, someone knocked on my front door, which opened into the veranda, from where one gets a panoramic view of the River Ganges. I wondered who it could be, for all the children who come to see me knock on the door on the other side that opens into the dorm. I knew it must be an outsider.

I opened the door, and to my surprise, I saw that it was Mr. Verma, the father of Jyotsna. I thought he had come to see me regarding disciplining his daughter. However, it turned out that Mr. Verma had indeed gone to see the principal to complain about my strictness in dealing with his daughter. This was what I learned from him that changed his mind.

After hearing his complaint, the principal told him that he, the principal himself, had put his two children into my care for a few weeks when his wife had been admitted to the hospital. Every day since then, his children ask if they can return to Auntie Salma's dorm, where they were happy and had lots of fun in the evenings!

The principal told Verma that he often went around the school to observe how school was functioning. When he did this, he found I gave the children tender, loving care. He also told Mr. Verma that I was an orphan. "She grew up in an orphanage so she understands the children's need for care and attention."

Mr. Verma was a kind-hearted man. After hearing from the principal, he thought of making amends for having misunderstood me, so he asked the principal if he could help me in any way. Then the principal told Mr. Verma that "Salma is trying to go abroad for studies and was trying to get her passport. However, she could not find a person to sign as her guardian, for she was an orphan." Mr. Verma immediately decided that this was his chance to help me and told the principal that he would see if he could help. He left the principal's office at once, came down the mountain from Allen school, and knocked on my door.

When I opened the door, Mr. Verma came straight to the point and said that he wanted to help me with my passport application and that he could sign as the guarantor! Totally surprised by this offer, I told him I did not need his help and that *my God would take care of it.* This may be hard for some readers to understand. However, at that time, according to the culture and my strict upbringing, unmarried women did not talk to a man alone or accept such gifts. I then gently closed the door.

At the end of summer 1977, children packed their summer clothes and put on their green blazers for school. I ensured everyone had a coat when they went down to the playground. I ensured they had enough warm blankets and quilts to cover themselves at night for the dormitories have no heating. I bought only one winter coat from a rummage sale with the little money I had saved, and I wore it every day. I was glad I did not need any winter clothes in South India. In November, all the students went home for the winter vacation. I, too, packed my trunk and went home to the Dohnavur Fellowship.

This winter at the fellowship, I was asked to work in the fiber workshop where we make placemats, dust brooms, small boxes, etc. So I went to work from 9:00 a.m. to noon. I enjoyed working with other Carunias. Most of them were older than me and had known me since my childhood. Potamari, who once took my colored ribbon from my hair when I was fifteen years old, was now working in the fiber room. She became my friend, asked me to sit beside her, and taught me how to weave fiber baskets and placemats. Working with my sisters, who had dedicated their lives to work in the fellowship, was lots of fun. As it says in Psalms 133:2: "Behold, how good and how pleasant it is for brethren (sisters) to dwell together in unity!"

I was still waiting for a reply from Bethany College, as it has been a year since I sent my application form to them. Bethany College only required *three reference letters from a friend, a pastor, and a teacher.* My friend Ruth Bradby, the pastor of the church I was attending, sent a good report. As for the teacher, I had given the name of my history and geography teacher, Alexandra Samuel, at Nazareth High School, who was now the principal of another high school. I had visited her the year before with my English friend from the Wynberg-Allen School. When she received the communication from Bethany College, she was overwhelmed, for it came from *America.* She was afraid of what the fellowship might say about her giving a reference to me, who was once her high school student for three years. So she decided to take it to Dohnavur Fellowship. Margaret Wilkinson, the leader of the fellowship, took the reference form from her, saying she would fill it out and send it to Bethany College.

I was home on my third winter vacation since I had first sent the application form to Bethany College two years previously. The college had offered me a seat, but the Dohnavur Fellowship had sent back the letter of acceptance. Not being told of this, I was waiting for an answer from Bethany College. When I was at home, Nura Sittie (Margaret Wilkinson) told me that my high school teacher Alex Samuel had come to the fellowship with the reference form she received from America. The fellowship did not want my teacher to complete the form. They felt that the fellowship should give any reference. Therefore, they took the document from my high school teacher, filled it out, and sent it to Bethany College.

Then she told me that she did not provide a good report about me, because I came home for vacation wearing jeans! There was no consideration for the difficulty of traveling. The fact was that I traveled three long days from my place of work to my home and changed trains and buses at four locations. I found wearing jeans safer and easier for travel than wearing a six-foot-long wraparound sari. However, this didn't matter, and there was no excuse. Little did they realize that I was becoming accustomed to wearing Western clothes.

November 23, 1977, was my birthday, and I turned thirty-three years old. My name was called on the next Sunday in the House of Prayer, and they prayed for all who celebrated their coming day during that week. Mala had passed away, but Seela celebrated her Coming Day with me. See picture on page 38.

By January 1978, I was still at Dohnavur waiting for the Lord's time, *trusting the unchanging God to help my prospects.* I was reminded of Numbers 23:19, "God is not a man, that he should lie; nor the son of man, that he should repent; hath he said, and shall he not do it? Or hath he spoken, and shall he not make it good?" One morning, at 10:00 a.m., in the middle of January 1978, Vimala Sittie (Hillary Rogers) came on her bicycle and gave me an envelope. (She was the missionary overseeing the unmarried girls who came home during the holidays.)

It was unusual that the envelope was not opened, for they opened all our mail in the office. I saw the letter from Bethany College! Vimala Sittie wanted to know what the letter said, and I read it aloud for her. It stated that *Salma Carunia is accepted and enrolled at the Bethany College of Theology and Missions.* Classes would begin in September 1978. Vimala Sittie, after hearing it, had a look of disapproval on her face. She went and told Nura Sittie. Immediately, Nura Sittie came on her bicycle and gingerly congratulated me.

However, I found out later that the leadership was unhappy about this news as they did not want the fellowship children to go abroad. So they refused to sign my passport form. I believed they knew that I would not be able to go overseas without a passport. Yet my faith was not shaken, for I trusted in the supernatural higher power of my Lord and Savior, Jesus Christ. Life is a kind of pilgrimage. "In Him, we live, move and have our beings" (Acts 7:28).

I went to the calligraphy room in what used to be the printing press. It now housed the weaving room on the ground floor, and the two upper rooms were used for soft-toy making and calligraphy. Sellamma was in charge of calligraphy, and she beautifully wrote Bible texts or verses on mahogany and teak wood. I asked Sellamma to write a verse for me to take to America. She told me to select a wood plank, so I chose the black ebony wood, twelve inches long and two inches wide. The verse I chose was Malachi 3:6, "I am the Lord; I do not change." This verse is still hanging in my living room even today!

I still had a few days remaining before my vacation ended. My very dear *sister, Dr. Ponnalari Carunia,* wanted to spend time with me in the evenings when she was off duty. She came to see me every day. We talked about my plans to go to America to study at the Bible college, as she and Mani Carunia were the only ones who believed me and my dream and calling from the Lord and gave me moral support.

The people in Dohnavur Fellowship and even those in Wynberg-Allen School, where I worked, thought my case was dead. *Hopelessly dead!* But they all proved to be like the witness who, in

John 11:14, said, "Lazarus is dead!" but I continued to pray for the resurrection of my hopeless case.

I went to bed on February 21, my last day at home. I woke up with a dream fading away from my eyes. I saw hundreds of stars standing around, folding their hands and paying respect to me in the Indian way of saying "namaskar" as I stood in the middle. I shared this dream with my friend Mani Carunia. She said, "Yes, Sal, one day, when you come back from America, all of the fellowship will come to say hi to you and namaskar with their hands folded, and God will make this dream come true." I just laughed. It sounds like Joseph's dream, and I dare not share the vision with anyone except my friend Mani. She was an eyewitness when, after ten years, I came home to Dohnavur Fellowship with my husband, Ben Michael Carter. All the people in authority and the missionaries came to welcome us home. They did namaskar to us with their hands folded! Of course, this was not really for me but for my American husband. "A prophet is not without honor except in his own home town, and in his own household (home)" (Matthew 13:57).

## Thinking Day

*Though you cannot visit sister Guides in France or Finland, in Austria or Australia, in Italy or Iceland, Canada or Chile, Ghana or Guatemala, USA or UAR, you can reach out to them there in your mind. And in this unseen, spiritual way, you can give them your uplifting sympathy and friendship. Thus, do we Guides, of all kinds and of all ages and nations, go with the highest and the best towards spreading true peace and goodwill on earth.*

—*Window on My Heart* by Olave Lady
Baden-Powell with Mary Drewery

For this reason, February 22, also the birthday of Lord and Lady Baden Powell, founders of the Boy Scouts and Girl Guides, is called Thinking Day and was celebrated at Dohnavur.

The Girl Guides were all wearing the blue Guide uniform with a white blouse and having fun, for it had been declared a holiday for the students. All the other children wore the blue sleeveless dress I used to wear in my childhood, and I rejoiced as I remembered my days playing in the green meadow of the children's compound. In 1978, as I was packing my things to return to work, I remembered my school days, playing tracking signs with Margaret Wilkinson.

She made me a patrol leader at the Guide camp when I was thirteen. How time flies, and now *I am thirty-three years old with bigger dreams of studying abroad.* But no one, in my home, except Dr. Ponnalari, supported me in my goal. It seemed impossible to all of them. However, *my faith in God, whom I believed more than ever before, was with me now all the more.* I said goodbye to Dr. Ponnalari and all the others and left home as the winter holidays ended.

March 1978, Jyotsna, now in sixth grade, had adjusted well to the disciplined boarding school life. She had matured since she had been with me in the third grade. I made her a prefect (leader) in the dormitory. She made friends with Harpawan, one of her classmates. I called her Pawanji; she joined the school in second grade and came from Thailand. She did not know any English then, but now spoke fluent English. They made a good pair and are still keeping in touch with each other. Today as I write this story in July 2020, it has been forty-five long years since I left them. I called Pawan on June 28, 2020, to wish her a happy birthday. She gave me Jyotsna's new phone number while I talked to her. I still feel that they are my precious sweet little kids whom I looked after once upon a time and cared for as my own children.

In spring, beautiful white, pink, orange, and yellow rhododendrons bloomed in bunches on the top of the trees against the blue skies. Spring turned into summer, and the weather changed. From my patio, I could see the mighty River Ganges flowing from the mountains to the plains, the panoramic view unobstructed by mist or clouds. Children changed into their summer uniforms. In June, it was time for the first break of school, and the children were going out for a two-week vacation with their parents.

Mr. Verma also came to take his children out, and Jyotsna bid goodbye for the summer along with her father. Mr. Verma asked me about my passport. When I told him nothing had moved in the matter, he said he was still willing to help me.

## Making of My Passport

I had been praying hard and doing much thinking about his offer. I could not find any Christian to come forward to help me. It seemed that I needed to drop my stubbornness or even the brainwashed thoughts that I cannot accept help or anything from anyone except the Christian community. I realized God could use anyone to fulfill His Word and plans. Acknowledging this miracle that God did according to His plan took time. I realized that if God used Cyrus, the king of Persia, to fulfill his purpose, He could do that for me as well, even in that which I had been blind to.

Then I saw that this help came from my God and Redeemer, Jesus Christ. I finally accepted Mr. Verma's help and gave him my passport application form. I had filled out the document, but the father's/guardian's signature box was still blank. I prayed about it that night and felt peace in my heart, knowing it was from the Lord. However, it had taken me two years to accept the help of the man who had come to my door, offering his support. That was God's way of showing me as in the cases of Cyrus, king of Persia, and King Artaxerxes and King Ahasuerus, when He used them to fulfill His purpose concerning His own people.

A month passed, and I still heard nothing from the passport office. Then on *July 13,* God prompted me to go down to New Delhi, and the voice was very clear to me through His words during my devotion—meditation quickens into the picture of imagination as the message came from meditating the Word of God! Then, I went to the principal and asked him if I could take some time off to visit New Delhi to see about my passport. He immediately granted me leave. That evening at bedtime stories, I informed the children that

I would be gone for some time but would return. The children were upset and asked me, "When will you come back?" I told them as soon as I got my passport.

Early the next morning, I went to the bus stand to catch the bus to Dehra Dun. I was seeking confirmation from the Lord for what now looked like a rash decision, but He had prompted me yesterday. I was learning to trust my Lord only. The journey started three years ago with a message from Mr. Thomas. Everything has a process to complete, step by step.

The bus departed at 9:00 a.m., and I opened the little Bible that I carried in my pocket. I found the verse in Revelation 3:8, "Behold, I have set before thee an open door, and no man can shut it." I was reassured and knew the Lord is with me in this. First Timothy 3:9, 4:10 says because we have fixed our hope on the living God and God's promises are everlasting—they never expire.

At Dehra Dun, I took another bus to New Delhi, which was almost an eight-hour journey. During that time, I sang: Hebrews 6:19

> Will your anchor hold in the storms of life?
> When the clouds unfold their wings of strife;
> When the strong tides lift and the cables strain,
> Will your anchor drift or firm remain?
>
> Will your anchor hold in the straits of fear?
> When the breakers roar and the reef is near;
> While the surges rave and the wild winds blow,
> Shall the angry waves then your bark overflow?
>
> We have an anchor that keeps the soul
> Steadfast and sure while the billows roll;
> Fastened to the Rock, which cannot move,
> Grounded firm and deep in the Savior's love.
>
> (*Evangelistic Services*, published 1923, song 285)

I arrived in New Delhi, went to Mr. Verma's house, and told him that my God prompted me to come here, so I came. He welcomed me into the large mansion he and his brother's family shared. The message of the Lord to me was: go to New Delhi. For what purpose, I did not know on that day. It was a real mystery, but was made known to me the very next day when something unimaginable and unexpected happened.

The next day, I told Mr. Verma that a month had passed since I submitted the application form and paid the required fees, but I had still not heard anything from the passport office. He told me to be patient because the passport takes time to be issued.

The same evening, a man came to Mr. Verma's house. He was not wearing any uniform but said he was from the police station and was sent to inquire about Salma Carunia. She had applied for a passport, as she had recorded this house as the address of her guardian. *What incredible timing—unequivocal proof of the Lord's work and omniscience!*

At once, Mr. Verma sent for me, so I joined them in the living room. The policeman asked me several questions. He also wanted to see my birth certificate and the acceptance letter from Bethany College, America, which I showed him, as I had brought all the documents with me. He was satisfied and told Mr. Verma that he would file the report in the passport office in New Delhi. In the end, Mr. Verma thanked him and gave him something for his visit, along with a bottle of nice cold Coca-Cola to enjoy in the hot Indian weather.

God's purpose in telling me to go down to New Delhi immediately was revealed, for none of us knew what would happen the next day after I arrived in New Delhi except God. God knew that the police verification for the passport issue would be done on that very day, and that if I were not in that house, the police would have sent an adverse report. How marvelous to hear God's voice prompting me to go down to New Delhi at the *right time* when I will be there at the *right place* when the investigation took place. See also Psalm 25:14; Daniel 2:28; and 1 Corinthians 2:10.

I was unaware that the police report would be sent from the local police station to the special branch and then sent to the passport office. This took several days before a passport would be issued. Naively, I thought that the passport would be ready immediately and went to the passport office every other day without success. Meantime, I ran out of money and called one of my friends, Chinammal Carunia, who was working near New Delhi, and she came to my aid. Chinna spoke four languages, including Malayalam. This came in handy because she made friends with the family who lived opposite to Mr. Verma's house, as they also spoke Malayalam.

One day, they asked her about me. She told them that I was having some problems with getting my passport. Immediately the head of the house, Mr. Iyer, who was working for the Goodyear tire company in New Delhi, told her he could help me, for he had a friend working at the passport office. Chinna gave my name and other particulars to him. The next day, Mr. Iyer called his friend and asked him to find out about Salma Carunia's passport.

One day, when I returned from that office empty-handed, Mr. Verma tried to cheer me up. He caught me crying and said, "Salma, I have given you all of the help that I can, and now *it is all in your God's hand.*" In the meantime, he received a letter from his daughter Jyotsna from the school saying, "Please send Auntie Salma soon with her passport, for all the children are missing her so much." She especially mentioned the evening time, as they have to go to bed right after dinner without bedtime stories, singing, or the fun they used to have with me. To tell you the truth, I missed my children, too, and wanted to return as soon as I got my passport.

In the third week of August 1978, I got a letter from the school supervisor asking me to return by the end of the month. I told Chinna Carunia, "Let us go to the passport office again. If I do not get it today, I will return to school work." Then, Chinna and I went to the passport office again and arrived at 10:00 a.m. We went around the office and made inquiries but got no answers, so we sat on the bench and prayed, holding each other's hands. We asked our heavenly Father to sign my passport. "(God is) the helper of the fatherless" (Psalm 10:14); "I will be a Father to you" (2 Corinthians 6:18).

It was almost 4:30 p.m., and since we had a long way to go home by taxi, we decided to leave. We both went out through the front door and noticed a large crowd coming inside. It was time to deliver new passports, and people were coming to collect theirs. Suddenly, a very tall man came out of the group, asking me if I was Salma Carunia. I said, "Yes," so he told me to come to the window. Then I went and stood in the line. When my turn came, I went forward with great confidence, for I remembered what Sirappan Annachie (Mr. Philip England) had told me on my fifteenth coming day: "In quietness and confidence shall be your strength" (Isaiah 30:15).

The man asked me if I could read and write, for I saw the woman standing before me just put her thumb impression and got her passport. I told him, "Yes. I can read and write in three languages." So he told me to sign, and I wrote Salma Carunia. *Then he gave me my passport.* After many years, the Indian government denied my passport renewal, because there was no father's/guarantor's signature on the old one. Now, I am an American citizen and I hold an American passport.

No man can see, as it is not visible to human eyes, that God has signed it, for He is the Father to an orphan! It is a supernatural miracle!

*This is the Lord's doing; it is marvelous to our eyes.*

—Psalm 118:23

I could not believe I was holding this miraculous blue Indian passport in my hand and showed it to Chinna, and we returned home. Mr. Verma was delighted to see the passport in my hand, and I gave it to him to see and *thanked* him for his help. This was a supernatural miracle from the Lord Jesus Christ on whom I put my trust and belief!

Now that I had it, I thought of going to the American embassy the next day to get a visa while I was still in New Delhi. Chinna and I took a taxi and went to the American embassy. There was a very large picture of President Carter, which was mounted on the wall. Deep in my heart, I wondered if I would ever *go to America.* Then we sat as I filled out the required form to get a *visa to go to America.* I had my acceptance letter from Bethany College with me, so I was sure there would be no problem getting a visa.

At about 10:00 a.m., my name was called to come to the window. I showed my acceptance letter from Bethany College, Minneapolis, Minnesota, USA. I submitted my application, and two Americans interviewed me. One of them told me, "Ma'am, you are a single lady and cannot go to America." It was that simple. I tried to tell him that *I am a nun and have no desire to get married, for I work among the children in the school, and I love taking care of them.* However, he ended the interview and gave my papers back and closed the window.

It was true that I considered myself a nun at that time and enjoyed working among the children at the school where I was working then. I also worked many years in the orphanage where I grew up, so I considered myself a nun. Well, I took my papers and returned to where I stayed in Delhi. I waited one more day, then went to the American embassy. There I filled out the visa application again and tried to explain that I was going to study at the missionary college, which I could prove with my acceptance letter. At about 11:30 a.m., my name was called. I went to the window again, pleading my case with the documents proving my admission to Bethany College. Unfortunately, it was the same man on the other side of the window. He remembered me from the last interview and said, "We already told you that you cannot go to America because you are a single lady." He ended the interview. But I was thinking of Revelation 3:11, "Hold fast what you have so that no one takes your crown."

## CHRIST IS IN ME

In my third year at Bethany College in America, I received this letter from Rama Krishna Iyer, a high-caste Brahmin who helped me with obtaining my passport and visa in New Delhi.

---

"BHAGAT KRISHNA JI"  
( R K IYER )

D-75 Panchsheel Enclave  
New Delhi-110017  
December 15, 1980

Dear Salama Cerunia,

    I am in receipt of your letter alongwith the X-Mas(Card) greetings. It is so nice of you to remember all of us even in your busy routine living in the Island Puerto Rico. I could very well understand that you are running a very busy life as a Book Store Secretary alongwith your other Warehouse job. I could very well understand what sincerity is and your letter is a proof that where there is a will there is a way. Human beings when guided by His Mercy always gets the purity and nobility. There is no day left passed without just remembering you and the passport incidence.

    Regaarding your writing of a book, and to mention my name, in this context, you may express the circumstances which led you to me and the Grace which was showered on you using me as an instrument in overcoming the obstacles in route, for your present achievement making special mention about the obstacles in a lighter vein. You may refer me throughout the entire context as "BHAGAT KRISHNA JI" as I continue to be a Bhagat (Devotee) of the Almighty God.

    The great sentiments express throughout your letter is praiseworthy quality of gratefulness and understanding of the merciful bounty and I really relish it and want you to continue your prayers to Almighty to keep you virtuous and in good health. May His Grace be showavered ever upon you.

    A line in acknowledgement of receipt of this letter willbe appreciated.

Your Loving Brother,

(R. Krishna Iyer)  
( R K IYER )

Salma's best friend, Chinnamal Carunia.

Salma celebrating her last Coming Day at Dohnavur Fellowship at thirty-three years of age on November 29, 1977.

## CHRIST IS IN ME

As I left the American embassy and found comfort in the words of a poem written by Amy Carmichael, as I wanted to be the ambassador for Christ:

> Rock of my heart and my Fortress Tower,
> Dear are Thy thoughts to me;
> Like the unfolding of leaf and flower opening
> silently,
> And on the edge of these Thy ways,
> standing in awe as heretofore Thee do I praise.
>
> God of patience and endurance, steadfast as the
> steadfast stars, stands Thy promise, Thine
> assurance,
> Unto Thine ambassadors, I Thy God will
> strengthen thee,
> Where I am, there thou shalt be.
>
> Let us welcome all life's weather whatsoever it
> may be,
> And or singly, or together,
> Find our hearts delight in Thee, Our Redeemer,
> our Adored,
> Lover and Beloved Lord.

The next day, the neighbors asked Chinna Carunia whether I got the visa. She told them no. They told Salma that she *was single* and *could not get a visa to go to America*. Then the wife told her that we should come back when her husband returned from work in the evening. We went back at 8:00 p.m. Mr. Ramakrishna Iyer told me his wife had informed him that I did not get my visa. He then asked me to bring an aerogram. He dictated a letter, pleading my case, addressed to Washington, DC, via the India desk. I had no idea at that time that an India desk in Washington, DC, existed. Then he wrote the address on it and told me to mail it the next morning. I came home at 10:00 p.m. and sang the vesper hymn.

> Let them that love Thee be as the sun when he
> goes forth in his might,
> Till the stars of evening kindle one by one, so let
> them run in light.
> Let them that love Thee breathe heavenly air, and
> refreshed in peace, be strong,
> Till the bells of the evening, joyful and aware,
> Call them to evensong.
>
> (Amy Carmichael)

On Saturday morning, I mailed the letter to Washington, DC. Mr. Verma told me he would take me back to the school in his car. On Sunday, August 27, early morning, we left for Mussoorie. I was very happy to return to my kids, whom I had left in the middle of July. On the way back to school, as we climbed the mountains, I remembered the book I had once read in my twenties, *Hind's Feet on High Places*, a novel by Hannah Hurnard and, feeling happy, began to hum a song

> As for God, His way is perfect. This is my
> song.
> When I called on Him, He heard me,
> For the battle did He gird me, in my weakness
> made me strong. This is my joyful song.
> And my way He maketh perfect, this is my song.
> Uphill, downhill, though it windeth,
> Often through a mist that blindeth—all day long
> and all night long. This is my joyful song.
> Perfect Leader of Thy people, Thou art our Song,
> Thine the love that never faileth,
> Thine the power that all prevaileth, Lord in
> Thee our hearts are strong. Thou art our joyful
> song.
>
> (Amy Carmichael)

We arrived at the school late afternoon, and I went to the supervisor's office to report to work. My darling Pawanji saw me first, came running, and hugged me, saying, "All the students missed you very much, and we are glad you are back." The news of my arrival went around the school like wildfire: Auntie Salma was back, and all the kids playing at the playground came running upstairs to Supervisor Rudling's office. It was a great welcome back as a hundred stood around me shouting, "Auntie Salma is back." Then they asked me, "Auntie, are you going to stay or go again?" I told them that I would tell them everything during story time that evening, and they all were very glad and told each other that Auntie was back.

My heart was glad to see the reaction of these children and the warm welcome I received at the entrance of my dormitory. They asked, "Are we going to have bedtime stories this evening?" I said yes, we will, and they all shouted with happiness, as they had to go to bed without bedtime stories for over a month. This tore my heart to see how much they had missed me, and I wondered what would happen *if* I were to get my visa to study in America.

Now I forgot to tell you that while I was in New Delhi, I appeared for an English proficiency exam called TOEFL (Test of English as Foreign Language), which is compulsory for studying abroad. It was held in a large hall, and the question paper was in two parts. The first part of the question paper had *one hundred questions*. I was surprised to see a very different kind of exam question paper. They were multiple-choice questions where you chose one answer from several and tick-mark the appropriate box. This was very easy compared to our Indian examination, where we wrote responses in paragraphs.

After an hour, the examiner gave the Part II question paper, which asked the student to write an *essay*. There were two topics, and one had to choose one. I decided, "Write about your train journey and explain the difference you noticed between North and South India." I could do this well, for I had traveled from north to south every year for the past five years. We were given one hour to complete the essay. When I returned from the exam hall, I thought I might have done well, but *one never knows what the result will be*. To pass the exam, one must score 70/100. Finally, my result came in the middle of September, and I scored 75 /100. I heaved a sigh of relief for having cleared one more hurdle.

I was supposed to join Bethany's first-year class of 1978 in September, but it was already October, and I still did not have a visa for travel. In November, the Wynberg-Allen School would close for the winter holidays. I would go down south to my Dohnavur home, far from the American embassy in New Delhi. This would effectively end my chance of getting a visa that year. Yet Isaiah 64:4 gave me courage, and the song by Amy Carmichael kept my hope alive.

Hal and Helen Strand from Bethany College worked with Washington, DC, to help Salma obtain her student visa.

Salma at age thirty-three, waiting to receive her visa to study abroad.

The Glory of the Lord

Thy ways by quiet waters and pleasant pasture land,
Lead on across the levels of tawny wastes of sand,
Through perilous mountain passes, in beating wind and rain,
Through valleys set with fountains, and on and on again
And I sing, yea, I sing in the ways of the Lord that Great is the Glory of the Lord.

# CHRIST IS IN ME

How often when outwearied, my force and courage spent,
I apprehend a Presence beloved, immanent;
Then colors wake about me, and living waters flow
The world moves on to music, the night is all aglow;
And I sing, yea, I sing in the ways of the Lord
that Great is the Glory of the Lord.

No mortal ear has heard it, No mortal eye perceived,
No swift imagination has ever yet conceived
How singular the beauty, How bountiful the Grace
Prepared for him who presses to Thy fair dwelling-place;
And I sing, yea, I sing in the ways of the Lord
that Great is the glory of the Lord.

(Amy Carmichael)

Salma at age thirty-three, getting ready to go and study abroad in America.

# CHAPTER 21

# Another Revelation: God's Intervention

On October 3, 1978, while everyone was sleeping, I heard someone call my name, Salma, loudly at about 2:00 a.m. Immediately, I woke up and went to the children's dormitory to check if any child was sick and had called for help. All of them were sleeping peacefully, so I went to the next dorm to check on the other fifty-five students. However, everything looked so quiet, and all the children were sound asleep. I checked bed by bed, as the night-lights shone above them, and I ensured all was well with my girls.

When this was finished, I returned to my room, closed the door, and eventually went to sleep. Suddenly, I awoke, very puzzled. It was as if a child had called me, but they would call *Auntie Salma,* and this voice called out, "Salma." Now I knew who called me as I knelt beside my bed and asked God, "Lord, did you call me?" Then I asked the Lord whether he had called to tell me that I was getting my visa. I ended this prayer with "Thy will be done!" When I finally went back to sleep, I dreamed that I got my visa and was showing it around to everyone in the school.

The next morning, I woke up at 6:00 a.m. I was out of my bed, light as a butterfly. Yes, this dream is the confirmation from God, who woke me up at 2:00 a.m. in the early morning *calling me by my name, Salma.* Only I knew deep in my heart that the dream was from the Lord revealing his secret. I knelt near my bed as it says in Psalm 95:6, "Let us bow down and kneel before the Lord our Maker for He is our God," and thanked the Lord for the confirmation through my dream on October 3, 1978.

I went to work at 7:00 a.m., woke the children up, and got them ready for school. Once they left the dorm and went downstairs for breakfast, I went to see Ammani Thomas. There I met Mr. Thomas, who had told me three years ago that he got a message from the Lord to say that I must go abroad to study at the Bible college. When he saw me, he started to tell me how much he was disappointed that I could not go abroad to study. Then I told him that God had told me this morning that my visa was on its way. Immediately, his wife said, "Oh! This Salma has a lot of faith and hope in the Lord." She then invited me to the South Indian breakfast that she had prepared.

The day went by quickly, and all the teachers gathered in the staff room at 3:00 p.m. for the afternoon tea. I went to have tea with them. While I was there for tea time, someone asked me about my visa prospect and said they were sad I did not get it. Then I asked myself whether I should tell them what had happened this morning. Yes, I can, for surely, I knew my Lord's voice. Then I told them the Lord had told me this morning that my visa was on its way! They all were wondering what does that mean and looked at me. Right then, the mail was delivered to the staff room. Everyone's eyes were on me when I got a white envelope with an American stamp! Suddenly, all shouted, "Open it! Open it!" I had just told them that God had told me this morning that my visa was coming today!

I then said to them that I had to pray over it, as I needed peace to accept whatever was written in the letter. Knowing this would be the final decision of the visa office, I prayed and opened it as all twenty teachers' eyes were on me as I read it quietly. Then I read it loudly at their request; the letter was from Washington, DC. The letter read, "Your request for the grant of a student visa has been approved." They were amazed by what they witnessed as a miracle of God had been performed right before their eyes. "Faith is the assurance of things hoped for, the evidence of things not seen" (Hebrews 12:1).

*This is the Lord's doing; it is marvelous to our eyes.*

—Psalm 118:23

That evening, I went to the principal to get permission to go down to New Delhi and showed him the letter from America. He immediately permitted me to go. I told my children I would be gone for two to three days and would be back soon, for I knew it would not take long to return with a visa. As I went down to Delhi from the Himalayas, watching the autumn leaves setting the forest and hills and mountains on fire with their glowing red color, I sang in my heart:

> O, the splendor of God's Will, Clear shining mystery, I worship and am still hushed by the thoughts of Thee,
> Thy great and noble ways lowland and mountain know; Fair flower bells chime their praise,
> And to Thee, the waters flow.
> O will most lovable, young budding trees aflame, And all things beautiful Illuminate Thy Name,
> Far hast Thou passed my prayer, Good hast Thou been to me;
> Thy lover everywhere, Blessed Will, make me to be.

(Amy Carmichael)

Early the next morning, I took the letter that I received from the Indian embassy in Washington, DC, with great confidence to the American embassy in New Delhi. I quickly submitted the application form along with the visa fees. I was told to wait there while this was reviewed, so I sat and patiently waited. When my turn came, I went to the window. As it happened, it was the same man who had twice rejected my visa applications earlier. I showed him the letter

I had received from Washington, DC, but he was still unwilling to grant the visa. I tried to convince him, but he did not listen. Hearing the commotion, another official came to the window and saw my letter. He then told the other man they could not deny the visa because they had an order from Washington, DC, to issue her student visa. He then politely asked me to wait in the lobby.

I sat for many hours, wondering what was going on. At 5:00 p.m., my name was called, and I went to the window. An Indian man at the counter pushed my passport through the gap without saying anything. I opened it and saw the American visa with its red, white, and blue seal issued by the Embassy of the United States of America, New Delhi. It was an F-1 m*ultiple entry student visa* issued in September 1978 and valid till June 30, 1982.

Before sunset, I reached Mr. Verma's house in the Panchsheel enclave, where I was staying. Everyone rejoiced when I showed them the student visa in my passport. I had a delicious North Indian dinner with the Verma family that I enjoyed. I went to my room, prayed, and fell asleep with a grateful heart.

Mr. Verma's daughter, Jyotsna, and her husband, Ashwani Sharma (CA by profession), with their son, Jatin Sharma (MB., working with JLL), and daughter, Garina (interior designer).

Left: Jyotsna Sharma and her mother, Kamal.
Center: Jagdish and Shiv Bhaya.
Right: Ashwani Sharma and Vinod Verma.

The next morning, Mr. Verma took me to the Wynberg-Allen School in his car. Since three of his children were studying in the same school, he was glad for the opportunity to see them, and he took some food and edibles for them. We arrived at the school by 5:00 p.m., and Mr. Verma enjoyed seeing his three children who lived in three different dorms.

I was excited with joy unspeakable. After all the trials and troubles that I faced over the last three years, the trips to Delhi, and the fears that getting it was next to impossible, now having my passport and visa in my hand filled me with joy and relief! I was glad I kept my *faith* in the living God and the *hope* on my Lord and Savior, Jesus Christ. This was a time of great witness, which I could show to those whom I lived among. Both Christians and non-Christians could now see this powerful miracle through the God I believed in, Jesus Christ, our Lord and Savior!

I told the school administration I would like to leave on October 15, and they agreed to let me go. Supervisor Irene said the school would not hire any staff in my place as the school would be closed for winter vacations in November before it began to snow. She wanted me to check the students' boxes and prepare them to go home. I wrapped up all my duties and submitted the reports to Supervisor Irene. She reassured me that she would take care of my children, assisted by the other staff, once I had left.

I packed my things in one suitcase, a last-minute gift from a dear friend, for I only possessed a steel trunk that I could not take to America. I still did not have winter clothes but just one coat that I packed and my saris. I knew I was going to a cold country in midwinter, but I had no idea how cold that place would be. I had never seen snow in my life!

On October 14, I spent the last bedtime story time with my children; some could not sing songs, for they were sad and crying at my departure. Afterward, I kissed them all good night, and they went to bed. After about half an hour, I heard a knock on my door and opened it. There stood two sixth-grade girls crying and asking me if they could spend the night in my room.

The hostel rules did not permit this, but these two students, Harpawan and Jyotsna, had been with me for the past five years. They had gotten attached to me and wanted to be with me for it was my last night in the school dorm. In the end, I gave it much thought and told them it would be okay. They quickly brought their mattress, still crying, and finally slept beside my bed in my room. I did not know what to think but felt I could break the rule on this special occasion. I had come to care so much for these children over the last six years and was quietly crying because I would soon have to leave them too.

In 2020, I wished Harpawan, who was in Thailand, a happy birthday by phone. She told me she would never forget the night I let her and Jyotsna sleep in my room. This was the last night that they could be with Auntie Salma at the Wynberg School. It made me happy that it gave them a lot of comfort as I was leaving them for good the very next day!

Some students have found me through social media after many years and occasionally communicate with me. As I write this, I have found a letter from Jyotsna, saying she was happily married to Mr. Sharma, a chartered accountant. This letter was written twenty years ago that I have kept and treasured, for they were my children forty-two years ago. At the end of the letter, she said, "Auntie, I want you to pray to God for me," I am sure she remembered her days in the evening prayers and Bible story time at the dorm in Wynberg-Allen School.

Mr. Verma's daughter, Jyotsna Verma (in pink), took Auntie Salma and her husband Mike, visiting the India gate in New Delhi. Later, they went to see the Parliamentary Building in New Delhi, 1991.

Jyotsna with her husband, Sharma, and their children.

CHAPTER 22

# At Last! A Visa to Study Abroad

*On October 15, 1978,* at 7:00 a.m., I got my students up and ready for school and sent them downstairs for breakfast, for I had to leave the school at 8:30 a.m. to catch the bus to New Delhi. To my surprise, Mr. Thomas came out and said, "Salma, I am going with you to Delhi." I was happy to have company. All the children, two hundred boys and girls, came rushing out from the dining room to walk me to the school gate. They sang, "I am not alone for my Jesus with me, with me wherever I go," the song I taught them. Then they sang another one and continued singing until we reached the school gate, which was a grand sendoff to me. Then I turned around, said goodbye to the children, and saw many were crying; it was heartbreaking and hard to leave them behind. However, I walked resolutely out of the gate to where God was leading me toward an adventurous future.

Mr. Thomas and I arrived at the bus stand and got on the bus going down to Dehra Dun. When the bus started to leave the bus stand, I took out the little New Testament from my pocket (I had no purse, for I could not afford such luxury) and opened it to read.

The impossible has become reality!

The verse in front of me was amazing and very appropriate. Matthew 28:20 says, "Lo I am with you always, even unto the end of the world." Amen! As God had confirmed, this plan of my study abroad is from the Lord. Yes, going to America from India seemed to be the end of the world, but my heart leaped with joy. Such great confidence came into my heart through this great promise that God gave me at that very moment.

I said goodbye to the lovely Himalayan Mountains as we descended. I have lived on these mountains for the past six years and was sad to leave them behind. Then I remembered the command I received from God when I graduated from the Bible seminary in *March 1972*. "Do the work of an evangelist, fulfill your ministry" (2 Timothy 4:2).

On my way down to New Delhi, I was thinking of my friends, Hindu, Muslim, Buddhist, and nonbelievers, and wondering who would tell them about the Savior of this world. These are my brothers and sisters with whom I lived in the same country, for it says in Hebrews 2:3–4, "How shall we escape if we neglect so great a salvation? After it was spoken through the Lord, it was confirmed to us by those who heard, God also bearing witness with them, both by signs and wonders and by various miracles and gifts of the Holy Spirit according to His own will." See also Psalm 90:10, "The days of our years are three score on this earth soon will be cut off, and we fly away!"

When we arrived in New Delhi, Mr. Thomas surprised me with a lovely South Indian lunch that his wife had packed for us. He was glad that his prophecy was now coming true. God, our Lord, worked a miracle after miracle when it seemed hard and impossible to human eyes to pursue this dream. We both thanked the Lord, who gave us the victory through Christ, our Lord and Savior. Job 19:25 says, "My Redeemer lives!" And I remember the text on the plaque that I packed in my suitcase, "I am the Lord, and I do not change" (Malachi 3:6), and was comforted by knowing the same *unchanging God is with me.* Then we bid goodbye to each other as he went about the school business, and I went to the house of Mr. Verma, who had promised to drop me at the airport.

> *May His beauty rest upon me as I seek the lost to win,*
> *And may they forget the channel, seeing only Him.*
>
> —Kete B. Wilkinson

# CHRIST IS IN ME

However, my problems were far from over. When I went the next day to book my flight ticket, I found that the cost of the cheapest ticket to New York via Rome, by Alitalia, was 6,303 rupees. All I had was 5,000 rupees, my provident fund the school paid me. I had no extra money except last month's salary, which I used for local travel. Now I need another thousand rupees, which will take another year or two of work, but I have left my job already!

I returned to Mr. Verma's house and told him. He then telephoned the travel agent. After negotiating the price, he paid the shortfall and purchased the ticket from New Delhi to Minneapolis.

In February 1991, I had the privilege to go and visit Mr. Verma, along with my husband, Dr. Ben Carter, as we passed through New Delhi. I had told my husband how Mr. Verma had helped me in 1976–78 during the troubled times when I was trying to get my passport. We stayed at their house, a large mansion, for two days. I noticed the large cross hanging in their living room and asked Mr. Verma about it, and he said that his daughter Jyotsna learned from Auntie Salma about Jesus Christ. Hence, he bought it and hung it on the wall, which is very unusual because his faith does not allow Christian displays.

I wondered whether he also started to believe after he eyewitnessed the great miracle that happened to me through Jesus Christ, the God in whom I believed, while I was under his roof. He also told me that his daughter wanted to put up a Christmas tree during that time of year. In this way, she could remember the days the children celebrated Christmas with Auntie Salma at Wynberg School. Ecclesiastes 11:1 says, "Cast your bread upon the waters: for thou shalt find it after many days."

I also hear from the girls from Thailand, who say they still remember Christmastime. It was a happy time for them to be in my dorm, as I decorated the dorm with stars made with tinsel and colored lights as we celebrated the Christmas pageant and invited the principal and all the staff. These are happy memories for me, too, that I took with me as I went across the ocean.

While I was writing this story, I recalled all the help Mr. Verma had given me, from signing my passport form as the guardian to paying for the ticket to make my flight to America in 1978 possible.

I wanted to thank him one more time today. I called his daughter Jyotsna today, July 26, 2020. She informed me sadly that Mr. Verma, her father, had passed away at the beginning of the month. I was saddened by the news and grateful for his help forty-two years ago. However, his daughter said she was happy to hear my voice and gave me all the family news. She also said, "Auntie Salma, you must come and see us sometimes," and the invitation stands. I hope to say goodbye to all my loved ones and family before it gets too late.

Mr. Om Prakash Verma with his family,
along with his brother's family.
With all my heart, I give many thanks again to
the Verma family for all their help.

*Since we have so great a cloud of witness surrounding us…let us run with patience (endurance) the race that is set before us… looking only unto Jesus, the Author and Finisher of our faith.*

—Hebrews 12:1–2

*May I run the race before me strong and brave to face the foe, Looking only unto Jesus as I onward go.*

—Kate B. Wilkinson

*The evidence of the indwelling God (I John 4:15) ... is the fundamental ground for our Faith and Victory. (I John 5:4)*

Salma Carunia with Ted Hegre, the president of Bethany Missionary College, and his wife Lucille.

# CHAPTER 23

## Arriving in America with Only One Dollar Left!

I sent a cable to the college informing of my flight details, and on October 21, 1978, I went to the airport in Delhi. I changed the remaining Indian rupees into American dollars, got twelve dollars, and went for check-in but found that my plane was indefinitely delayed. I worried about the extra money it may cost me. However, they announced that Alitalia passengers would be accommodated on a Pan American flight to New York via London. I had no time to inform the college about the change in my flight schedule. When I entered the security gate, the man who stamped my passport asked me whether I was going alone (Hindi Alag). I feared he might stop me, so I rushed into the terminal, where everyone awaited boarding their plane. Then when the time came to board the plane, I went inside and sat on my seat and could not believe that this big object (a house-like place where one spent hours) could lift up and fly. I started to sing:

> What room is there for troubled fear? I know my
>     Lord, and He is near;
> And He will light my candle, so that I may see
>     the way to go-

> There need be no bewilderment to one who goes
>     where he is sent;
> The trackless plain by night and day is set with
>     signs, less he should stray-
> O Love, O Light, I sing to Thee and in my heart
>     make melody.
>
> (Amy Carmichael)

The Pan Am flight stopped for fuel in Tehran, Frankfurt, and London. I went to a phone booth in London and talked to Evu Sittie (Evelyn Bowden). She then worked as the secretary at the Dohnavur Fellowship, Wimbledon office. This was the very Evu Sittie, who was my English teacher from fifth to seventh grade and knew me very well. I wondered what she would think now, for this little (naughty as they labeled me) Salma, who used to be punished often and sat at the detention table for many hours. She was indeed surprised to hear from me. We had a very nice talk, remembering my childhood years. In 1970, Evu Sittie went to our Wimbledon office in London from Australia to work as the Dohnavur Fellowship secretary from 1970 to 1980. She passed away in July 1996. The captain of the plane announced that the aircraft was going to fly over the vast Atlantic Ocean, and I started to sing again:

> My path may cross the lonely sea, but that need
>     never frighten me;
> Or rivers full to the very brim, but they are open
>     ways to Him;
>
> Lord, grant to me a quiet mind, that trusting
>     Thee for Thou art kind,
> I may go on without fear, for Thou my Lord art
>     always near;

> O Love, O light, I sing to Thee and in my heart make melody.
>
> (Amy Carmichael)

Once the plane left Heathrow Airport, London, they served coffee, which tasted very bitter. I missed the Indian jaggery, the sweetener we got from the palmyra palm tree. I asked the steward four times for more milk and sweetener. The fifth time, she told me, "Ma'am, this is American coffee." I got the message that they drink very strong black coffee that I do not like, even today, because it is too strong for me as I do not need or crave that kind of caffeine. At almost eighty, my mind is sharp and very alert all day long without it.

When I arrived in New York, I visited the immigration officer sitting inside a glass booth. I was very surprised to see a great big man with a uniform. He looked so dignified that I was afraid, and my hand shook as I gave him my passport. He stamped it, smiled at me, and said loudly, "Welcome to America," and returned my passport. God was with me every step of the way, and now I am in America and am happy and grateful to the Lord who led me through fire and high waters!

Then I went to pick up my luggage because I had to catch the next plane to Minnesota. I asked people where I should go to catch the next plane and could not find anyone speaking in English. Everyone was saying something in Spanish, Italian, or other languages. I was very disappointed because I thought everyone in the West spoke English, and I was coming to Bethany to study mission work in English only.

Since I was put on a Pan Am flight at the last minute, the person who was to meet me at the Alitalia terminal sent a message from New York to Bethany College Minneapolis, saying I did not arrive on the Alitalia flight. So those from Bethany Missionary College, who were to meet me at St. Paul Minneapolis Airport, received the message and returned to the college, thinking I was still in India!

Somehow, I managed to find my connecting flight and arrived in Minneapolis at 11:30 p.m., and no one was at the airport to meet me. I saw that everyone was lining up for a taxi, and I, too, lined up with them, dragging my suitcase behind me, for there were no wheels on suitcases in those days. I was amazed to see how orderly everything was in America. The roads were supersmooth for travel. It looked like heaven on earth to me!

Eventually, my turn in line came, and I told the taxi driver to take me to Bethany College. Now oddly, I could always hear someone talking when I was in the taxi. I thought it was the taximan talking to someone, but later, I found that it was his car radio. I was from a very primitive part of South India and lived a very protected life in an orphanage for many years. These normal things in the outside world, like a radio in a car, would shock me.

When I reached the college, it was midnight, and we met a watchman on duty on his golf cart doing his rounds on the campus. It was a Saturday night, and his name was Jay, a student, for the students took turns as night guards. At first, Jay told the taxi driver that the gates were closed, and he could not enter. Then the taximan told him he had brought someone who said she was a student at this school. Jay still did not open the gate, so I spoke to Jay, and he asked, "Are you Salma Carunia from India?"

I said, "Yes!"

Then he told me to get out of the taxi immediately, as the whole school awaited my arrival!

At this point, the taxi driver asked me to pay eleven dollars, so I carefully gave him that money. After the taxi driver had gone, *I raised my hands toward heaven* and said, "Lord! Here is one dollar left for me to live the rest of my life, where you have brought me to, according to your will and divine guidance. Take it and use it for Thy glory!"

Jay carried my suitcase to the school building. He also told me there was a group who went to meet me at the airport, but they got a message from New York that I was not on the Alitalia flight, so they returned. I said God brought me safely, and I landed here in person after two long days of journey and many hours of flying.

*I am the Lord; I do not change.*

—Malachi 3:6

On October 21, 1978, midnight, I arrived at my destination, the Bethany College of Mission and Theology in Minneapolis, Minnesota, USA. It seemed like an unrealistic dream, but I knew and was sure that this plan for my life was from God. Hallelujah!

The next day was Sunday, October 22, 1978, and I went to Bethany Church with the other students. Pastor Hegre, president of Bethany College, came to the pulpit to give the Sunday message. I did not recognize him, for it was years ago that I had seen him when he had come to God's Garden in Dohnavur fellowship with John Risk, the fellowship leader. I was fifteen years old and working there when I was detained from middle school in *1959*. To my surprise, he said today's text is from Malachi 3:6, "I am the Lord, I do not change." *Wow!*

This is the same text carved on a wooden plaque I brought from home. This choice of text by Pastor Hegre confirmed that the same unchanging God, the Lord Jesus Christ, who was with me in India, is also with me here in the faraway land of America. My faith grew more and more in the Lord Jesus, my Redeemer. He had brought me to this place to prepare me to be his witness in the future by studying his Word in Bethany School of Mission and Theology. The universe is divided into four faculties: art, law, medicine, and theology. I now have a chance to study theology (the study of God's law; Latin: jurisprudence, *juris* meaning "law," and *prudence* meaning "knowledge")! I learned later in my life that my father was a judge; the desire for wisdom and knowledge runs in my family!

My call to the mission field came to me on April 26, 1972, when I graduated from the South India Bible Seminary at Bangarapet. Now, here at Bethany, I will be equipped with four years of instruction to become a missionary for Christ and His kingdom.

*Bible reading is an education in itself.*

—Lord Tennyson

# CHRIST IS IN ME

Here I conclude part 1 of my story of the miracles, blessings, and faith that allowed me to come to study in America. The next story in my life will tell of my first missionary journey as an evangelist and then my second and third missionary journeys to many countries. In this, you will learn of my joy when I married Ben Michael Carter, who found Christ and met me while I was doing my internship in Puerto Rico. We traveled together, teaching and witnessing for Christ. He earned an MA in Theological Studies from the Billy Graham Center, Wheaton College, Illinois; an MTh from the University of Aberdeen in Scotland, UK; and a PhD in Christianity in the non-Western world from the University of Edinburgh in Scotland, United Kingdom. These gave him the intellectual tools to challenge commonplace thinking, and he wrote many insightful books, which will be available from now on at www.christianfaithpublishing.com.

This story started with the one dollar I had when I arrived in America on October 21, 1978. I rejoice for all the miracles along the way and for God's providence and faithfulness in my life as I have lived throughout all these eighty (80!) years in good health.

*And the end of all our exploring*
*Will be to arrive where we started*
*And know the place for the first time.*

—T. S. Eliot

Amy Carmichael

*For whatsoever is born of God overcometh the world: and this*
*is the victory that overcometh the world, even our faith.*

—1 John 5:4

Salma with Margaret Wilkinson, who was like a mother to the second to eighth generations, and provided education for us to get ahead and advance in our lives. Thank you, Nura Sittie!

This ends the story for now.

# NOTES AND ENDNOTES

## Amy's First Children Become Leaders and My Relationship to Them

In 1926, Amy Carmichael chose Arulai, her loved convert from nearby village Pannaivilai, to be the leader after her since Arulai was already helping Amy in her work, but Arulai died before Amy. Amy wrote the story of this family in a book called *Mimosa*. This family faithfully served in Dohnavur Fellowship, and even today, Mimosa's great-grandchildren of the fourth generation are still leading the Dohnavur family. I have told you about the girl named Devarul with whom I was growing up. She also came from the Mimosa family. Her older sister was Paramananthie. They both resided with Lola's family. Shanthie Aruldasan's father was a cousin of Arulai and had been sent to Ceylon/Sri Lanka by Amy, where he married Kanmani, who was rescued as a child by Amy from a very dangerous situation.

Kanmani had been sent to Sri Lanka with a missionary friend, then on to China where she was protected by China Inland Missions. (When Mike and I were teaching in Nanchang, China, in 1990–1992, we were able to visit her place of refuge: the China Inland Mission.) When Kanmani was eighteen years old, she returned to Sri Lanka where Mr. Aruldasan was sent to marry her. They had two children born at Dohnavur, named David and Shanthie. Shanthie Aruldasan and Rajamacottie, both from the Mimosa family, became my beloved house mothers in my teen years. See more information at www.amycarmichael.org or www.friendsofdohnavur.org

1. Even though I had a keen desire to learn music, we were not allowed to play the piano or taught to read music. So I decided to develop my voice instead and sang soprano in the choir at South India Biblical Seminary, Bangarapet, South India. In the upcoming chapters, I will tell you about the great miracle which happened in my life and how faith in Christ got me to America. Once there, I had the opportunity to join the choir at Plymouth Park United Methodist Church, Irving, Texas. I gladly joined and enjoyed singing the hymnals and other songs in the church, wearing the choir robe. In summer 1997, we went on a tour of Europe, Switzerland, Austria, Czech Republic. We ended up in Prague singing at all the cathedrals. I enjoyed it very much. The song that I still remember and was singing even yesterday in my kitchen goes like this: "And when I'm dead and free I'll sing on, I'll sing on, and when I'm dead and free I'll sing a song of praise for Christ laid aside his life for my soul…I'll sing along." This is a joyful thing for me to depart one day from this earth into God's kingdom, singing his praise till the last breath, saying, "Christ is in me, the Hope of Glory." This is the Lord's doing. It is marvelous to our eyes. In the autumn of 2000, we went to New York to sing at Carnegie Hall. It was my dream that came true. God is *great*! I say thanks to Mellial Sittie (Alice Roberts) who trained my voice to sing.

2. In June 2018, on my way back to the USA from France, I stopped in England to attend the farewell of Hanna Tahany, our secretary of the London office of Dohnavur Fellowship located in the Leprosy Mission building. Hanna Tahany from Egypt has been working as the secretary for the past fifteen years. It was sad to say goodbye to her, but she moved on to minister and help people who spoke the same language as her. Jackie Woolcock (Kiruba Sittie) was there and gave her thanks to Hanna. We, the Dohnavur family, appreciated her work greatly and sent her off with blessings. At her farewell gathering, I said that the Dohnavur family appreciated her work and thanked Hanna Tahany for the help she gave us while working at our London office for the past fifteen years. Besides me, Tarie and Leelabai, who are children of Dohnavur missionaries, were also present at the farewell function representing the whole Dohnavur family.

3. On June 11, 2018, I flew to Geneva, Switzerland, and was met by Urani, with whom I went to high school. She was with her Swiss husband, whom she had married fifteen years ago. They live in France, and it takes five hours to drive down the Swiss mountains to where they lived. The next day, her husband took us to Paris, where we stayed for four days in a hotel near the Eiffel Tower. We spent a week touring the city, and it was a dream come true for both of us to climb up to the top of the Eiffel Tower together hand in hand as we remembered our history and geography and the English teachers who taught us. Next week, he drove us back to Geneva, where he was born and raised. There we went to see a famous reformed church, with a museum attached. As a theologian, I was excited to see the first edition of the Vulgate Bible, printed at Mainz before

1456 and ascribed to Gutenberg. There was another large book, one of the first printed with movable type. And with them was the large wooden first printing press! Seeing it reminded me of the first time I was taken to a printing press when I was six years old in the Dohnavur Fellowship.

In November of 2000, Salma sang at Carnegie Hall in New York with the Plymouth Park Methodist church choir from Irving, Texas.

Salma's story will continue in part 2.
Here is a brief preview.

Salma in Puerto Rico at age thirty-seven, where she was an intern with the Bethany Missionaries. This is where Ben Michael (Mike) Carter met her.

Salma with Harold and Cathy Brokke on her graduation day, May 1982.

Salma working in the tape department at
Bethany Missionary College.

Salma's graduation day at Bethany Missionary College, May 1982.

Salma Carunia in the Bethany College garden, 1978–1982.

Salma Carunia with Ted Hegre, the president of Bethany Missionary College, and his wife Lucille.

Ben Michael Carter

North Korea DMZ, 1972–1974.
Panama Canal Zone, 1974–1976.

Salma and Mike after they became engaged to be wed.

# CHRIST IS IN ME

The Carter family: Terri, Patrick, Hilda (mom), Salma, Mike, Benny (dad).

Mike and Salma, June 10, 1982.

```
Dearling, to me thou art most fair
    I purpose thee to love
With thee I would thine own life share
    Mine own is not enough

I think thou art my missing part
     Torn from me long ago
Thou holdest now my very heart
    Dearling, I love thee so
```

Mike Carter.

Mike and Salma's wedding day on July 3, 1982.

# POSTSCRIPT

## Changes at Dohnavur Fellowship

Readers may be glad to know that the fellowship is still in existence as of this writing. Some of the hardships that I endured are no longer inflicted upon the children. Since 2015, Dohnavur has been a very different place from what it was when I was a child. Things have changed as now the Child Welfare Committee, a governmental organization, has the final say in matters of how children are treated and fed with nutritious food. They must also be provided with mattresses for their beds.

Social Services now control all children's homes and try to get *all orphans* adopted; therefore, babies no longer come to Dohnavur Fellowship. Gone are the days when orphans or children whose parents or relatives could no longer care for them could bring a child to their door. The fellowship, after establishing that a child was at risk, could then accept the child and become responsible for all of that child's needs. *It was a family with strong ties* and a home to which we old girls could come if we were in distress after moving out to hold a job or were given in marriage. Old boys and girls went home to Dohnavur to celebrate Christmas and Easter along with our great family.

It is sad to see that now the old girls who lived outside were stipulated with many rules, such as they must fill out some kind of form to return home to see beloved friends and family. Also, a hefty price (fees) must be paid, even to stay only as a guest. Most of the girls do not earn much, cannot afford to come home anymore, and miss seeing others with whom they grew up as a family. Now, even though communication is done via cell phones, many times it is intercepted.

Now, the District of Child Protection Office (DCPO) and Child Welfare Committee (CWC), who oversee NGOs like Dohnavur Fellowship are responsible for placing children aged five to sixteen from poor and vulnerable backgrounds in Dohnavur Fellowship to receive an education until the age eighteen. As of today, only twenty-nine children remain at Dohnavur. At the end of each semester, and on any school breaks, they are sent home to their families. Once they reach eighteen years of age, they will be sent back to their families by the fellowship as they are no longer protected by the DCPO. They keep their family names, and no more children will be named Carunia (this was Amy Carmichael's Tamil name). Also, religious instructions are not permitted, as they are to retain their family's cultural identity.

By the end of this year, the old girls aged sixty to eighty, the remaining Carunias of Amy's children who gave their service to the fellowship, soon will be sent to the newly built retirement home with individual rooms. Their view of the outside world has been blocked by the construction of a high wall with a small lattice at the top. Their freedom of movement is also curtailed. This is being done to empty all the houses and facilities in the compound to be rented to the other organizations. If God is willing, I hope to return home to see all of my sisters one more time before it is too late.

> "On Christ the solid rock I stand, all other ground is sinking sand."

If anyone has questions about my stories of faith (Titus 1:9), please contact the author by email at cartersalma49@gmail.com. My mailing address is 363 E Las Colinas Boulevard, Apartment 343, Irving Texas, 75039, USA.

My future address is in John 14:2–3.

## In Bethany Missionary College

I received a BTh and missions degree and was able to do mission work for Christ in several countries. I met my husband when I was doing an internship in San Juan, Puerto Rico. That started his pursuit of me, but more importantly, his conversion to accept Christ as his Savior. This story can be read in the book *The Clay Supper: Confessions of a Born-Again Christian* by Ben M. Carter. It is available at www.christianfaithpublishing.com.

God of the universe broke into history and made Jesus Christ known to us (Ephesians 1:13–14, the longest sentence in all scripture).

Since its establishment in 1948, Bethany Global University (formerly known as Bethany College of Missions) has trained over three thousand missionaries to take the church to where it is not. Students spend sixteen months training overseas and working alongside seasoned missionaries while they earn their degrees.

Dan Brokke, son of Harold and Cathy Brokke, served as the president of Bethany Global University, as well as its parent organization Bethay International, from 2006 until 2022. He now serves as the vice president of communications at GO Movement.

The history of Bethany's missionary work from 1946-1996 has been documented as a Ph.D thesis by Salma's late husband, Dr. Ben Michael Carter. It is called "A Study of Bethany Fellowship as an Example of Conservative North American Evangelical Missions.", and will be available in part 2 of Salma's book.

In June 2024, due to the transition to a primarily online/remote learning model, Bethany Global University has listed its thirty-two-acre campus in Bloomington, Minnesota, for sale.

These changes to two of my favorite communities in which I lived remind us that "this world is not my home, as I am a pilgrim, and just passing through." So lay up your treasures somewhere beyond the blue skies. Here I sing:

> Swift to its close ebbs out life's little day;
> Earth's joys grow dim; its glories pass away;
> Change and decay in all around I see;
> O Thou who changest not, abide with me.

My current address is: 385 Las Colinas Blvd E, Irving, TX 75039.

My future address is found in John 14:2-3:
"In my Father's house are many mansions…that where I am, there ye may be also."

# PUBLISHED WORKS AND ARTICLES

## Five Books

Available at Christian Faith Publishing, 832 Park Ave., Meadville, Pennsylvania 16335

1. *The Depersonalization of God: A Consideration of Soteriological Difficulties in High Calvinism* (1989)
2. *Unity in Diversity: A New Christian Paradigm* (1991)
3. *The Defective Image: How Darwinism Fails to Provide an Adequate Account of the World* (2001)
4. *The Door* (a novel about a Christian wizard who does battle with an evil demon, with the fate of the world hanging in the balance) (2004)

## Thesis and Doctorial Papers

Attended August 1984–1985.
Received an MTh.
Thesis: University of Aberdeen, Scotland, UK, 1986. "An Examination of the Concept of Salvation by Faith as It Developed and Was Articulated in Pure Land Buddhism by Shinran Shonin with a Comparison of Shinran's Concept with That of Martin Luther."

Attended August 1992–December 1995.

Received a PhD in Christianity in the non-Western world.

Doctorial paper: University of Edinburgh, Scotland, UK, October 1995.

"A Study of Bethany Fellowship as an Example of Conservative North American Evangelical Missions."

## Poetry Chapbooks

*In the Day of the Voice of the Seventh Angel*, circa 1991, 23 pages.
*Standing on the Shores of Glass*, 2000, 10 pages. This work has pictures with poems

## Articles

Mike authored and published intellectual papers for symposiums, articles, and book reviews. He engaged in active correspondence on several websites, such as New Scientist, and MSNBC's Discussion Board.

The list of such published articles and reviews is incomplete. The papers were published by such well-respected journals and magazines as: *Perspectives on Science and Christian Faith: Journal of the American Scientific Affiliation; Journal of Evangelical Theology Society; First Things.*

The following articles are known and in the collection. It is not known where or if all of these were published:

(The works in this presentation are not in a particular order.)

1. "The Problem of Epistemology and Comic Models," *Perspectives on Science and Christian Faith: Journal of the American Scientific Affiliation*
2. "Salvation of Souls, But What Is a Soul?"
3. "The Limitations of Mathematics in Assessing Causality"
4. "The Epistemological Effects of Sin" from *Philosophia Christi*, Volume 6, Number 2, 2004

5. "Chaos Theory as an Evangelical Theological Tool"
6. Critique paper: "Richard Dawkins and the Infected Mind"
7. Critique paper: "New Age Thinking about the Soul: The Postmodern Metaphysics of Gary Zukav"
8. "Is a New Christendom Emerging in the Non-Western World? Philip Jenkin's and Lamin Sanneh's Contrasting Visions"
9. "God as Omnipotent Creator"
10. "Jesus as Logos: A Defense of the Instrumentalist View of Science as the Best Christian Options"
11. Conference paper: "Truth Is the Agreement of Cognition with Its Object"

## Book Reviews

1. A Fundamentalist Responds to Daniel C. Dennett's *Darwin's Dangerous Idea*. (February 1997 (Simon & Schuster, New York, 1995)
2. The Real Issue Is God: *The Measure of Man* by Stephen J. Gould (W.W. Norton & Company, NY, London, 1996)
3. *Nonzero* by Robert Wright (Pantheon Books, 2000)
4. *Religion Explained* by Pascal Boyer (Basic Books, 2001)
5. *The Bit and the Pendulum* by Tom Siegfried (John Wiley & Sons, Inc., 2000)
6. God in Stephan Wolfram's *A New Kind of Science* (Wolfram Media, 2002)

SECRETARIAT OF STATE

FIRST SECTION - GENERAL AFFAIRS

From the Vatican, 19 September 2017

Dear Ms Carter,

I am writing to acknowledge the gift of inscribed copies of Dr Ben Michael Carter's writings, which you presented to His Holiness Pope Francis.

In expressing appreciation for this kind gesture, I am pleased to assure you of His Holiness's prayers for your late husband and for you and your intentions.

Yours sincerely,

Monsignor Paolo Borgia
Assessor

Ms Salma Carunia Carter
363 E Las Colinas Blvd, Apt 343
Irving, TX 75039
USA

In the summer of 2017, Salma traveled to Italy and stayed in Rome, near the Vatican. She presented her scholarly husband's books and writings to the Vatican Library. In September 2017, she received a thank-you letter from Pope Francis, expressing appreciation, acknowledging the gift of inscribed copies of Dr. Ben Michael Carter's writings with his personal photo with the papal seal.

## ABOUT THE AUTHOR

The untold story of the pilgrimage of Salma Carunia Carter, B.Th & Missions from Dohnavur Fellowship orphanage in South India to America, to whom the Colossians 1:27, "Christ is in me, the hope of glory," mystery was revealed at the age of fifteen. She was detained from middle school and punished with hard labor for a year, working in the garden. The first day of this labor, she was weeding in the garden; as the sun's beautiful yellow rays fell upon her face, through a large mango tree, her body, mind, and soul were groaning, travailing together, along with the whole of creation around her (Romans 8:22). Something was happening to her body when her mind was processing this fate of that whole year, and her spirit was crying, "Abba, Father," who is the only father who she knew, for she was an orphan. There in the garden, she felt her mind, body, and soul were working together; even though God has made us in three parts that function differently, but our bodies are mortal (man as subject to death), there is another part that is immortal and lives forever, eternally: the spirit! While carrying water buckets to water the plants daily. She felt great shame because of this separation from her fellow students. Her education was resumed after these trails and tribulation. It is an astounding odyssey of faith and determination, which is enlightening and edifying to the reader. All this occurs in a location and era very foreign to today's western people. India transformed from a British colony into a new nation during this time. She continued her journey of faith in America, arriving at the age of thirty-three with just one dollar to her name, only by the help of the supernatural God, her Lord Jesus Christ who had redeemed and restored her life. Amen.

www.ingramcontent.com/pod-product-compliance
Lightning Source LLC
LaVergne TN
LVHW021548120125

800879LV00014B/639